D1551978

GILES OF ROME'S *DE REGIMINE PRINCIPUM*

*Reading and Writing Politics at Court
and University,* c. *1275–*c. *1525*

From the time of its composition (*c.* 1280) for Philip the Fair of France until the early sixteenth century, Giles of Rome's mirror of princes, the *De regimine principum*, was read by both lay and clerical readers in the original Latin and in several vernacular translations, and served as model or source for several works of princely advice. This study examines the relationship between the didactic political text and its audience by focusing on the textual and material aspects of the surviving manuscript copies, as well as on the evidence of ownership and use found in them and in documentary and literary sources. Briggs argues that lay readers used *De regimine* for several purposes, including as an educational treatise and military manual, whereas clerics, who often came first into contact with it at university, glossed, constructed apparatus for, and modified the text to suit their needs in their later professional lives.

CHARLES F. BRIGGS is Assistant Professor of History at Georgia Southern University. He has published articles in *Scriptorium, Manuscripta, English Manuscript Studies, 1100–1700,* and *Medieval Perspectives.*

Cambridge Studies in Palaeography and Codicology

This new series has been established to further the study of manuscripts from the Middle Ages to the Renaissance. It includes books devoted to particular types of manuscripts, their production and circulation, to individual codices of outstanding importance, and to regions, periods and scripts of especial interest to scholars. Certain volumes will be specially designed to provide students in the field with reliable introductions to central topics, and occasionally a classic originally published in another language will be translated into English. The series will be of interest not only to scholars and students of medieval literature and history, but also to theologians, art historians and others working with manuscript sources.

GILES OF ROME'S
DE REGIMINE PRINCIPUM

Reading and Writing Politics at Court
and University, c. 1275–c. 1525

CHARLES F. BRIGGS

Georgia Southern University

CAMBRIDGE
UNIVERSITY PRESS

PUBLISHED BY THE PRESS SYNDICATE OF THE UNIVERSITY OF CAMBRIDGE
The Pitt Building, Trumpington Street, Cambridge CB2 1RP, United Kingdom

CAMBRIDGE UNIVERSITY PRESS
The Edinburgh Building, Cambridge CB2 2RU, United Kingdom
40 West 20th Street, New York, NY 10011-4211, USA
10 Stamford Road, Oakleigh, Melbourne 3166, Australia

© Charles F. Briggs 1999

First published 1999

Printed in the United Kingdom at the University Press, Cambridge

Typeset in Adobe Garamond 11¼ on 13½pt in QuarkXPress™   [SE]

A catalogue record for this book is available from the British Library

Library of Congress cataloguing in publication data
Briggs, Charles F.
Giles of Rome's *De regimine principum*: Reading and Writing
Politics at Court and University, *c.* 1275–*c.* 1525 / Charles F. Briggs
p.   cm. (Cambridge Studies in Palaeography and Codicology, 7)
Includes bibliographical references and index.
ISBN 0 521 57053 0
1. Giles, of Rome, Archbishop of Bourges, *c.* 1243–1316. De
regimine principum.   2. Political science – Study and teaching –
History.   3. Didactic literature, Medieval and Modern – History and
criticism.   4. Learning and scholarship – History – Medieval,
500–1500.   5. Manuscripts, Latin (Medieval and modern)   6. Education
of princes.   7. Education, Medieval.   I. Title.   II. Series.
JC393.G573B75   1999
97-47553   CIP

ISBN 0 521 57053 0 hardback

For Jane, Mary Fair, and Clio

Contents

Plates

Acknowledgments

Throughout the eight years spent bringing this project *a semine ad florem*, I have received help and encouragement from many quarters. I owe a special debt of gratitude to Dick Pfaff, who as my dissertation director at the University of North Carolina at Chapel Hill, and as friend and colleague since, has unfailingly encouraged (or at least suffered) me to steer my own course, while expertly indicating the flaws in my navigation. Other scholars whose assistance and advice have been invaluable are François Avril, Fred Behrends, Charles Burnett, Janet Coleman, Francesco Del Punta, Ian Doyle, Tony Edwards, David Fowler, David Ganz, Jean-Philippe Genet, John Headley, Don Kennedy, Roberto Lambertini, Concetta Luna, Michael McVaugh, Ezio Ornato, Malcolm Parkes, Alan Piper, Richard Rouse, Kathleen Scott, Jenny Stratford, and Giuseppe Zivelonghi. Through the years, my conversations and correspondence with these learned associates have been a constant reminder to me of how much our pursuit of the past is the effort of a group, each of whose members offers something unique and precious.

I could not, of course, have conducted the research on which this book is based without the generous and expert assistance of the staffs of the numerous libraries and archives in which I have worked, or with whom I have corresponded. Special thanks go to those who have granted permission to publish photographic reproductions of portions of manuscripts under their care. These include the Archbishop of Canterbury and the Trustees of Lambeth Palace Library; the Bodleian Library, Oxford; the British Library; the Dean and Chapter of Hereford and the Hereford Mappa Mundi Trust; the Dean and Chapter of York; the Master and Fellows of Corpus Christi College, Cambridge; the Master and Fellows of Gonville and Caius College, Cambridge; the Master and Fellows of Jesus College, Cambridge; the Syndics of Cambridge University Library; and the Walters Art Gallery, Baltimore.

Generous support in the way of funding was provided by the Georgia Southern University Faculty Research Committee and the American Philosophical Society, which defrayed the costs of travel to collections in the United Kingdom and France in the summer of 1994 and autumn of 1996. The latter trip could not have been accomplished without a sabbatical leave funded by the Georgia Southern University Foundation. The comments and criticisms of the editors of Cambridge Studies in Palaeography and Codicology, Rosamond McKitterick and Albinia de la Mare, as well as of the Cambridge University Press's two anonymous readers, have gone a long way toward transforming the dissertation into the book; and at the Press, Kate Brett, Hilary Gaskin, Alison Gilderdale, and Victoria Sellar have patiently shepherded the book into publication. Peggy Brown, Paul Remley, Patricia Stirnemann, and Siegfried Wenzel were all kind enough to read through earlier drafts, and I thank them for suggesting many essential changes. As for any errors in fact or interpretation, or any stylistic infelicities that must, I am afraid, unavoidably remain, I bear full responsibility.

Several of my colleagues in the Department of History at Georgia Southern have offered much needed encouragement, and allowed me to bend their ears on numerous occasions regarding what to them must have seemed a rather obscure topic. In particular, George Shriver read and commented on (usually over coffee, and sometimes over doughnuts) the drafts of several articles and papers, which in some way or another have been related to this project, while Tim Teeter has helped me construe some troublesome passages of Latin. Other assistance has come in the way of free lodging, not to mention meals and camaraderie from Margie Pfaff in Chapel Hill, Don Smith in Oxford, and Dominique and Odile Le Bris, and Nora Sardi in Paris, while Jim Jennings came through with crucial information that time limitations precluded me from accessing myself. Lastly, words cannot begin to express my gratitude for the love, support, and encouragement lavished upon me by my family. In partial recompense, I dedicate this book to them.

Abbreviations

BL	British Library, London
BN	Bibliothèque Nationale, Paris
BRUC	A. B. Emden, *A Biographical Register of the University of Cambridge to 1500*
BRUO	A. B. Emden, *A Biographical Register of the University of Oxford to 1500*, 3 vols. and Appendix
BRUO 1501–40	A. B. Emden, *A Biographical Register of the University of Oxford, A.D. 1501–1540*
CCR	*Calendar of Close Rolls*
CCUL	*Catalogue of the Manuscripts Preserved in the Library of the University of Cambridge*
CPR	*Calendar of Patent Rolls*
De Ricci	S. de Ricci and W. J. Wilson, *Census of Medieval and Renaissance Manuscripts in the United States and Canada*
DNB	*Dictionary of National Biography*
DRP	*De regimine principum*
EETS	Early English Text Society
MLGB	N. R. Ker, *Medieval Libraries of Great Britain*
MLGB Supplement	A. G. Watson, *Medieval Libraries of Great Britain: Supplement to the Second Edition*
MMBL	N. R. Ker and A. J. Piper, *Medieval Manuscripts in British Libraries*
SC	*Summary Catalogue of Western Manuscripts in the Bodleian Library at Oxford*

Introduction

HERE ENDS THE BOOK ON THE RULE OF PRINCES BROUGHT FORTH BY BROTHER GILES OF ROME OF THE ORDER OF FRIARS HERMITS OF SAINT AUGUSTINE, which ought to be read often at table, just as it is said at the end of the second book.

The duke, in accordance with the theory of Master Giles and by order of the king, had a ditch of good depth and breadth dug between him and the enemy, and the soil that had been excavated, following the same Master Giles, thrown up on the inside towards his men.

The conventional explicit and much less conventional exhortation to the reader in the first passage above was penned by the scribe of a copy of Giles of Rome's *De regimine principum* which belonged to John Lecche, an Oxford graduate, official at the court of Canterbury, and king's clerk.[1] The scribe, who wrote in the Anglicana script used both by university scribes and Chancery clerks during the middle years of the fourteenth century, was referring to a passage in the last chapter of the second book of *De regimine*, wherein Giles, in the course of recommending a minimum of speech at table, suggests:

if at the tables of kings and princes some useful things were read aloud continually, so that at the same time as the throats of those reclining take food their ears might receive learning, this would be altogether fitting and proper. Therefore kings and princes ought to ordain that praiseworthy customs of the kingdom, if such have been collected in writing, be read at the table; or also praiseworthy deeds of their predecessors, and especially of those who have comported themselves in a sacred manner and religiously with respect to divine things, and who have ruled the kingdom justly and in due fashion; or that there be read at the table the book *on the rule of princes*, both so that princes themselves might be instructed in how they should rule, and that others might be taught how to be obedient to princes. These things, then, or other useful things, reported in the common idiom so that all could

---

[1] "Explicit liber De regimine principum editus a fratre Egidio Romano ordinis fratrum here-mitarum sancti Augustini, qui deberet frequenter legi in mensa ut dicitur in fine secundi libri": London, Lambeth Palace Libr. 150, fol. 98v. On Lecche see *BRUO* 2, pp. 1118–19.

be instructed through them, would be the things to be read at the tables of kings and princes.[2]

In the second passage, the anonymous author of the *Gesta Henrici Quinti* relates how during the siege of Harfleur in 1415 Henry V and his brother Thomas, duke of Clarence, applied the techniques of siege craft they had drawn from chapter 17 of the third part of the third book of *De regimine*.[3] Each passage presents testimony of a different way of reading. The first would have recommended itself to Lecche and, presumably, to the scribe, who, like Giles, would have been familiar with the old monastic practice of reading at the evening meal;[4] as for the second, Henry and his brother were men raised for war who, at least in the mind of the *Gesta's* author, looked to *De regimine* for advice on how to defeat their enemies in France.

What follows is a history of the relationship between *De regimine* and its audience from the time of its composition in the late thirteenth century until the beginning of the sixteenth century, when the use of *De regimine* appears to have declined as the medium of texts shifted from manuscript to print. It argues that this mirror of princes was read in a variety of ways, for many different reasons, and by a wide array of those people who belonged to the literate classes of the later Middle Ages. The most important source for this history is the extant *De regimine* manuscripts themselves, which subsist as the most "authentic witnesses" of the attitudes, needs, and intellectual habits of those who copied, illuminated, translated, read, and indeed often added subsidiary apparatus to, or substantially altered the form and content of the text inscribed on their parchment or paper leaves.[5] Indeed, these manuscripts are particularly eloquent artifacts of important intellectual currents that were running through medieval society from the thirteenth to the fifteenth century. Giles belonged to the first generation of scholars exposed to the corpus of Aristotle's moral philosophical works, and drew extensively from them and from some of their Arabic and medieval commentaries, as well as from several other works of classical and late antique authorship. Thus the *De regimine* attests to one

---

[2] "Immo si ad mensas regum semper autem utilia loquerentur ut simul cum fauces recumbentium summunt cibum earum aures doctrina perciperent, esset omnino decens et congruum. Ordinare igitur deberent reges et principes ut laudabiles consuetudines regni si tales sunt in scripto redacte, vel etiam laudabilia gesta predecessorum suorum, et maxime eorum qui sancte et religiose se habuerunt ad divina et qui iuste et debite regnum rexerunt, legerentur ad mensam. Vel etiam ad mensam legeretur liber de regimine principum ut ipsi principantes instruerentur qualiter principari deberent et alii edocerentur quomodo est principibus obediendum. Hec igitur vel alia utilia tradita secundum vulgare ydioma, ut omnes per ea doceri possent in mensis regum et principum legenda essent": *DRP* 2.3.20.

[3] *Gesta Henrici Quinti: The Deeds of Henry the Fifth*, ed. and trans. F. Taylor and J. S. Roskell (Oxford, 1975), p. 43.

[4] On aural "reading" in the Middle Ages, see J. Coleman, *Public Reading and the Reading Public in Late Medieval England and France* (Cambridge, 1996). Less apposite to this study, but still worth consulting is D. H. Green, *Medieval Listening and Reading: The Primary Reception of German Literature, 800–1300* (Cambridge, 1994).

[5] M. A. Rouse and R. H. Rouse, *Authentic Witnesses: Approaches to Medieval Texts and Manuscripts* (Notre Dame, Ind., 1991), p. 1.

aspect of the process through which classical learning was transmitted to the Middle Ages. And *De regimine* would in turn be a model, or at least an important source, for many late medieval mirrors of princes and other works of advice for rulers. Furthermore it was popular, at least in so far as one can use this term in the context of manuscript culture. Some 350 copies are extant, one of the most numerous survivals of a non-religious work from the Middle Ages. It circulated widely in Latin and in several vernacular translations among a diverse group of lay and clerical readers, including royalty, aristocracy, the gentry and urban bourgeoisie, and a large assortment of scholars and clerics. Consequently, by mapping the course of its reception one should be better able to determine the contours of the linguistic and cultural appropriation of learned Latin discourse by a lay audience.

Ideally, perhaps, a study of this nature would be based on a thorough examination of all the surviving manuscripts. Yet in the case of *De regimine* such a project would be too vast for one person and the results too cumbersome to fit in one slim volume – a state of affairs brought about by the two somewhat contrary phenomena of, on the one hand, *De regimine*'s popularity and influence in the Middle Ages and, on the other, the relatively scant attention given it by modern scholars until very recently. At this time, a comprehensive study would involve the examination of a plethora of manuscripts in libraries scattered throughout Europe and North America, several of whose collections have not been adequately catalogued. The estimated corpus of nearly 300 Latin manuscripts is only now beginning to be catalogued with the goals of reconstructing *De regimine*'s textual transmission and producing a first critical edition of it – a result still perhaps decades from completion.[6] As for the translations into most of the European vernaculars, many of the manuscripts are described only in outdated catalogues; and though several versions have been edited, many are still accessible only in manuscript.[7]

[6] A series of monographic catalogues is being prepared under the direction of Francesco Del Punta. The first of these, devoted to the manuscripts in Italian libraries, has recently appeared: F. Del Punta and C. Luna, *Aegidii Romani Opera Omnia: I.1/11, Catalogo dei manoscritti (1001–1075) "De regimine principum": Città del Vaticano – Italia* (Florence, 1993). The catalogue of manuscripts in France is nearing completion, but those devoted to the manuscripts in German, Central and Eastern European, Iberian, British, and North American libraries are still only in the planning stage. The planned critical edition will not be undertaken until all the catalogues have been published. Aware of the likelihood that this outcome is many years away, the editors of *Aegidii Romani Opera Omnia* intend in the next decade to publish a kind of "best text" edition with a facing-page modern Italian translation.

[7] D. Van den Auweele, "Un abrégé flamand du 'De regimine principum' de Gilles de Rome," in *"Sapientiae Doctrina": Mélanges de théologie et de littérature médiévales offerts à Dom Hildebrand Bascour O.S.B.*, ed. R. Hissette, G. Michiels, D. Van den Auweele (Louvain, 1980), pp. 327–58; F. Corazzini (ed.), *Del Reggimento de' principi de Egidio Romano, volgarizzamento trascritto nel MCCLXXXVIII* (Florence, 1858); S. P. Molenaer (ed.), *Li Livres du Gouvernement des Rois: A XIIIth Century French Version of Egidio Colonna's Treatise De regimine principum* (New York and London, 1899); *The Governance of Kings and Princes: John Trevisa's Middle English Translation of the "De regimine principum" of Aegidius Romanus*, ed. D. C. Fowler, C. F. Briggs, and P. G. Remley (New York, 1997); J. B. Perez (ed.), *Glosa Castellana al "Regimiento de Príncipes" de Egidio Romano*, 3 vols. (Madrid, 1947); A. Mante (ed.), "Aegidius Romanus: De regimine principum" [Middle Low German translation of Johann von

Intimately connected to the dearth of adequate manuscript descriptions and editions is the relative scarcity of modern scholarship devoted to Giles and *De regimine*. Giles, the most prolific and original thinker of the Augustinian order of friars (with the possible exception of Martin Luther, who did most of his writing after leaving the order), has not fared nearly so well at the hands of modern scholars as the intellectual luminaries of the Augustinians' rival mendicant orders, despite the clear importance of Giles's works in the curriculum of the late medieval universities.[8] As for *De regimine*, although it has long been recognized as a seminal work in the mirror of princes genre, only very recently has its doctrine been subjected to the kind of exhaustive and sympathetic analysis that it deserves.[9] And while *De regimine*'s reception, transmission, and use in the Middle Ages appear to have fared somewhat better at the hands of modern scholarship, this does not mean these topics have been adequately explored. The work of Gerardo Bruni, published over sixty years ago, remains the only concerted attempt to tackle these issues.[10] Yet Bruni's efforts, though impressive (indeed, the present study is deeply indebted to them), were nevertheless constrained by the limitations of the printed sources

Brakel], Ph.D. dissertation, Lund, 1929; J. V. McMahon (ed.), "Das Puech von der Ordnung der Fuersten: A Critical Text-Edition of Book I of the MHG Version of the De regimine principum of Aegidius Romanus," Ph.D. dissertation, University of Texas at Austin, 1967; M. Menzel (ed.), *Die "Katharina divina" des Johann von Vippach: Ein Fürstenspiegel des 14. Jahrhunderts* (Cologne and Vienna, 1989); U. Störmer (ed.), "Der ostmitteldeutsche Traktat *Welch Furste Sich vnde syne Erbin wil in synem Furstethum festin* nach Aegidius Romanus, *De regimine principum*," in *Zwei ostmitteldeutsche Bearbeitungen lateinischer Prosadenkmäler* (Berlin, 1990); A. Tille (ed.), "Aegidius Romanus: De regimine principum" [fragment of lower Rhenish German translation], *Zeitschrift für die gesamte Staatswissenschaft* 57 (1901), pp. 484–96.

[8] By way of example, a look at the general index of the *International Medieval Bibliography* for the period July–December 1994 turned up fifty-seven entries for Aquinas, four each for Bonaventure and William of Ockham, six for Duns Scotus, and none for Giles: *International Medieval Bibliography*, vol. XXVIII (Leeds, 1995). On Giles and Luther, see J. R. Eastman, "Relating Martin Luther to Giles of Rome: How to Proceed!" *Medieval Perspectives* 8 (1993), pp. 41–52. For the importance of Giles's works in the curriculum, see L. Thorndyke (ed. and trans.), *University Records and Life in the Middle Ages* (New York, 1972), p. 355.

[9] Among the several surveys of medieval political philosophy which discuss *De regimine*, the best and most recent is Jean Dunbabin's chapter "Government," in *The Cambridge History of Medieval Political Thought, c. 350–c. 1450*, ed. J. H. Burns (Cambridge, 1988), pp. 477–519. The first work entirely devoted to *De regimine*, but now very outdated, is V. Courdaveaux, *Aegidii Romani de Regimine Principum Doctrina* (Paris, 1857). The study that scholars most often refer to is that found in Wilhelm Berges' still useful *Die Fürstenspiegel des hohen und späten Mittelalters* (Leipzig, 1938). The most thorough treatment by far can be found, however, in three recent articles by Roberto Lambertini: "A proposito della 'costruzione' dell'*Oeconomica* in Egidio Romano," *Medioevo* 14 (1988), pp. 315–70; "'Philosophus videtur tangere tres rationes.' Egidio Romano lettore ed interprete della *Politica* nel terzo libro del *De regimine principum*," *Documenti e studi sulla tradizione filosofica medievale* 1 (1990), pp. 277–325; "Il filosofo, il principe e la virtù. Note sulla ricezione e l'uso dell'*Etica Nicomachea* nel *De regimine principum* di Egidio Romano," *Documenti e studi sulla tradizione filosofica medievale* 2 (1991), pp. 239–79.

[10] G. Bruni, *Le opere di Egidio Romano* (Florence, 1936), pp. 75–108; "Il *De regimine principum* di Egidio Romano," *Aevum* 6 (1932), pp. 339–70.

upon which he almost exclusively relied. The numerous other studies that mention *De regimine* do so only in the course of investigating their own principal subjects, be they mirrors of princes, education, politics, or literary tastes.[11] So, as far as *De regimine* is concerned, they reveal facets, but no comprehensible whole.

Convinced, then, of the need for a study focused on *De regimine*, but aware of the obstacles that at this time stand in the way of an exhaustive history of this text and its readers in all of medieval Europe, I have obeyed the dictates of prudence and confined my attention primarily, but by no means exclusively, to medieval England. This choice has been made for several reasons, many of them purely practical. To begin with, I needed to be able to lay much of the groundwork from my base in the United States, a long way from most of the collections. Thus I had to have access to a critical mass of reasonably good manuscript catalogues, and this was something the British Isles could provide. Moreover, several of the English collections have been microfilmed and the contents of many of England's medieval libraries, both institutional and private, have been, and continue to be, the subject of considerable investigation. Yet if pragmatic considerations guided my initial decision, the ensuing investigation has shown it to have been a fortuitous one. The group of sixty surviving manuscripts of demonstrable medieval (pre-Dissolution) English origin and/or provenance is large and varied enough to support a number of general findings, without being so numerous as to prove unwieldy. Likewise, the manuscripts and other evidence of ownership have rendered an audience that was both large and diverse in terms of education, social status, gender, and profession, yet still tied together geographically, linguistically, politically, and institutionally. I have, however, tried to keep the English heart in its European body by personally examining a "control group" of some forty manuscripts of French and Italian origin, while also consulting Francesco Del Punta and Concetta Luna's monographic catalogue of the manuscripts in Italian libraries and Adolar Zumkeller's study of the *De regimine* manuscripts in Germany and Central Europe.[12] This lends some contrast to the English situation and also encourages general observations regarding the reception of *De regimine* throughout later medieval Europe.

In preparing this study I have received considerable guidance from the works, and sometimes the spoken words, of textual historians and students of the manuscript book, like Richard and Mary Rouse, Neil Ker, Malcolm Parkes, and Ian Doyle. Nevertheless, the job of researching an *histoire de texte* that looks at so many manuscripts and crosses the frontiers of both language and readerly milieu has

---

[11] See, for example, Berges, *Fürstenspiegel*, 320–8; N. Orme, *From Childhood to Chivalry: The Education of the English Kings and Aristocracy, 1066–1530* (London, 1984); R. H. Jones, *The Royal Policy of Richard II: Absolutism in the Later Middle Ages* (Oxford, 1968); R. F. Green, *Poets and Princepleasers: Literature and the English Court in the Late Middle Ages* (Toronto, 1980), pp. 135–67.

[12] A. Zumkeller, *Manuskripte von Werken der Autoren des Augustiner-Eremitenordens in mitteleuropäischen Bibliotheken*, Cassiciacum, Band 20 (Würzburg, 1966).

obliged me, a historian by training, to cobble together bits and pieces of methodology from the fields of codicology, art history, and literary studies, as well as from my own discipline. Telling the story of this text and its readers has also forced me to grapple with several problems of terminology, and to come up with an *ordo narrationis* for this study that has no close precedents. Before getting started, then, it seems prudent to discuss the norms and structure that I have imposed herein. The entire work is composed, really, of four distinct parts. In the first, which comprises the first two chapters, I take a broad view of *De regimine*'s audience and manuscripts, throughout Europe, in order to establish the general trends and characteristics of *De regimine*'s production, reception, transmission, and use.

The focus then shifts to England for the remainder of the study, first looking at the lay audience of *De regimine*, then turning to the clerical readership, and concluding with a battery of appendices. Chapter 3 reconstructs the late medieval lay audience, which included kings, queens, nobles, gentry, and urban bourgeoisie, and argues that the portions of the text they read and their interpretations of the text differed from time to time and from reader to reader, according to their various needs and agendas. The following chapter remains in the lay milieu, though here the focus shifts from the audience to the vernacular translations, both French and English, that they read. Particular attention is given to John Trevisa's Middle English translation, and to why this version did not flourish. Chapters 5 and 6 have as their subject the clerical audience, who often made their first acquaintance with *De regimine* while at university, where they used it as a textbook of moral philosophy, but then often continued to refer to it in their later professional life, whether as administrators, confessors and preachers, or lawyers. This group has left particularly revealing evidence of their uses of the text, thanks to the ways they glossed and modified it to suit their needs.

At the outset, it must be said that establishing the medieval audience of any text is a tricky business, and doing so for *De regimine* can on occasion be particularly so.[13] A work's audience could, after all, be associated with the text and its manuscripts in several ways. The text could be read from beginning to end or partially, once or repeatedly; it could be recited to a group of listeners, a practice common to both the university classroom, the monastic or college refectory, or the royal or noble hall.[14] Someone might have possessed but not read it, using it rather as a kind of talisman or symbol of status or power, or indeed not using it at all.[15] Here *De*

---

[13] Much of my discussion on the limitations and biases of the sources for audience has been derived from N. R. Ker's "Revised Preface" in *MLGB*, pp. vii–xxiii; and K. Harris, "Patrons, Buyers and Owners: The Evidence for Ownership and the Role of Book Owners in Book Production and the Book Trade," in *Book Production and Publishing in Britain, 1375–1475*, ed. J. Griffiths and D. Pearsall (Cambridge, 1989), pp. 163–99.

[14] Coleman, *Public Reading*, pp. 88–97; Green, *Medieval Listening*, pp. 210–25.

[15] V. J. Scattergood, "Literary Culture at the Court of Richard II," in *English Court Culture in the Later Middle Ages*, ed. V. J. Scattergood and J. W. Sherborne (London, 1983), p. 36.

regimine's audience has been fairly broadly construed to encompass everyone who seems to have had some meaningful association with the text. These meaningful associations or relationships were largely of three kinds: patronage; possession, whether ownership or borrowing; and use or study. These associations were not, of course, mutually exclusive, since many of those who patronized the production of manuscripts were also their original owners. Also, those for whom evidence of use alone survives may have been owners; if not, they were almost certainly borrowers of one sort or another, or were members of institutions whose libraries contained the book they consulted. Scribes could also be readers, either because they copied a text for their own use, or because in the act of copying they simultaneously read it with some degree of comprehension.[16]

Three kinds of evidence have been adduced here to reconstruct *De regimine*'s audience. The first of these can be characterized as internal, and is taken to mean both the raw total number of manuscripts, which is used to determine the text's overall popularity, its patterns of diffusion, and the kinds of reader toward which manuscripts would have been aimed; it also includes the more discrete signs of ownership, provenance, and use which reside in the manuscripts, usually in the form of *ex libris* inscriptions, colophons, or coats of arms. This internal evidence is practically unimpeachable, *when it exists*. Yet it must also be remembered that there is a great deal about which it can say nothing, owing to the overall loss of manuscripts over the centuries. And because the patterns of loss have by no means been even, the collections of some individuals and institutions have ended up appearing far larger or smaller in relation to one another than they in fact were.[17]

The other two types of evidence are external, derived either from documents – be they wills, book bequests, inventories, or library catalogues – or the borrowings from and references to *De regimine* in other texts. Whatever form the evidence takes, however, it must be used with caution. This is especially true of books mentioned in the documentary sources for which there is no corroborating evidence in the way of surviving manuscripts. One must be particularly wary with wills and inventories of moveables, for they are usually incomplete, careless, and arbitrary in their treatment of books. The compilers of inventories were more likely to regard books as commodities than as repositories of texts, while wills frequently single out only the titles of liturgical and devotional books, or those that were particularly valuable, and even these often receive but the barest of descriptions.[18] And though medieval library catalogues tend to be much more reliable witnesses, many of these

---

[16] On scribes as owners, see M. B. Parkes, "The Provision of Books" in *The History of the University of Oxford*, vol. II, ed. J. I. Catto and R. Evans (Oxford, 1992), pp. 426–7.

[17] Ker, *MLGB*, p. xi; N. R. Ker, "Oxford College Libraries in the Sixteenth Century," *Bodleian Library Record* 6 (1957–61), p. 463, and "The Migration of Manuscripts from the English Medieval Libraries," *The Library*, 4th ser., 23 (1942–3), pp. 1–11; C. E. Wright, "The Dispersal of the Libraries in the Sixteenth Century," in *The English Library before 1700*, ed. F. Wormald and C. E. Wright (London, 1958), pp. 148–75. [18] Harris, "Patrons, Buyers and Owners," pp. 163–5.

have been lost, making it impossible to put together anything like a complete picture of institutional ownership. Moreover, the titles *De regimine principum*, *Gouvernement des rois et des princes*, or *Government of Kings and Princes* were used generically in the Middle Ages for several distinct texts, thus occasionally causing confusion both in the Middle Ages and today. The Latin title was used for the pseudo-Aristotelian *Secretum secretorum*, Thomas Aquinas's and Ptolemy of Lucca's *De regimine principum*, and sometimes even Thomas Hoccleve's *Regement of Princes*;[19] the French could apply equally to Henri de Gauchy's translation of *De regimine*, Jean de Vignay's translation of the anonymous *Liber de informatione principum*, or Jean Golein's translation of *De eruditione principum*, a Latin mirror by either Vincent of Beauvais or Guillaume Peyraut;[20] the English could also designate John Lydgate and Benedict Burgh's *Secrets of Old Philosophers*, a work that itself was derived from the *Secretum secretorum*.[21] Consequently, a fair degree of circumspection must be used in those cases in the documentary sources where a title appears unaccompanied by the author's name.

Despite these caveats and my having had to wear so many methodological hats, it is hoped that this study's treatment of evidence of varied kinds of human association with *De regimine* – whether consulting it to storm Harfleur or to compose a sermon – has been sufficient to set the text and its manuscripts in a social and cultural context that is at once clearly delineated yet sufficiently broad. I also hope my efforts will go some way toward explaining what accounted for the rise and eventual decline of *De regimine*'s popularity and influence in the later Middle Ages and early Renaissance, and towards a more complete understanding of what "politics" meant for *De regimine*'s readers.

---

[19] Bishop William Rede bequeathed an "Aristoteles Liber de regimine principum" to Balliol College in 1385 (*BRUO* 3, p. 1559), and the scribe of the list of contents in Bodleian Laud Misc. 645 (fol. 1) mistakenly assigns to Aristotle the authorship of the manuscript's copy of *De regimine*. Bruni, Berges, and Zumkeller mistakenly identify Hoccleve's *Regement* as an English translation of *De regimine*: Bruni, *Le opere*, pp. 99–100; Berges, *Fürstenspiegel*, p. 326; Zumkeller, *Manuskripte*, p. 40.

[20] L. Delisle, *Recherches sur la librarie de Charles V*, pt. II (Paris, 1907), pp. 88–90; J.-Ph. Genet (ed.), *Four English Political Tracts of the Later Middle Ages*, Camden Fourth Series 18 (1977), pp. 12–13.

[21] G. A. Lester, *Sir John Paston's "Grete Boke": A Descriptive Catalogue, with an Introduction, of British Library MS Lansdowne 285* (Woodbridge, Suffolk, 1984), p. 12; R. A. B. Mynors, *Catalogue of the Manuscripts of Balliol College, Oxford* (Oxford, 1963), p. 339.

I

Giles of Rome and De regimine principum

Giles of Rome (alias Aegidius Romanus, Egidio Colonna) was born at Rome *c.* 1243.[1] By the time he was fifteen he had entered the convent of Augustinian friars at Santa Maria del Popolo in Rome, where he remained some two years before being sent to the order's new *studium* at Paris. After completing his studies in arts, he proceeded by the late 1260s to theological studies. Because the Augustinians did not yet have their own regent master in theology, he studied instead under Thomas Aquinas, whose teaching would have a major impact on Giles's later work. Giles's own scholarly activity got under way in 1270, when he embarked on writing a considerable number of Aristotelian commentaries and theological treatises. His career at the university was temporarily suspended in 1277, when several of his doctrines were censured in the wake of Bishop Etienne Tempier's condemnation of Aristotelian and Averroistic heterodoxy in the faculty of arts.

Giles's whereabouts cannot be documented with certainty from the end of 1277 until the attestation of his presence at the Augustinians' chapter general at Padua in 1281. The traditional assumption that he spent these years as the tutor of the heir to the French throne, Philip the Fair, can be neither proven nor disproven. Elizabeth Brown, for instance, seems to favor the idea of some kind of teacher/student bond, whereas, according to Joseph Strayer, "Egidius was a busy man . . . he could not have had time to supervise the details of Philip's education."[2] There can be little doubt, however, that whatever his other activities may have been, he did during these years compose the *De regimine*, a work which he dedicated to the young Philip, whose father, Philip III, took enough of an interest in *De regimine* to commission a French translation by 1282.[3] Certainly Giles had returned to Italy by

---

[1] Unless otherwise noted, the material for Giles's life and career is drawn from F. Del Punta, S. Donati, and C. Luna's entry for "Egidio Romano" in *Dizionario biografico degli italiani*, vol. XLII, pp. 319–35.

[2] E. A. R. Brown, "Persona et Gesta: The Image and Deeds of the Thirteenth-Century Capetians: The Case of Philip the Fair," *Viator* 19 (1988), pp. 232–5.

[3] The earliest copy of the French translation (Dôle, Bibl. mun. 157, fol. 1) contains the following ascription: "Ci commence li livres du gouvernement des rois et des princes, estrait de politiques, que

9

1281, where he would remain, occupied with matters relating to the promotion and welfare of the Augustinian order, until 1285, when he was given leave to return to Paris following the favorable outcome of a reexamination of those propositions of his that had been censured by Tempier eight years previously.

In 1287 the Augustinians' chapter general designated him the official doctor of the order and installed him as their first regent master of theology at Paris. His pre-eminence in the order was further confirmed when he was appointed to the post of general of the order, a duty he was able to perform while still remaining at Paris. Thanks in large part to his friendship with Benedetto Caetani, he assumed the archiepiscopal see of Bourges immediately after Caetani became pope in 1295. His allegiance to Caetani, now Pope Boniface VIII, brought him a short time later into conflict with Philip the Fair when Boniface promulgated the bull *Clericis laicos*. Giles spent the next several years at the papal curia, where in 1302 he wrote the uncompromisingly pro-papal tract *De ecclesiastica potestate*, a work whose influence can be clearly seen in Boniface's inflammatory bull *Unam sanctam*, issued against Philip in November 1302.[4] Boniface's capture at Anagni and subsequent death in the following year signaled the end of Giles's rise to prestige and power. Bereft of his chief protector and now long out of favor with the king of France, Giles sought the patronage of Philip's uncle Robert, count of Clermont-en-Beauvaisis, and of Robert of Anjou, king of Sicily. His fortunes did improve somewhat, however, when his participation in the suppression of the Templars in 1311–12 partially reconciled him with Philip. Giles died at Avignon on December 22, 1316.

There can be no doubt that Giles's course of study at Paris and his earlier work on Aristotle's moral philosophy had prepared him well for the task of composing *De regimine*. Not only did he belong to the first generation of scholars who had access to the entire corpus of the Latin Aristotle and pseudo-Aristotle translations (with the exception of the *Economics*), he had also been exposed to and indeed partaken in the ferment of interpretive activity that attended the early reception of Aristotle's works on moral philosophy and rhetoric.[5] The influence of Aquinas's *Sententiae* on the *Ethics* and *Politics*, as well as his *De regno* and *Summa theologica* is particularly apparent in *De regimine*.[6] Moreover, in the years just prior to composing his mirror

---

frere Gile de Rome, de lordre de saint Augustin a feit pour monseignour Phelippe, aisne filz monseigneur Phelippe, tres noble roi de France . . . . et est translatez de latin en francois par maistre Henri de Gauchi par le comandement au noble roi devant dit en lan M.CC.IIIIxx.II.": Bruni, *Le opere*, pp. 85, 97.   [4] Burns (ed.), *Cambridge History of Medieval Political Thought*, pp. 400–2.

[5] William of Moerbeke translated the *Politics* and *Rhetoric* during the 1260s. The full text of the *Ethics* was translated by Robert Grosseteste *c.* 1246, but it was a revision of his translation, done in the 1250s, perhaps by Moerbeke, that proliferated. The *Economics* would not be translated until the 1290s. N. Kretzmann, A. Kenny, and J. Pinborg (eds.), *The Cambridge History of Later Medieval Philosophy* (Cambridge, 1982), pp. 77–8.

[6] Lambertini, "'Costruzione' dell'*Oeconomica*," pp. 335–57; Lambertini, "Il filosofo, il principe e la virtù," pp. 243–68; Lambertini, "Egidio Romano lettore ed interprete della *Politica*," pp. 287–304.

of princes, Giles himself had wrestled with several of the issues he was to confront in that work in his *Expositio in libro Rhetoricorum* and in a treatise entitled *De differentia ethicae, politicae et rhetoricae*.

The careful scholarship that earned Giles the sobriquet *Doctor Fundatissimus* is readily apparent in the *De regimine*. No other work of the medieval mirrors of princes genre is nearly as lengthy (approximately 155,000 words compared to the roughly 20,000 of the *Secretum secretorum*), nor do any come close to approaching the depth and breadth of its command of classical sources, especially Aristotle's *Politics*, *Ethics*, and *Rhetoric*. Giles cites the *Politics* by name approximately 230 times, the *Ethics* 185 times, the *Rhetoric* 88 times, and the *De re militari* of Vegetius 23 times. And though no other named source appears nearly so frequently, a count of these reveals an impressive seventy-eight citations from thirty-two distinct sources.[7] Conversely, *De regimine*'s studious avoidance of Scripture or the writings of the Fathers – the Old Testament, Solomon, and St. Augustine are each referred to but once – is unique among medieval mirrors. The profound influence of Aristotle on Giles is apparent in the very structure of *De regimine*, whose division into three books, devoted respectively to the conduct of the individual (ethics), the rule of the family and household (economics), and the governance of the city and kingdom (politics), is based on a division of the moral sciences derived from the moral philosophy of Aristotle and formulated at Paris during the twelfth and thirteenth centuries.[8] Each of these books is in turn divided into parts, which are further subdivided into chapters. The first book has four parts, the first of which deals with happiness and the proper goal of human life (13 chapters), the second with virtues (34 chapters), the third with the passions (11 chapters), and the fourth with the habits of men, as determined by their age and condition (7 chapters). The second book has three parts, treating respectively marital relations and the proper conduct of women (24 chapters), the raising of children (21 chapters), and the management of the household, i.e. property, finances, and servants (20 chapters). In the three parts of the final book the opinions of ancient philosophers regarding the

[7] Aristotle/Ps.-Aristotle: *Metaphysics* (12), *De anima* (8), *Magna moralia* (7), *Physics* (4), *De animalibus* (2), *De causis* (2), *Posterior Analytics* (1), *De generatione* (1), *De fortuna* (1), *Meteorologica* (1), *De memoria* (1), *Sophistici elenchi* (1), *De interpretatione* (1), *De eligendis* (1); Valerius Maximus, *De factis memorabilibus* (6); Paladius, *De agricultura* (4); Plotinus (3); Alfarabi (2); Andronicus Peripateticus (2); Averroes, *Commentary on the Metaphysics* (2); Boethius, *De consolatione philosophiae* (2); *The Institutes* (2); Ps.-Dionysius, *De divinis nominibus* (2); "Commentator super libris Ethicorum," (not Averroes, but perhaps one of the ancient Greek Aristotle commentators via Albertus Magnus's *Super Ethica commentum* [see Lambertini, "Il filosofo, il principe, e la virtù," pp. 254–6]) (1); Boethius, *De arithmetica* (1); Justinus (1); Livy (1); Macrobius (1); Proclus (1).

[8] J. A. Weisheipl, "The Classification of the Sciences in Medieval Thought," *Mediaeval Studies* 27 (1965), pp. 65–6. Lambertini, "'Costruzione' dell'*Oeconomica*," pp. 318–24. The threefold division of moral philosophy seems first to have been formulated in the Middle Ages by Hugh of St. Victor: C. J. Nederman, "Aristotelianism and the Origins of 'Political Science' in the Twelfth Century," *Journal of the History of Ideas* 52 (1991), p. 185.

nature and organization of the state are considered, and in many cases refuted (20 chapters), followed by discussions of the rule of the state in peacetime (36 chapters) and wartime (23 chapters).

The narrative of *De regimine* is patterned on the discourse of the schools; every subject is treated in the same disciplined, methodical, and closely reasoned manner that Giles as well as the university-educated readers of *De regimine* would have expected in a university lecture or textbook. The typical chapter begins with a brief reiteration of the subject of the previous chapter, followed by the statement of a general proposition. A summary of *rationes* for the proposition are then enumerated and explained one after the other, with each of the *rationes* often being further subdivided and discussed. The chapter concludes with a restatement of the original proposition, followed by a transition to the topic of the next chapter. This application of learned discourse would explain in part the work's wide dissemination in a clerical milieu. Nevertheless, one suspects that for lay readers, its very strengths were also its weaknesses, since there is nothing in the way of the rhetorical and stylistic devices to which most of them would have been accustomed, like, for instance, versification, allegory, or direct discourse. Granted, when translated into the vernacular such a text had the advantage of being clear and easy to follow. Moreover, the gravity of the narration is occasionally relieved by the insertion of illustrative analogies or instructive stories, as when Giles in book 2, part 1, chapter 19 warns that women should be

sobre and war of to moche drynke. For superfluyte boþe of mete and of drynke is cause of lust and of likynge of lecherie. þerfore in olde tyme among wymmen of Rome, as Valerius Maximus seith, libro ii, capitulo De Institutis Antiquis, how it was not laweful to drynke wyne. þerfore he seith þat vse of wyne was vnknowe to wymmen of Rome lest it scholde brynge hem to schame and velanye, for ofte vse of wyne was next to þe most venus.[9]

In a recent series of penetrating articles, Roberto Lambertini has suggested several other features that would have recommended *De regimine* to both clerical and lay readers. It was, for example, the first and most successful attempt to construct a manual on the management of the household and education of children based on Aristotelian principles. Moreover, its form of discourse, though academic in nature, was sufficiently vulgarized to appeal to lay audiences and, unlike most other princely mirrors, it addressed itself not just to the prince but to all citizens, thus substantially widening the scope of its intended target audience.[10] And, perhaps most importantly, Giles succeeded in composing a work that at one and

---

[9] *The Governance of Kings and Princes: John Trevisa's Middle English Translation of the "De regimine principum" of Aegidius Romanus*, ed. D. C. Fowler, C. F. Briggs, and P. G. Remley (New York, 1997), pp. 200–1.

[10] Lambertini, "'Costruzione' dell'*Oeconomica*," pp. 317–18, 334–5, 366–8. Christine de Pizan's *Livre de corps de policie* is also addressed to all citizens: Christine de Pizan, *The Book of the Body Politic*, trans. K. L. Forhan (Cambridge, 1994).

the same time rested on the substantial authority of the Stagirite while simultane-ously bending, pruning, or superseding Peripatetic doctrines when they neither served the ends nor conformed to the ideological framework of Giles or his audi-ence. The sharpest points of divergence are Giles's rejection of the practice of usury, an uncompromising preference for kingship, and for that matter inherited king-ship, over other forms of government, the assertion that kingdoms are usually a better form of government than city-states, and the insistence that the king is above the law.[11] Finally, for all its profane trappings, the *De regimine*'s primary goal was the formation of a Christian prince.[12]

Given the incomplete state of scholarship on *De regimine*'s textual history, the brief overview that follows attempts no more than to trace the barest outlines of its trans-mission and use in the pan-European context. A handful of surviving manuscripts dated or dateable to the late thirteenth century show that the propagation and diffusion of *De regimine*, both in Latin and the vernacular, started shortly after Giles had finished it. The earliest extant manuscript, Dôle, Bibl. mun. 127, dated 1282, contains the French translation prepared at the request of Philip III by Henri de Gauchy, a canon of Saint-Martin, at Liège;[13] several other copies of this transla-tion were very likely produced before 1300, both in France and Italy.[14] Nor was the early vulgarization of the text limited to French, since by 1288 Gauchy's version had itself been translated into Italian.[15] The diffusion of the Latin original seems to have gotten off the ground right at the end of the thirteenth century, since very few Latin manuscripts can be securely dated much before 1300.[16]

During the first half of the fourteenth century, however, the production and dis-semination of Latin copies increased precipitously, thanks in large part to the agency of the university book trade. Fifteen manuscripts bear marks of having been copied from pecia exemplars provided by university stationers.[17] The pecia system was in use at several universities in the first half of the fourteenth century. Nevertheless most of the *De regimine* pecia copies probably descend from Parisian exemplars, since almost all the manuscripts originated in France (though one, Bibl. Apost. Vat. Chig. B.V.68, is clearly in an Italian hand), and Toulouse, the only other French university besides Paris where the utilization of the pecia system has been

---

[11] Lambertini, "'Costruzione' dell'*Oeconomica*," pp. 357–66; Lambertini, "Egidio Romano lettore ed interprete della *Politica*," pp. 304–13, 316–25.

[12] Lambertini, "Il filosofo, il principe e la virtù," p. 279.   [13] Bruni, *Le opere*, p. 94.

[14] New York, Pierpont Morgan Libr. M. 122; BN fr. 1203 and fr. 24233 (both of Italian origin); Bibl. Apost. Vat. Ross. 457.

[15] Florence, Bibl. Naz. Centrale II, IV, 129 bears the colophon "Facto et compiuto mettedima XVI di digiugno en anno domini MCCLXXXVIII": Bruni, *Le opere*, p. 101. Another very early Italian version, dated *c.* 1300 is contained in BN it. 233.

[16] Bern, Burgerbibl. Bong. 182; Paris, Bibl. Mazarin 838, and BN lat. 15101 and lat. 15449 (both *c.* 1300); Bodleian Libr. Laud Misc. 702 (*c.* 1300); Troyes, Bibl. mun. 989 (1301); Bibl. Apost. Vat. Borgh. lat. 360 (*c.* 1300).   [17] Del Punta and Luna, *Catalogo*, pp. 341–50.

demonstrated, is far less likely than Paris to have been a major center of *De regimine*'s dissemination.[18] Fully ten of the manuscripts were derived from the so-called exemplar in forty-three peciae, and the other five manuscripts descend from at least three, and as many as five, other exemplars. The earliest copies from each of these exemplars have been assigned dates ranging from *c.* 1300 to about 1350.[19] The exemplar in forty-three peciae was in circulation by 1304, in which year it is listed among the books of philosophy that stationers were expected to make available to scholars studying at Paris.[20] By the beginning of the fourteenth century, then, *De regimine* had become a textbook for the arts curriculum at Paris, whose stationers responded by creating several pecia exemplars, which in turn promoted the use of the text.[21]

Nevertheless, the many early Latin copies that bear no pecia marks are evidence that the avenues and nodes of diffusion quickly spread beyond the confines of the quarters of the Paris stationers. Dated manuscripts of Italian origin survive from 1310, 1317, and 1318.[22] The text had very likely reached England no later than 1313, when Bishop Ralph de Baldock of London bequeathed a copy of *De regimine*, which he may well have obtained on the continent, to his cathedral chapter.[23] The process of diffusion there had begun by the first quarter of the fourteenth century, to which period belongs the earliest copy of English origin. *De regimine* had probably reached Germany by the middle of the fourteenth century and was known in Spain by the 1340s, when it was translated into Castilian from the Latin.[24] The production of Latin copies throughout Europe increased during the second half of the fourteenth century. In the first half of the fifteenth century the rate of production in England, Germany, and the Iberian peninsula remained high or grew, while it fell off in Italy and France. The same decline occurred elsewhere in Europe beginning in the mid fifteenth century.[25]

Throughout the fourteenth and fifteenth centuries the universities and the book trade connected with them, at Paris and elsewhere, continued to play an important role in the propagation of the Latin *De regimine*. Several manuscripts bequeathed

[18] G. Pollard, "The *Pecia* System in the Medieval Universities," in *Medieval Scribes, Manuscripts and Libraries: Essays Presented to N. R. Ker*, ed. M. B. Parkes and A. G. Watson (London, 1978), p. 148.

[19] Del Punta and Luna, *Catalogo*, pp. 341–50.

[20] H. Denifle and A. Chatelain, *Chartularium Universitatis Parisiensis*, vol. II (Paris, 1891; reprint, Brussels, 1964), p. 111.

[21] On the pecia system at Paris, see Rouse and Rouse, *Authentic Witnesses*, pp. 259–338.

[22] Del Punta and Luna, *Catalogo*, p. xi.   [23] *BRUO* Appendix, pp. 2147–9.

[24] Berges, *Fürstenspiegel*, p. 325; Perez (ed.), *Glosa Castellana*, vol. I, pp. xxvi–xxvii.

[25] The estimates for England and Italy are the most reliable, being derived from my research and that of Del Punta and Luna (*Catalogo*, pp. x–xi). Somewhat less trustworthy are my estimates for France; I have been able to examine just under half of these, though Concetta Luna has kindly assisted me with the dating of most of the other manuscripts. The figures for Iberian and Central European libraries are the least reliable, as for these I have had to rely entirely on the work of Bruni (*Le opere*, pp. 92–5) and Zumkeller (*Manuskripte*, pp. 36–41).

by university alumni to the libraries of their cathedral chapters and collegiate churches bear the marks of having originally been produced for the university market.[26] Yet it must be remembered that in the medieval book trade the university environment was just part, albeit a very important part, of a complex pattern of exchanges and contacts within and between several other institutional structures. The Augustinian friars were particularly involved in copying, preserving, studying, and disseminating the *magnum opus* of their *Doctor Fundatissimus*. Not only did their libraries hold several copies, but two fourteenth-century Italian Augustinians, Bartholomeo da Urbino and Leonino da Padova, drafted abridgments of *De regimine*, while in England a number of Augustinians compiled or copied alphabetical indexes for use with the text.[27] In Germany, the Augustinians were responsible for preparing several translations for the nobility.[28] In the 1370s, Johann von Vippach, an Augustinian from Erfurt, composed the *Katharina divina*, an East Middle German mirror, largely derived from *De regimine*, for the margravine of Meisen, Katharina von Henneberg.[29] At about the same time, Friar Johann von Brakel of Osnabruck (d. 1385) made a Middle Low German translation, while an Austrian member of the order, probably Leopold of Vienna (d. 1385), prepared a version for either Albert III or Albert IV of Austria.[30] Other mendicant and monastic orders, however, also had a hand in these processes. Several manuscripts belonged to the Franciscans, Dominicans, Cistercians and Benedictines, with a much smaller number being found in the libraries of several other orders.[31]

[26] The evidence of the English manuscripts will be discussed in chapters 5 and 6 below. Two surviving continental examples are Bibl. Apost. Vat. Pal. lat. 727 (to Mainz Cathedral by 1479), Reims, Bibl. mun. 883 (to Reims Cathedral in 1471). This was probably also the case with two *De regimine* manuscripts, now lost, listed among the books of the collegiate church of Saint-Paul, Liège in 1460: A.-C. Fraeijs de Veubeke, "Un catalogue des manuscrits de la collégiale Saint-Paul à Liège au milieu du XVe siècle," *Revue d'histoire des textes* 4 (1974), pp. 387, 399.

[27] Toulouse, Bibl. mun. 740 and Bibl. Apost. Vat. Urb. lat. 1376 are both Augustinian manuscripts, and the scribe of BN lat. 10207 was an Augustinian as well. For Bartholomeo da Carusi (fl. s. xiv¹), see *Dizionario biografico degli italiani*, vol. VI, pp. 779–80; a manuscript of this abridgment has not been identified. Leonino da Padova's abridgment, made in the later fourteenth century, has been edited by H. Müller, "Aegidii Romani de regimine Principum libri III, abbreviati per M. Leoninum de Padua," *Zeitschrift für die gesamte Staatswissenschaft* 36 (1880), pp. 96–114, 568–78, 673–749. The involvement of the English Augustinians will be discussed below, pp. 100–3.

[28] For a general survey of the German aristocracy's literacy and its relationship with the clergy, in a slightly earlier period than this, see Green, *Medieval Listening*, pp. 204, 211–15, 222–5, 270–315.

[29] Menzel (ed.), *Die "Katharina divina"*, pp. 4–12.   [30] *ibid.*, p. 15.

[31] The English manuscripts belonging to these religious orders will be discussed in chapters 5 and 6 below. For manuscripts belonging to religious in Italy, see Del Punta and Luna, *Catalogo*, pp. xxxi–xxxii. In France, manuscripts belonged to the Victorines (BN lat. 15101) and Celestines (Paris, Bibl. de l'Arsenal 744) of Paris. The Cistercians of Cîteaux (Turin, Archivio di Stato J.a.VII.29), Clairvaux (Troyes, Bibl. mun. 989 and 1602), Cysoing (Lille, Bibl. mun. 321), Morimond (Besançon, Bibl. mun. 433) and Salvanes (Grenoble, Bibl. mun. 869) all had copies; so also did the Benedictines of Saint-Bertin (Saint-Omer, Bibl. mun. 517) and Saint-Denis (BN fr. 1201 belonged to Richard le Scot, one of the authors of the *Grandes chroniques de France*), and the Dominicans of Avignon (Avignon, Bibl. mun. 763, and possibly 764).

Moreover, the Dominicans Bartolomeo da San Concordio and Bartolomeo Capodilista prepared abridgments of *De regimine* to be utilized by their confreres.[32]

Like the universities, the papal curia furnished an important venue for the exchange and propagation of books. After writing *De regimine*, Giles himself had sojourned for extended periods there, both in Rome and in Avignon. During these times he no doubt kept his own copy with him, which he may have lent out for copying; he probably also presented a copy to the pope. One of the earliest Latin copies, Bibl. Apost. Vat. Borg. 360, resided in the papal library at Avignon.[33] In later years, ecclesiastical dignitaries and officials could have obtained copies of *De regimine* while on business at the curia. This appears to have been the case with the English cardinal Simon Langham, who, upon his demise at Avignon in 1376, had among his considerable possessions there a copy of *De regimine*, which his will directed to be left to Westminster Abbey, where he had formerly been abbot.[34]

Thanks to the agency of clerics who translated *De regimine*, the text experienced a less extensive but still considerable diffusion among the royalty and nobility. The early translations into French and Italian have already been mentioned. These, however, were only the first of many. Though Henri de Gauchy's was by far the most prolific of the French versions with its thirty-one extant copies, either of the full text or abridgments, others followed by a clerk named Guillaume, who may have been a Dominican friar, for a burgher of Orleans (c. 1330), by Gilles Deschamps (1420), and "par ung frere de l'ordre des freres Prescheurs par le commandement de tres puissent seigneur le conte Laval" (1444).[35] This profusion of copies and versions of the French *De regimine* shows how closely the French royalty and nobility identified with this text. The Capetians and their Valois successors continued to own and commission copies of *De regimine* in Latin and in the French translation of Henri de Gauchy. Indeed, from the middle of the thirteenth century, the rulers of France, joined in the fifteenth century by members of cadet branches of the royal family, seem to have made the composition, translation, and propagation, not to mention the reading of texts belonging to the mirrors of princes genre, of which *De regimine* was the most successful example, into what amounted to a matter of policy.[36] Louis X's widow, Clemencia of Hungary, owned a *De regimine* in French, and several copies, both inherited and newly made, were kept in the royal library at the Louvre during the time of Charles V and his succes-

---

[32] Bartolomeo da San Concordio's abridgment will be discussed in chapter 5. Nothing is known of Bartolomeo Capodilista, beyond the ascription to him of the abridgment found in Reims, Bibl. mun. 884.   [33] Del Punta and Luna, *Catalogo*, p. xxxii.   [34] See below, p. 106.

[35] The manuscripts of the French translations are listed in Appendix C. Each of the three later translations is represented by a single manuscript, respectively Paris, Bibl. de l'Arsenal 2690, London, BL Egerton 811, and Bibl. de l'Arsenal 5062. These are briefly discussed in Berges, *Fürstenspiegel*, pp. 321–2; and Genet (ed.), *Four English Political Tracts*, p. x.

[36] Genet (ed.), *Four English Political Tracts*, pp. xii–xv.

sor.[37] Copies could also be found in the libraries of the Valois Philip the Bold of Burgundy and his wife Margaret, John duke of Berri, Charles d'Orléans, and a duke of Bourbon, probably Peter II.[38] A beautiful illuminated French translation belonged to Beraud III, count of Sancer, while another decorated French manuscript bears an inscription of the count of Mortain.[39] Nor does *De regimine*'s utility seem to have been exhausted in these circles at the end of the fifteenth century, as the royal counselor Jean Budé commissioned an abridgment of it for his personal library.[40]

Several French *De regimine* manuscripts made their way into the libraries of English kings and nobles, and this may partially explain why the English translation which the secular clerk John Trevisa made *c.* 1400 for his patron Thomas Lord Berkeley never flourished.[41] The demand for *De regimine* in Italy and Germany was also considerable. Five more Italian versions would appear before the end of the Middle Ages, and between the early fourteenth and early fifteenth centuries a total of six German versions in almost as many dialects would be produced.[42] In the Iberian kingdoms, *De regimine* was first vernacularized in the 1340s in a Castilian version by the Franciscan Juan Garcìa de Castrojeriz, who also prepared an extensive vernacular commentary. Castrojeriz was working under the commission of Bernabé, bishop of Osma, who presented the translation and commentary to the infante, Pedro the Cruel.[43] This version survives in some nine manuscripts and was printed at Seville in 1494.[44] A letter of the Aragonese infante, Juan, written in 1381, records a Catalan translation commissioned by the count of Urgel. This can probably be identified with the translation by the Carmelite friar Arnau Stanyol which survives in an incomplete copy, now in the Escorial, and was printed at Barcelona in 1498.[45] The existence of a Portuguese version is rendered problematic by the

---

[37] L. Douët d'Arcq (ed.), *Nouveau recueil de comptes de l'argenterie* (Paris, 1874), p. 64 (Clemencia of Hungary). Nine copies are listed among the books of the royal library: Delisle, *Recherches*, pt. 2, pp. 87–8.

[38] P. M. de Winter, *La bibliothèque de Philippe le Hardi, Duc de Bourgogne (1364–1404)* (Paris, 1985), pp. 23, 42, 50, 152, 289. H. de Beauvoir (ed.), *La librarie de Jean duc de Berry au Chateau de Mehun-sur-Yevre, 1416* (Paris, 1860), p. 42. Charles d'Orléans had a French *De regimine* in his library by 1440 (Green, *Poets and Princepleasers*, p. 140) and received a second Latin copy (BN lat. 6695) in 1445 from the abbot of Saint-Aurelian, Epernay. The duke of Bourbon's manuscript is BN lat. 6482.

[39] The manuscripts are, respectively, BN fr. 1202 and fr. 581.

[40] BN lat. 6697. This book was copied for Budé sometime between 1483 and 1487: M.-C. Garand, "Les copistes de Jean Budé (1430–1502)," *Bulletin de l'Institut de Recherche et d'Histoire des Textes* 15 (1967–68), pp. 293, 304, 307–8. [41] This will be discussed in considerable detail in chapter 4.

[42] For the Italian translations, see Bruni, *Le opere*, pp. 101–4; Bruni failed to mention an earlier copy of the sixth translation he discusses. This is BN it. 233, a late thirteenth-century translation directly from the Latin that in the fourteenth century belonged to Niccolo Pallavicini. By the fifteenth century, Latin copies were also kept in the libraries of the dukes of Milan (BN lat. 6477) and Aragonese kings of Naples (BN lat. 10107). The German translations are listed in Störmer (ed.), "Der ostmitteldeutsche Traktat," p. 197. [43] Perez (ed.), *Glosa Castellana*, pp. xxvi–xxix.

[44] *ibid.*, pp. xxx–xxxvi; Bruni, *Le opere*, pp. 96–7.

[45] Berges, *Fürstenspiegel*, pp. 324–5; Bruni, *Le opere*, p. 97.

want of even a single extant manuscript. Nevertheless, the chronicler Ruy de Pina attested that a member of the royal family, Don Pedro, made such a translation; and the record of a *De regimine* "em vulgar" in the library of King Duarte I (1433–8) seems to verify Pina's report.[46] A Flemish abridgment appeared in the first half of the fourteenth century, while a portion of Giles's mirror was even translated into Hebrew.[47]

Given the considerable diffusion of *De regimine* among both clerical and noble readers, it is not surprising to find a number of references to and echoes of this text in late medieval political literature. Already in the early fourteenth century, Dante in the *Convivio* mentions the first part of the *De regimine* in the same breath with Cicero and Virgil, and the Italian jurist Bartolus of Sassoferrato cites Giles in his *De regimine civitatis*.[48] A few years later, in the *Libro de los Estados* Juan Manuel recommended the reading of *De regimine* to those trying to distinguish the difference between monarchy and tyranny; it also seems likely that another fourteenth-century Castilian political work, the *Castigos e documentos del rey don Sancho* also borrowed from Giles.[49] The work most heavily indebted to *De regimine*, however, was the anonymous *Avis aux roys*, written for the Valois court around the middle of the fourteenth century, which "ne paraît être qu'une reprise du traité de Gilles de Rome."[50] In the later fourteenth and fifteenth centuries, Honoré de Bouvet, Philippe de Mézières, Christine de Pizan, and Jean de Gerson either drew material from or cited *De regimine* as required reading for the well-tutored prince.[51] Beyond the confines of the French royal court, the Castilian Pedro López de Ayala recommended reading "Egidio el romano, omne de grant saber / in regimini principum," a course that Thomas Hoccleve in the *Regement of Princes* assumed Henry, the prince of Wales, had already taken by 1411.[52] And though they do not cite *De regimine* explicitly in their works, both Nicholas of Cusa and Guillaume Fillastre kept copies of it.[53]

For a number of reasons, then, *De regimine* became, as Wilhelm Berges has put

---

[46] Berges, *Fürstenspiegel*, p. 325.

[47] Auweele, "Un abrégé flamand," pp. 339–41; Bruni, *Le opere*, pp. 86, 96.

[48] Dante, *Convivio*, IV, 24, quoted in Perez (ed.), *Glosa Castellana*, p. xix. For Bartolus and *De regimine*, see H. G. Walther, "'Verba Aristotelis non utar, quia ea iuristae non saperent.' Legistische und aristotelische Herrschaftstheorie bei Bartolus und Baldus," in *Das Publikum politischer Theorie im 14. Jahrhundert*, ed. J. Miethke (Munich, 1992), p. 119.

[49] Perez (ed.), *Glosa Castellana*, p. xxiii; H. L. Sears, "The *Rimado de Palaçio* and the 'De regimine principum' Tradition of the Middle Ages," *Hispanic Review* 20 (1952), p. 22.

[50] D. M. Bell, *L'Idéal éthique de la royauté en France au Moyen Age* (Geneva and Paris, 1962), p. 61.

[51] Bell, *L'Idéal éthique*, pp. 79, 93, 116, 122, 139; *The Tree of Battles of Honoré Bonet*, ed. G. W. Coopland (Liverpool, 1949), p. 61.

[52] Perez (ed.), *Glosa Castellana*, p. xxiii; *Hoccleve's Works, The Regement of Princes*, ed. F. J. Furnivall, EETS, extra ser. 72 (1897), pp. 77–8.

[53] For Cusa's glosses on *De regimine*, see Berges, *Fürstenspiegel*, p. 37. By 1412 Fillastre owned Bartolomeo Capodilista's *De regimine* abridgment in Reims, Bibl. mun. 884.

it, "der am weitesten verbreitete abendländische Fürstenspiegel und überhaubt eines der meistgelesenen Bücher des späten Mittelalters."[54] There was its own inherent utility and appeal, which probably resulted in large part from its successful assimilation of Greek thought with the ideology of the later medieval lay and clerical elites, coupled with its early placement in three of the most fertile sites of textual propagation and literary patronage in the West: the University of Paris, the Capetian court, and the papal curia. But these, of course, are only the broad outlines of this story in which *De regimine* plays the protagonist.[55] Now it is time to unpack the evidence of the manuscripts and texts of *De regimine*, and then situate these same books and their contents in their proper historical context, for only after having done so can the story be fully comprehended.

[54] Berges, *Fürstenspiegel*, p. 211.
[55] On the notion of the text as the protagonist in history, see Rouse and Rouse, *Authentic Witnesses*, p. 1.

2

Books, contents, uses

In the dedicatory prologue Giles explains that in response to Philip's request he has written his "book on the education of princes or rule of kings in order that you might be mighty in natural rule, having the more diligently considered governing the realm in accordance with reason and law."[1] On the face of it, then, the *De regimine* was first and foremost a book for kings and princes. And so it was. But a short time later Giles points out that the text's utility was not limited to a royal audience, since "although this book is entitled On the Education of Princes, nevertheless the entire populace can be educated by it; for despite the fact that not just anyone can be a king or a prince, each person should nevertheless make great efforts to be such a one as would be worthy to rule a kingdom or principality."[2] The large number of surviving manuscripts suggests Giles's words here were premonitory in so far as his manual would be read by an audience that extended far beyond the circle of kings and princes. While one must bear in mind the several factors that urge caution when reckoning a medieval text's popularity based on the total number of surviving manuscripts, the approximately 350 extant copies of *De regimine* can be favorably compared with the survivals of other mirrors of princes, like the *De regimine principum* of Thomas Aquinas and Ptolemy of Lucca (twenty-seven MSS), the *De morali principis instructione* of Vincent of Beauvais (Berges lists three MSS, "among others"), or the anonymous *Liber de informatione principum* (six MSS), later translated into French for King Charles V by Jean Golein (ten MSS).[3]

One work of advice for princes, however, did far outstrip the *De regimine* in

---

[1] "[U]t de eruditione principum, sive de regimine regum, quendam librum componerem, quatenus gubernatione regni secundum rationem et legem diligentius circumspecta polleretis regimine naturali": *DRP* prol.

[2] "Nam licet intitulatus sit hic liber de eruditione principum, totus tamen populus erudiendus est per ipsum. Quamvis enim non quilibet possit esse rex vel princeps, quilibet tamen summopere studere debet, ut talis sit, quod dignus sit regere et principari": *DRP* 1.1.1.

[3] Thomas Aquinas, *On Kingship to the King of Cyprus*, trans. G. B. Phelan and I. T. Eschmann (Toronto, 1949; reprint, 1982), p. xxii; Berges, *Fürstenspiegel*, pp. 306–7, 336–7.

popularity, this being the pseudo-Aristotelian *Secretum secretorum*, extant in some 600 Latin copies, as well scores of copies in vernacular translations.[4] There were several reasons for this. To begin with, the *Secretum secretorum* had more time to proliferate, since it was first translated from Arabic into Latin in the twelfth century, long before the composition of *De regimine*, while a second translation was made in the first half of the thirteenth century. Second, it was much shorter than *De regimine*, and thus could be copied much faster and more cheaply, especially given that a large percentage of *Secretum* copies are abridgments. Moreover, there is the varied contents of the *Secretum*, which ranges from ethical and political advice, to prescriptions for diet and hygiene, to astrological lore.[5] And finally, of course, the work was purported to be a letter from Aristotle, the prince of the philosophers, to Alexander the Great, one of the medieval West's paragons of ancient pagan kingship and knighthood.[6]

DATES AND PLACES OF ORIGIN

If the total number of manuscripts speaks volumes about the degree to which *De regimine* succeeded in proliferating, the patterns of its reception, transmission, and use will begin to appear upon closer examination of the manuscripts' dates and places of production, and of their form and contents. The dates and origins of the sixty manuscripts of demonstrable pre-1530s English origin or provenance (hereafter referred to as the English Group) appear in tables 1 and 2.

Despite an unavoidable lack of precision in dating some of the manuscripts and the added problem of manuscripts lost owing to accidental or willful destruction, the overall pattern in the rate of production is clear. The distribution between manuscripts of English origin (in Latin, French, and Middle English) produced in the fourteenth and the fifteenth centuries is nearly even, with very few manuscripts from either end of the two-hundred year period, and a bulge in production running from the second half of the fourteenth through the first half of the fifteenth century. The most accelerated proliferation occurred in the half-century between 1380 and 1430, and the lowest rate of production can be assigned to the last fifty years of the fifteenth century. These trends in production can be related to both the supply of and demand for manuscripts. The earliest supply came from the continent, owing to the demand of a few English scholars and lay patrons. As more people and institutions became aware of the text and wanted access to it they made or ordered their own copies until there were enough of these in circulation and in

---

[4] C. B. Schmitt and D. Knox, *Pseudo-Aristoteles Latinus: A Guide to Latin Works Falsely Attributed to Aristotle before 1500* (London, 1985), p. 56.

[5] M. A. Manzalaoui (ed.), *Secretum Secretorum: Nine English Versions,* vol. 1, EETS orig. ser. 276 (1997), pp. ix–xlvi. [6] M. H. Keen, *Chivalry* (New Haven, 1984), p. 121.

Table 1. *Chronology of English Group MSS*

Fourteenth century	26	first quarter	4 (3 from France)
		first half	5 (2 from Italy)
		middle	3
		second half	6 (1 from France)
		last quarter	7
		unspecified	1
Fourteenth/fifteenth century	4		
Fifteenth century	30	first quarter	8 (1 from France, 1 from Germany)
		first half	13 (1 from France)
		middle	6 (1 from France)
		second half	1
		unspecified	2 (1 by Italian scribe with English decoration)

institutional libraries to satisfy the need, at which point the rate of production dropped off.[7] The virtual cessation of production in the last quarter of the fifteenth century was probably due to what became an oversupply of manuscripts in relation to demand, resulting from the shift toward a market for printed books, as well as changes in literary tastes and the academic curriculum.

The preponderance of manuscripts from France and Italy among the earliest copies of English provenance suggests that production there outstripped that of England during the half-century after the composition of *De regimine*. This is a sensible supposition, given that the text originated in France and that its author spent the remaining thirty-five years of his life either there or in Italy. An examination of the surviving Latin *De regimine* manuscripts of French and Italian origins bears out this suspicion (see table 3). Not only was the overall level of production higher (sixty-nine French and sixty-five Italian MSS versus forty-six Latin MSS of English origin) but the highest rates of production occurred earlier, that is from the late thirteenth through the middle years of the fourteenth century only, dropping off substantially after the turn of the fifteenth century.[8] Conversely, Zumkeller's ninety-one dated or dateable Latin manuscripts of German origin, or that are now in German and Central European libraries (some of which were probably imported from France and Italy), point to a pattern of production closer to that found in England, though peaking somewhat later, since at least sixty-five of the manuscripts, and possibly more, date from after *c.* 1390.[9]

[7] Cf. C. Bozzolo and E. Ornato, *Pour une histoire du livre manuscrit au Moyen Age* (Paris, 1983), p. 94.
[8] Del Punta and Luna, *Catalogo*, pp. x–xi, xxiv–xxv. The Latin manuscripts of French origin are listed below in Appendix B.
[9] Zumkeller, *Manuskripte*, pp. 36–41. A manuscript not listed by Zumkeller, Pierpont Morgan Libr. M. 123, was copied in Bohemia in 1412.

Table 2. *Dates and origins of English Group MSS*

Manuscripts	Date	England	France	Italy	Germany
Baltimore, Walters Art Gallery W. 144	xiv^1	*			
Bethesda, Nat. Libr. of Medicine 503	xiv^{ex}	*			
Cambridge Univ. Libr. Dd.3.47	xv^1	*			
Cambridge Univ. Libr. Ee.2.17	xv^{in}		*		
Cambridge Univ. Libr. Ff.3.3	xiv^{in}	*	*		
Cambridge Univ. Libr. Ff.4.38	xv^{med}	*			
Cambridge Univ. Libr. Ii.2.8	xv^{in}	*			
Cambridge Univ. Libr. Ii.4.22	xiv^2	*			
Cambridge Univ. Libr. Ii.4.37	xiv^1	*			
Cambridge Univ. Libr. Kk.2.11	xv^{in}	*			
Cambridge, Corpus Christi Coll. 283	xv^{in}	*			
Cambridge, Gonville & Caius Coll. 113/182	xv^1	*			
Cambridge, Gonville & Caius Coll. 508/387	xiv^{in}	*			
Cambridge, Jesus Coll. Q.B.9	xiv^2		*		
Cambridge, Pembroke Coll. 158	xv^1	*			
Cambridge, Peterhouse 208	xv^2	*			
Cambridge, Peterhouse 233	xiv^1			*	
Cambridge, St. John's Coll. A.12	xv^1	*			
Cambridge, Trinity Coll. B.15.20	xiv^2	*			
Canterbury Cath. Libr. B.11	xiv/xv	*			
Chicago, Univ. of Chic. Libr. 533–v	xiv^{in}	*			
Durham Cath. Libr. B.III.24	xiv^{ex}	*			
Durham Cath. Libr. B.IV.31	xiv^1			*	
Durham Univ. Libr. Cos. V.I.9	xiv^{ex}	*			
Edinburgh Univ. Libr. 106	xiv^{ex}	*			
Glasgow Univ. Libr. Ham. 141	xv^1		*		
Hereford Cath. Libr. P.V.7	xiv^{ex}	*			
London, BL Ar. 384	xv^1	*			
London, BL Roy. 4 D.iv	xv^1	*			
London, BL Roy. 5 C.iii	xv^{med}	*			
London, BL Roy. 6 B.v	xv^1	*			
London, BL Roy. 10 C.ix	xv^1	*			
London, BL Roy. 12 B.xxi	xv^1	*			
London, BL Roy. 15 E.vi	1445		*		
London, Lambeth Pal. Libr. 150	xiv^{med}	*			
London, Lambeth Pal. Libr. 184	1460–1	*			
London, Lambeth Pal. Libr. Arc. L.40.2/L.26	xv^1	*			
New York, Pierpont Morgan Libr. M. 122	xiv^{in}		*		
Oxford, All Souls Coll. 92	xv^{med}	*			
Oxford, Balliol Coll. 146a	xv^{in}	*			
Oxford, Balliol Coll. 282	xiv^{med}	*			
Oxford Bodleian Auct. F.3.2	xiv^2	*			
Oxford, Bodleian Auct. F.3.3	xiv^{med}	*			

Table 2. (*cont.*)

Manuscripts	Date	England	France	Italy	Germany
Oxford, Bodleian Bodl. 181	xv	*			
Oxford, Bodleian Bodl. 234	xiv^{ex}	*			
Oxford, Bodleian Bodl. 544	xv^{med}	*			
Oxford, Bodleian Bodl. 589	xv^{1}	*			
Oxford, Bodleian Digby 233	xv^{in}	*			
Oxford, Bodleian Hatton 15	xiv^{2}	*			
Oxford, Bodleian Laud misc. 645	xv^{in}	*			
Oxford, Bodleian Laud misc. 652	xiv/xv	*			
Oxford, Bodleian Laud misc. 702	xiii/xiv		*		
Oxford, Jesus Coll. 12	1416				*
Oxford, Lincoln Coll. Lat. 69	xv^{1}	*			
San Marino, Huntington Libr. EL 9.H.9	xiv^{2}	*			
Vatican, Bibl. Apost. Vat. Ottob. lat. 1102	xiv^{ex}	*			
Vatican, Bibl. Apost. Vat. Ottob. lat. 1166	xiv	*			
Vatican, Bibl. Apost. Vat. Ottob. lat. 2071	xiv/xv	*			
Verona, Bibl. Capitolare 234	xv	*		*	
York Minster Libr. XVI.D.5	xiv/xv	*			

For the most part, the reasons for these trends in production in England explain those in the rest of Europe. Of course the chief consumers of these Latin manuscripts would have been *litterati*, that is, those who could read Latin. Consequently most would have been clerics. As has already been mentioned in the introduction, several of the manuscripts produced during the first half of the fourteenth century were copied from pecia exemplars, and therefore would have been produced for a university audience. Thus, without having recourse to a single owner's inscription or contemporary library catalogue, one can surmise that during those years there was a significant demand for this text at Paris and perhaps at some other universities where the pecia system was employed. This further suggests that the reading of *De regimine* became related in some way to the university curriculum.

Such a circumstance would help explain the different chronologies of production in different parts of Europe. At Paris, where Giles taught as the Augustinians' regent master of theology during the later 1280s and perhaps into the early years of the next decade, *De regimine* became associated with the curriculum by *c.* 1300, and experienced its highest rate of production for a university audience over the next fifty or sixty years. The adoption of the text by students and faculty at the Italian universities seems to have occurred a bit later, since the highest rate of production there seems to have been during the middle to later years of the fourteenth century. These high rates of production in France and Italy during the fourteenth century,

Table 3. *Chronology of Latin MSS of French and Italian origin*

	France	Italy			France	Italy
Late thirteenth century	3	0				
Thirteenth/fourteenth century	4	3				
Fourteenth century	43	45		first quarter	5	3
				first half	12	5
				middle	2	1
				second half	6	5
				last quarter	1	5
				unspecified	17	26
Fourteenth/fifteenth century	1	0				
Fifteenth century	18	17		first quarter	0	2
				first half	8	2
				middle	1	3
				second half	0	5
				last quarter	2	2
				unspecified	7	3

followed by the precipitous decline in the fifteenth, are particularly striking when one recalls that, in France at least, overall levels of book production increased dramatically at the beginning of the fifteenth century, after a long trough in production during the middle fifty years of the fourteenth century brought about by a glut of thirteenth-century academic and religious books coupled with severe demographic, political, and economic crises.[10] In England the text's use at the universities seems to have begun during the second quarter of the fourteenth century, though its more general use had to wait until the second half of the century. In Germany and Central Europe the increase in numbers of copies of *De regimine* can be directly linked to the chronology of university foundations. Two fourteenth-century copies are now in Prague (university founded 1347), four are in Vienna (university founded 1365); and at Crakow (university founded 1364, re-established 1397) all six of the *De regimine* manuscripts in the present-day cathedral and university libraries were copied in the fifteenth century. In general, the later dates of the manuscripts in the German and Central European libraries can reasonably be tied to the later founding of universities there, most of which did not come into being until the fifteenth century.[11]

The role of France, and especially of Paris, in the proliferation and dissemination of manuscripts was not only limited to *De regimine*'s early years. Several of the Latin copies now in England and Italy can be assigned a French origin, and many of these

[10] Bozzolo and Ornato, *Pour une histoire*, pp. 85–98.
[11] H. de Ridder-Symoens (ed.), *A History of the University in Europe* (Cambridge, 1992), pp. 62–5.

date to the second half of the fourteenth or to the beginning of the fifteenth century. This is also true of the French translations, three of which were acquired by Englishmen during the fifteenth century.[12] Conversely, foreign-produced copies of *De regimine* are virtually absent from the collections of French libraries today; and almost all the few that are there did not arrive until after the end of the Middle Ages. The few manuscripts that did make their way to France are of Italian origin. None comes from England or Germany. France, then, was and continued to be the principal *fons et origo* of *De regimine* manuscripts, followed by Italy. England, the lands to the east of France, and presumably Spain, on the other hand, were consumers of some of these French and Italian products, but then established their own native manuscript traditions.

SIZE AND MATERIAL SUPPORT

The form of surviving manuscripts is a useful guide to their intended use. Here I define form as a combination of the size, composition, and quality of a manuscript's material support, as well as the quality of its workmanship. Large books imply some sort of ceremonial function or the desire on the part of the patron to impress those who beheld them, medium-sized books can often be associated with university and communal libraries, while small volumes suggest personal, private use. The quality of script, and extent and quality of illumination also provide a good measure of what would have originally been expected of a manuscript book. In the case of the *De regimine*, the form of the Latin copies suggests that for the most part they were made for the communal or private use of scholars, whereas, not surprisingly, that of the vernacular copies is more consonant with books produced for the upper ranks of lay society.

This can be illustrated by looking at the formal characteristics of size (dimensions and height + width), material support, and illumination of the sixty manuscripts in the English Group (see table 4). The manuscripts' mean size in height + width is 503 mm. Thirty-six of the manuscripts fall below this average and twenty-four above it, yet the dimensions of the great majority of them do not vary greatly from it. Just over half have a height + width that ranges within 100 mm of the mean (24 MSS > avg. − 50 mm, 7 MSS < avg. + 50 mm), while fully three-quarters fall within 200 mm (28 MSS > avg. − 100 mm, 17 MSS < avg. + 100 mm). Thus most of the manuscripts approximate each other in size, with the greater number being somewhat smaller than the average. To put it another way, most of the manuscripts are of a size consonant with use at a desk or lectern and storage in a bookpress, i.e.

---

[12] A fourth which has not been included in this study, BL Harley 4385, an early fourteenth-century *de luxe* copy of Henri de Gauchy's translation, may also have come to England in the fifteenth century. Its earliest attested English owner was Elizabeth I's principal secretary William Cecil, Lord Burghley.

communal use in institutional libraries. A comparison of the dimensions of these manuscripts with those of the books of philosophy and theology produced for a university audience surveyed by Destrez bears this out, since thirty-seven have a height that falls within his range of 280–360 mm.[13] As for the books of the English Group whose size falls at the extremes, the very smallest were likely originally produced for individual use.[14] At the other extreme, the three largest books have dimensions substantially greater than the average, and are adorned with rich illumination and fine display scripts; two of them are in the vernacular.[15] They bear, then, all the marks of being expensive *de luxe* manuscripts prepared for wealthy lay readers, which indeed they were.[16]

The relative quality of a manuscript's parchment is usually commensurate with the quality of the book's other formal characteristics. Thus books treated in this study that use poor parchment are usually not illuminated and are written in highly current scripts, while those that are composed of high-quality vellum are often sumptuously illuminated and written in display scripts. In this sense, then, the quality of parchment tends to confirm what is already evident from other features of our manuscripts but offers little else, at least to someone as inexpert as I am in scientific codicology. There is, however, also the matter of the incidence of paper versus parchment manuscripts. On the one hand, the choice of paper or parchment in itself tells us little beyond the fact that both materials were available to those that made the book, since both fine and humble workaday books could be made from the same paper stocks. On the other hand, watermarks on paper can be used to help date and locate a manuscript's origin, while tracing changes in the ratio of paper to parchment books can elucidate the relative abundance or scarcity of paper in a given place. It has long been known that in the later Middle Ages England lagged well behind the rest of Europe in the manufacturing of paper, a state of affairs very evident in our manuscripts.[17] Whereas only three manuscripts of English origin are composed of paper, of the twenty-two Latin *De regimine* manuscripts of French origin conserved in the Bibliothèque Nationale in Paris, eight are made of paper. Looked at in another way, only one of the fifteenth-century Latin *De regimine* copies in the Bibliothèque Nationale is written on parchment. Thus in the fifteenth century paper virtually replaced parchment as the preferred material for making Latin *De regimine* manuscripts in France, while parchment continued its reign in England.

[13] J. Destrez, *La pecia dans les manuscrits universitaires du XIIIe et XIVe siècles* (Paris, 1935), p. 89.

[14] The three smallest are Bodleian Bodl. 544; Bibl. Apost. Vat. Ottob. lat. 1166; and Bodleian Laud Misc. 702.   [15] BL Roy. 15.E.vi; Lambeth Palace Libr. Arc.L.40.2/L.26; Bodleian Digby 233.

[16] See below, pp. 65–6, 68–70.

[17] L. Febvre and H.-J. Martin, *The Coming of the Book: The Impact of Printing, 1450–1800*, trans. D. Gerard (London and New York, 1990), pp. 30–43.

Table 4. *Formal characteristics of English Group manuscripts*

Manuscripts	Dimensions (mm)	Height + Width (mm)	Support	Illumination
Baltimore, Walters Art Gallery W. 144	300 × 205	505	parchment	illustration
Bethesda, Nat. Libr. of Medicine 503	275 × 185	460	parchment	illustration
Cambridge Univ. Libr. Dd.3.47	270 × 185	455	parchment	
Cambridge Univ. Libr. Ee.2.17	280 × 210	490	mixed	illustration
Cambridge Univ. Libr. Ff.3.3	295 × 205	500	parchment	illustration
Cambridge Univ. Libr. Ff.4.38	260 × 185	445	parchment	
Cambridge Univ. Libr. Ii.2.8	335 × 230	565	parchment	decoration
Cambridge Univ. Libr. Ii.4.22	290 × 190	480	parchment	
Cambridge Univ. Libr. Ii.4.37	255 × 190	445	parchment	
Cambridge Univ. Libr. Kk.2.11	265 × 200	465	parchment	
Cambridge, Corpus Christi Coll. 283	260 × 185	445	parchment	illustration
Cambridge, Gonville & Caius Coll. 113/182	263 × 185	448	parchment	
Cambridge, Gonville & Caius Coll. 508/387	285 × 200	485	parchment	
Cambridge, Jesus Coll. Q.B.9	245 × 170	415	parchment	illustration
Cambridge, Pembroke Coll. 158	360 × 250	610	parchment	
Cambridge, Peterhouse 208	290 × 200–10	490–500	mixed	
Cambridge, Peterhouse 233	225 × 160	385	parchment	
Cambridge, St. John's Coll. A.12	330 × 225	555	parchment	
Cambridge, Trinity Coll. B.15.20	285 × 205	490	parchment	decoration
Canterbury Cath. Libr. B.11	270 × 195	465	parchment	
Chicago, Univ. of Chic. Libr. 533–v	280 × 190	470	parchment	illustration
Durham Cath. Libr. B.III.24	335 × 235	570	parchment	decoration
Durham Cath. Libr. B.IV.31	295 × 190	485	parchment	
Durham Univ. Libr. Cos. V.I.9	290 × 190	480	paper	illustration
Edinburgh Univ. Libr. 106	300 × 195	495	parchment	
Glasgow Univ. Libr. Ham. 141	280 × 200	480	mixed	
Hereford Cath. Libr. P.V.7	330 × 240	570	parchment	
London, BL Ar. 384	225 × 160	385	parchment	
London, BL Roy. 4 D.iv	367 × 260	627	parchment	

London, BL Roy. 5 C.iii	330–5 × 230	560–5	parchment	
London, BL Roy. 6 B.v	300 × 215	515	parchment	
London, BL Roy. 10 C.ix	340 × 260	600	parchment	
London, BL Roy. 12 B.xxi	215 × 160	375	parchment	
London, BL Roy. 15 E.vi	470 × 330	800	parchment	illustration
London, Lambeth Pal. Libr. 150	285 × 205	490	parchment	
London, Lambeth Pal. Libr. 184	288 × 195	483	parchment	decoration
London, Lambeth Pal. Libr. Arc. L.40.2/L.26	405 × 275	680	parchment	decoration
New York, Pierpont Morgan Libr. M. 122	345 × 230	575	parchment	illustration
Oxford, All Souls Coll. 92	280 × 190	470	parchment	
Oxford, Balliol Coll. 146a	300 × 215	515	parchment	
Oxford, Balliol Coll. 282	305 × 205	510	parchment	
Oxford, Bodleian Auct. F.3.2	290 × 185	475	parchemnt	
Oxford, Bodleian Auct. F.3.3	305 × 190	495	parchment	decoration
Oxford, Bodleian Bodl. 181	300 × 205	505	parchment	
Oxford, Bodleian Bodl. 234	260 × 170	430	parchment	illustration
Oxford, Bodleian Bodl. 544	190 × 135	325	parchment	
Oxford, Bodleian Bodl. 589	235 × 135	370	parchment	
Oxford, Bodleian Digby 233	460 × 325	785	parchment	illustration
Oxford, Bodleian Hatton 15	350 × 230	580	parchment	
Oxford, Bodleian Laud misc. 645	360 × 250	610	parchment	decoration
Oxford, Bodleian Laud misc. 652	355 × 240	595	parchment	
Oxford, Bodleian Laud misc. 702	200 × 145	345	parchment	illustration
Oxford, Jesus Coll. 12	210 × 155	365	mixed	
Oxford, Lincoln Coll. Lat. 69	295 × 210	505	paper	
San Marino, Huntington Libr. EL 9.H.9	345 × 245	590	parchment	
Vatican, Bibl. Apost. Vat. Ottob. lat. 1102	300–4 × 205–10	505–14	parchment	decoration
Vatican, Bibl. Apost. Vat. Ottob. lat. 1166	198 × 135	330	parchment	
Vatican, Bibl. Apost. Vat. Ottob. lat. 2071	358 × 270	628	parchment	
Verona, Bibl. Capitolare 234	280 × 197	477	parchment	decoration
York Minster Libr. XVI.D.5	290 × 190	480	parchment	

ILLUMINATION

The total cost of a new manuscript book was the sum of the costs of the material and labor that went into making it. Some expenses were unavoidable: there had to be a writing surface as well as, of course, the writing itself, and often an exemplar had to be rented. Anything beyond this, in quantity or quality, materials or labor, was optional and, of course, would add to the overall cost.[18] The presence or absence of illumination, here defined as any kind of decoration or illustration above the level of rubrics and the basic colored initial, with or without flourishing, can serve as a rough indicator of a manuscript's original value, and thus of the patron's status as well as his or her intended uses.[19] Books purchased by university masters and students usually lacked illumination or were minimally adorned. Those destined for wealthy lay or ecclesiastical readers tended to be illuminated, often extensively.

Here it must be stressed that this treatment of illumination is based on a survey of 180 of the 350 estimated surviving manuscripts. Included are, on the one hand, the manuscripts I have personally examined, these being the sixty manuscripts of the English Group and another four manuscripts now in English libraries, as well as a further forty-four manuscripts conserved in French libraries; on the other hand are seventy-two of the Latin manuscripts in Italian libraries catalogued by Del Punta and Luna. Consequently, most of my conclusions are to some extent preliminary. This will be especially the case for the Latin copies in German, Central European, and Iberian libraries, which are entirely ignored here. The same holds true to a greater or lesser degree for all the vernacular traditions except the English. All the Spanish vernacular manuscripts have been excluded, as well as the manuscripts of three of the six German translations, and all but one of the Italian translations. Manuscripts of the French versions are much better represented, though even here I have only had the opportunity to examine twenty-one of the thirty-four extant copies. Still, while this survey misses several illuminated manuscripts, as well as possible lines of continuity in types of representation in the Spanish and German manuscripts, I am reasonably confident that the overall findings will still be valid. After all, most of the manuscripts not covered here are later copies, which makes it more likely that the visual representations found in them would have been drawn from the manuscripts that I have surveyed here.

[18] J. J. G. Alexander, *Medieval Illuminators and Their Methods of Work* (New Haven, 1992), pp. 36–7.

[19] English-speaking scholars are still hampered by the lack of an established terminology for the manuscript book. The French term for the basic black or colored initial is *initiale*, whereas an initial of the next grade above this, i.e. one "tracée sur un fond peint, qui sert d'encadrement, et rehaussé d'or ou d'argent" is called a *lettrine*. My definition of illumination includes all decoration from the *lettrine* to the most elaborate border, as well as illustration in the form of miniatures (including historiated initials), but excluding *figurae*, i.e. sketches in pen or pencil drawn into the margins by a scribe, *libraire*, or later reader: J. Lemaire, *Introduction à la codicologie* (Louvain-la-Neuve, 1989), pp. 186–91.

Viewed in aggregate, without regard to their language, the manuscripts of *De regimine* without illumination greatly outnumber those that have it. If, however, the Latin manuscripts are separated from those containing translations, the picture changes dramatically. Just over a third of the manuscripts of the English Group are illuminated, and only thirteen of these have miniatures; yet all seven of the vernacular copies are illustrated, whereas merely six of the fifty-three Latin copies are. A look at the manuscripts containing Latin and French copies in several continental libraries yields similar results. Only fifteen of the seventy-five Latin manuscripts in Italian libraries contain miniatures; and of the thirty-three Latin manuscripts in French libraries that I have had the opportunity to inspect, only eight are illustrated, though another five are adorned with some kind of decoration. On the other hand, nine of the ten copies of the French translation now conserved at the Bibliothèque Nationale and the Bibliothèque de l'Arsenal in Paris are illuminated, eight of them with miniatures. There is, then, a kind of inverse relationship between the Latin and vernacular manuscripts of *De regimine*, in so far as illumination is concerned. The patrons of vernacular manuscripts tended overwhelmingly to prefer illustrated copies of *De regimine*, while there was a tendency almost as pronounced to forgo such ornamentation among the readers of the Latin *De regimine*. Conversely, then, a vernacular manuscript without illumination may point to a different kind of reader than the norm, while ornate Latin copies may well have been destined for readers beyond the confines of the scholarly milieu. Nevertheless, one should keep in mind that at least in the case of the English Group manuscripts, the proportion of illuminated *De regimine* manuscripts is still quite high when measured against the overall proportion of illuminated manuscripts produced in late medieval England, which is estimated at one in forty for illustrated manuscripts and one in twenty for those with decoration alone.[20]

The decoration and illustration in the *De regimine* manuscripts vary considerably in quantity, quality, and iconography. Although the illumination of several individual manuscripts will be discussed in much greater detail in later chapters, it will be useful here to establish a basic taxonomy of illumination. To begin with, there is the basic distinction between manuscripts with decoration only and those with decoration and illustration. Among the manuscripts bearing decoration only there is a subcategory of books bearing coats of arms and other devices that were meant to identify a book's owner and/or donor. Since owners and donors were usually keen to make themselves known to readers immediately, their arms tend to appear right at the beginning of the book, on a frontispiece or the incipit page. Sometimes, however, a more ambitious program of coats of arms could be arranged in order to signify the familial and political relationships of the manuscript's owner.

---

[20] K. L. Scott, "Design, Decoration, and Illustration," in *Book Production and Publishing in Britain, 1375–1475*, ed. J. Griffiths and D. Pearsall (Cambridge, 1989), p. 31.

Illustrations played many roles in medieval manuscripts. They could, like coats of arms, identify an owner or donor. They also increased the value of a book, marked its textual divisions, and amused, delighted, and impressed the reader. But illustrations could in addition provide visual cues to and commentary on the text, thus influencing a reader's experience of it. And because these illustrations were designed to convey meaning, they can also help the modern scholar interpret how those readers read the text.[21] Kathleen Scott has demonstrated four principal types of pictorial matter used in late medieval English manuscripts. These are the "narrative" illustrations which depict an event or moment in the action of the text, the "utilitarian" pictures that provide visual descriptions and instructions, especially in technical and medical manuals, the "static" representations of the author of, or main actor in, the text, and the patron/original intended owner portrait.[22] Illustrations of another type, often found in French manuscripts, and usually in the form of personifications, serve, according to Claire Richter Sherman, as "visual definitions and re-presentations of abstract ideas." These are sometimes situated at the beginning of a textual division, to act as "laconic subject guides."[23] To these should be added a sixth type, which is in fact closely related and sometimes identical to Sherman's visual definition, and which I call "synoptic," that is, a miniature that conveys to the reader the main theme or subject of an entire text or some part thereof. In playing this role, the synoptic illustration is also intimately associated with the marking of textual divisions.

The illustrations in *De regimine* tend to fall into the static and synoptic categories. Whether a copy has one or several illustrations, the miniature on its opening page is without exception of the static type, and most frequently represents Giles presenting his book to a prince, whom the first sentence of the prologue identifies as Philip the Fair. Less commonly it depicts Giles alone, usually holding his book, or, even less frequently, just the prince. It should be pointed out, however, that the presentation scene probably originates from the original Latin copy, now lost, which Giles would have presented to Prince Philip. Here the presentation scene would also have functioned as an owner portrait. Indeed, thanks to the efforts of one skilled artist, it played this role once again in Besançon, Bibl. mun. 434, a copy of Henri de Gauchy's French translation of *De regimine* presented to Charles V of France in 1372. Although the presentation scene is utterly conventional in

[21] L. Lawton, "The Illustration of Late Medieval Secular Texts, with Special Reference to Lydgate's 'Troy Book'," in *Manuscripts and Readers in Fifteenth-Century England: The Literary Implications of Manuscript Studies*, ed. D. Pearsall (Cambridge, 1983), pp. 41–6.

[22] Scott, "Design," pp. 45–7, and K. L. Scott, "*Caveat Lector*: Ownership and Standardization in the Illustration of Fifteenth-Century Manuscripts," *English Manuscript Studies, 1100–1700* 1 (1989), pp. 19–63.

[23] C. R. Sherman, *Imaging Aristotle: Verbal and Visual Representation in Fourteenth-Century France* (Berkeley, 1995), p. 42.

composition, the features of the prince in the miniature are clearly those of Charles himself.[24]

In the typical presentation scene, Giles, wearing the habit of an Augustinian friar, and occasionally a bishop's miter as well, kneels or stands and presents his book to the prince, who is usually seated (plates 1 and 8).[25] And although most artists would have employed this illustration simply on account of convention and the models available to them, such a scene would still have had the power to authenticate the text by identifying it with its venerated author and with the prestige and authority of rulership. Giles's authority is particularly evident in a manuscript produced in Italy in the second half of the fourteenth century, where in place of the normal presentation scene one finds Giles standing at a lectern and reading from his book to an enthroned prince and a group of people, meant to represent the populace, who are seated between friar and prince on the ground.[26] Such a scene could have resulted from the conflation of the presentation scene with that found in another, and much earlier, manuscript of Italian origin, wherein Giles sits and lectures to a group of friars.[27] In both cases, the peculiar emphasis on Giles's authority could be the result of Augustinian involvement.[28] A much more frequent variation on the presentation theme is one wherein either Giles, the prince, or both are accompanied by members of their respective milieus – in Giles's case fellow Augustinians, and, in the prince's, members of the court.[29] There is a surprising amount of variation in these group scenes. For example, in BN fr. 19920 (fol. 2v), produced in the early fourteenth century, probably at Paris, a philosopher, who is presumably meant to represent Aristotle, presents the book to the prince, while Giles is relegated to the background. This is an interesting inversion of the central and authorial role Giles plays in the two Italian manuscripts just mentioned. Another kind of displacement occurs in BN fr. 213 (fol. 3), a manuscript produced at Paris in or shortly after 1469. Here Giles and the prince are both displaced, Giles

---

[24] Photo in J. Glenisson (ed.), *Le livre au Moyen Age* (Paris, 1988), p. 104.

[25] Baltimore, Walters Art Gallery W. 144, fol. 2; Besançon, Bibl. mun. 433, fol. 1, and 434, fol. 103; Durham Univ. Libr. Cosin V.I.9, fol. 2 (mitred Giles); New York, Pierpont Morgan Libr. M. 122, fol. 1 (mitred Giles); BL Harley 4385, fol. 1; Bodleian Bodl. 234, fol. 1 (standing prince), Digby 233, fol. 1, and Laud Misc. 702, fol. 2; Bibl. de l'Arsenal 2690, fol. 5 (mitred Giles); BN lat. 6477, flyleaf facing fol. 1 (F. Avril and M.-Th. Gousset, *Manuscrits enluminés d'origine italienne*, vol. II [Paris, 1984], p. 21; pl. X), lat. 18428, fol. 1; Toulouse, Bibl. mun. 741; Tours, Bibl. mun. 764, fol. 1. Illuminated manuscripts that have lost their original opening leaves, like Cambridge University Libr. Ee. 2.17 and Ff.3.3, and Jesus Coll. Q.B.9, may all originally have had an initial illustration of this type. This is also probably the subject of the badly damaged miniature at the beginning of Avignon, Bibl. mun. 763 (fol. 1). The eight manuscripts in Italian libraries that contain this scene are listed in Del Punta and Luna, *Catalogo*, p. xxx.   [26] BN lat. 10207, fol. 2.

[27] BN fr. 24233, fol. 1: Avril and Gousset, *Manuscrits*, p. 181; pl. CXXVII.

[28] The scribal colophon in BN lat. 10207 (fol. 198v) reads "Frater Augustinus Papiensis fuit scriptor libri presentis. Georgica natione atque heremitica [*sic*] religione."

[29] Arras, Bibl. mun. 586/688, fol. 1; BL Harley 4385, fol. 1; Bodleian Digby 233, fol. 1; BN fr. 573, fol. 195.

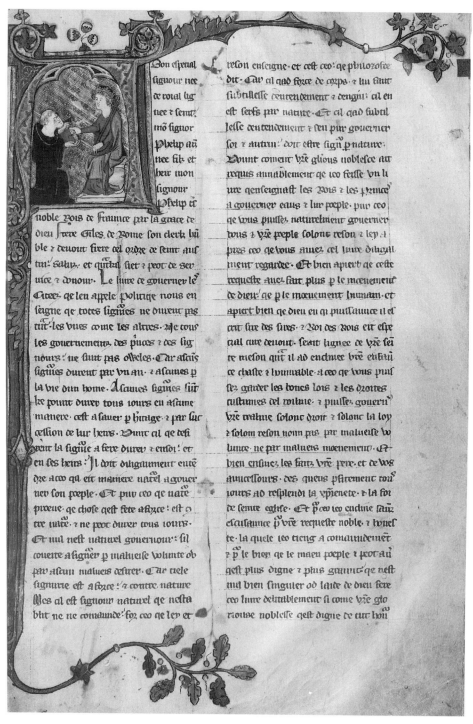

I Presentation scene. Baltimore, Walters Art Gallery, MS W. 144, fol. 2r

not being in the scene at all, while the central figure of authority is not a prince but rather the pope, on either side of whom are seated two royal personages; and all are surrounded by courtiers and servants.[30] In other cases there is no acknowledgment of Giles's membership in the Augustinian order, as for instance in BL Roy 15.E.vi (fol. 327) where the presenter of the book is clearly a layman (plate 2), and BN fr. 1202 (fol. 1) where a university master lectures to a prince and his court.

Sometimes, however, Giles appears alone, represented either as a simple friar or as a friar and bishop. I know of nine manuscripts that use this motif, seven of them Italian, and two English.[31] It could well be that one of the English copies (Nat. Libr. of Medicine, 503) was influenced by an Italian exemplar, since it belonged to an Augustinian convent, and the English Augustinians maintained close ties to their Italian counterparts.[32] Indeed the apparent emphasis on Giles's authority conveyed by this image suggests to me that the model, as well perhaps as several of the manuscripts, have an Augustinian origin. The other English manuscript, probably of Benedictine origin, is different enough from the Italian model to suggest that it may have derived its inspiration from another, perhaps English, model (plate 3).[33] Certainly the introductory miniature representing Giles alone began in Italy and largely remained there. I do not know of any manuscript of French origin wherein it occurs. It should further be mentioned that none of the manuscripts that contain this illustration appear to have been produced in the first few decades after *De regimine*'s composition, whereas the presentation scene can be found in the very earliest illustrated manuscripts.

Another introductory scene, depicting the prince alone, has a particularly intimate association with Italy. Both of the manuscripts in which it is found were illustrated in Italy, one very early (*c.* 1300) and the other in the second half of the fourteenth century. Yet the two are different enough that there does not appear to be any direct filiation. The earlier manuscript depicts a prince holding a book, while the figure in the latter, whose rich attire could signify either a prince or nobleman, neither wears a crown, sits upon a throne, nor holds a book.[34] A similar scene appears in one other manuscript produced in Italy, though at the beginning of the third book.[35] This manuscript is particularly interesting, because although it was almost certainly written and, a few years later, illustrated in Italy, it nevertheless

[30] BN MS fr. 213, fol. 3.

[31] Bethesda, Nat. Libr. of Medicine 503, fol. 1; Cambridge, Corpus Christi Coll. 283, fol. 1; BL Harley 3022, fol. 1. The remainder are listed in Del Punta and Luna, *Catalogo*, p. xxx.

[32] A. Gwynn, *The English Austin Friars in the Time of Wyclif* (London, 1940).

[33] The model could have been the author portrait, as seen in some late medieval English frontispiece miniatures: E. Salter and D. Pearsall, "Pictorial Illustration of Late Medieval Poetic Texts: The Role of the Frontispiece or Prefatory Picture," in *Medieval Iconography and Narrative: A Symposium*, ed. F. G. Andersen (Odense, 1980), pp. 115–16.

[34] BN n.a.l. 73, fol. 1; Bologna, Bibl. Universitaria 1512, fol. 1: Avril and Gousset, *Manuscrits*, p. 182; pl. CXXVIII; Del Punta and Luna, *Catalogo*, pp. xxx, 102.

[35] BN fr. 1203, fol. 93v. Avril and Gousset, *Manuscrits*, pp. 149–50; pls. CIV and CV.

2 Presentation scene. London, British Library, MS Royal 15.E.vi, fol. 327r

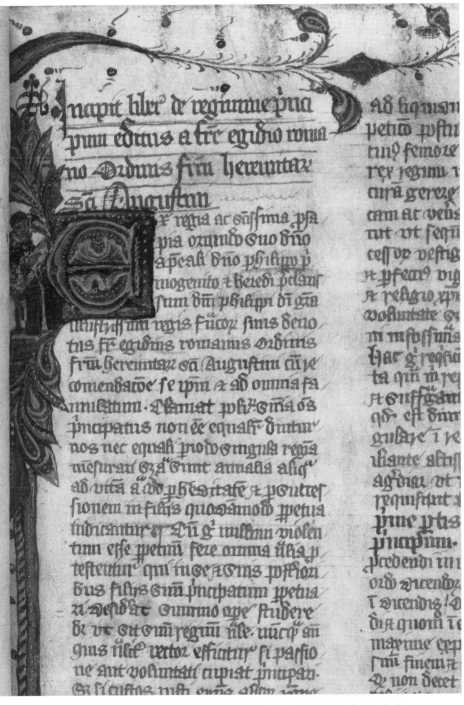

3 Author portrait in border beside initial. Cambridge, Corpus Christi College, MS 283, fol. 1r

contains one of the earliest copies of Henri de Gauchy's French translation. Very likely it was copied by a French scribe in Bologna, which would explain the French "look" of the script. Perhaps he had been commissioned by one of the many French scholars who studied and taught at Bologna in the late thirteenth century.[36]

Manuscripts with a single miniature far outnumber those with multiple illustrations. Moreover, just as the Latin manuscripts are far less likely than vernacular manuscripts to contain illumination, so too are they lacking in multiple illustrations. I know of only six Latin copies with multiple illustrations, two from France and four from Italy. None is related to another, and only three present a program of illustration that is related to the text.[37] Again one must turn to the vernacular manuscripts to find an abundance of illustrations. In them also, however, one observes considerable variety in the choice of subjects; likewise, no one program is exactly like any other. Nevertheless, some common traits can be observed in these manuscripts, both Latin and vernacular. First, there is some regularity in the number and placement of illustrations, with them often occurring either at the beginning of each of the three books, or each of the ten parts. Clearly, then, the illustrations function as markers of textual divisions.

Because there is so much variation in the subjects and programs of illustration, it seems likely that the teams of artisans who worked on these different manuscripts rarely, if ever, had the opportunity to consult other copies with multiple illustrations. Bereft of such models, the designers and artists of these manuscripts seem to have practiced two different strategies, sometimes within the same manuscript. On the one hand they could simply employ some stock scene which could be repeated over and over with just enough variation to distinguish one miniature, and thus one textual division, from another.[38] Or some attempt could be made to relate the subject matter of miniatures to the content of the textual divisions they introduced. Book 1, part 2, whose subject is the virtues, might be prefaced by a scene inhabited by personifications of the four cardinal virtues: prudence, justice, fortitude, and temperance.[39] The same strategy could also be used to introduce both of the next two parts, on the passions and on the habits associated with the different ages and stations of men.[40] Personifications are also used in one manuscript to signify the subject matter of the second and third parts of book 3, where the figure of a woman stands for peace and thus for the rule of the city in peacetime, and that of a knight symbolizes rule in time of war.[41] Very often miniatures depicting the management

---

[36] My thanks go to Patricia Stirnemann for her expert help with this manuscript. On French scholars in Bologna, see Ridder-Symoens (ed.), *History of the University*, pp. 286–7.

[37] Cambridge Univ. Libr. Ff.3.3; Florence, Bibl. Medicea Laurenziana S. Croce Plut. XVI sin. 11; Milan, Bibl. Ambrosiana I 194 inf.; BN lat. 6477, lat. 6482, and lat. 10207. Only the first three of these have illustration programs that are integrated with the text.

[38] See, for example, the miniatures accompanying the French *De regimine* translation in BN fr. 573.

[39] BN fr. 1202, fol 12.   [40] Bibl. de l'Arsenal 5062, fols. 58v, 71.

[41] Florence, Bibl. Medicea Laurenziana S. Croce Plut. XVI sin. 11, fols. 70v, 86v.

of the household and the instruction of children are associated with the textual divisions of book 2, which treats the various aspects of governing the family and household.[42] In the first two parts of the third book, where the focus is on the theory and practice of governing the city, it is common to find miniatures showing the prince in the city with his subjects, who are sometimes distinguished by their different ranks and occupations;[43] whereas the final part, on warfare, might depict the prince, or indeed Giles, with a group of knights.[44] These programs of illustration, however, could also be used to drive home some kind of message to the intended reader, through the repeated representation of some figure or figures accompanying the prince. This person could be Giles himself, a counselor, or a philosopher.[45] In all these cases it seems likely that the reader was being urged to pay close attention to advice given him by the book he was reading but also by wise counselors who had his/her interests at heart. On the other hand, the prince might repeatedly stand alone, his power and authority unmediated.[46]

It is little wonder that there is such diversity in these illustration programs. First, there is the scarcity of the manuscripts containing multiple illustrations, coupled with the variety in places and times of execution. And even when two or more manuscripts can be assigned roughly the same time and place of production, it is clear that they were executed neither by the same team of artisans nor for the same patron. One suspects, then, that more often than not the exemplars available to these artisans either had no illustration at all or, perhaps more frequently, had only the one presentation scene at the beginning of the text. Nevertheless, there are those rare instances when the same scene or scenes occur in the same place in different manuscripts. Two possible explanations for these convergences come to mind. For one thing, the topics of the different textual divisions often would have been clear enough and the probable choices of representational models limited enough to the designers of different illustration programs, that they might independently have chosen the same kinds of representational material. Indeed, most of the scenes that at first sight look so much alike, in fact contain enough small differences in their composition and details to quickly dispel any certainty of them having been derived from a common source.

[42] Baltimore, Walters Art Gallery W. 144, fols. 41v, 51v, 63v; Cambridge Univ. Libr. Ff.3.3, fol. 67; Florence, Bibl. Medicea Laurenziana S. Croce Plut. XVI sin. 11, fols. 34v, 45; BL Harley 4385, fols. 59v, 76v; Milan, Bibl. Ambrosiana I 194 inf., fol. 56; BN fr. 573, fol. 226, fr. 1202, fols. 59, 77v, 96, and it. 233 (Avril and Gousset, *Manuscrits*, p. 127; pls. I, LXXXIII, LXXXIV).

[43] Cambridge Univ. Libr. Ff.3.3, fol. 119v; BL Harley 4385, fol. 108v; Bodleian Digby 233, fol. 62; Bibl. de l'Arsenal 5062, fol. 168v; BN fr. 1202, fols. 112, 125, and it. 233, fol. 148.

[44] BL Harley 4385, fol. 149v; Milan, Bibl. Ambrosiana I 194 inf., fol. 86v; BN fr. 1202, fol. 157.

[45] BL Harley 4385; Bodleian Digby 233 (Giles and counselor/s); Baltimore, Walters Art Gallery W. 144 (philosopher).

[46] Though I have not seen the entire illumination program, this seems to be the message imparted by the four panels that introduce the French *De regimine* in Bibl. Apost. Vat. Ross. 457, fol. 1: Bruni, *Le opere*, p. 77.

There are three manuscripts, however, in which the similarities in one of the illustrations are so striking as to suggest some sort of affiliation, even if it is very likely a mediated one. It occurs in the miniature that introduces the second book in Walters Art Gallery W. 144 (fol. 41v), Cambridge Univ. Libr. Ff.3.3 (fol. 67), and BL Harley 4385 (fol. 59v). The central composition in each case shows a prince addressing his queen and their two children. This, in fact, is all one finds in Cambridge Univ. Libr. Ff.3.3 (plate 4), whose approximate date of production in the first quarter of the fourteenth century makes it the earliest of the manuscripts. The illustration in the Walters manuscript (plate 5), which dates from just a short time afterwards, is almost identical to its counterpart in Cambridge; the same prince addresses the same queen and two children, and all display the same gestures and expressions. The only differences are that the figure of a servant with a staff has been added to the scene in Walters, and the relative positions of the figures in the two miniatures are reversed as in a mirror's reflection. More differences have made their appearance in the much later Harley manuscript, which dates from the early fifteenth century. A tree has been inserted between the prince and a group composed of the queen, children, and servant, while the prince himself is accompanied by Giles and a counselor. The addition of the author and counselor was necessitated by the designer's overall program, rather than by his model, and the tree was probably included to set off and balance the two groups in the scene (and perhaps to suggest that the prince ought to keep counsel with Giles and his counselor, rather than with the queen, whose very femininity, as Giles makes pains to point out in the same book, renders her virtually incapable of giving sound counsel).[47]

The similarities between these three miniatures certainly suggest that they all derive from the same model, and that, indeed, elements tended to get added to the model over time. This model was probably of northern French origin, since Cambridge Univ. Libr. Ff.3.3 almost certainly was produced there, and Harley 4385 is undoubtedly Parisian. And though the Walters manuscript was produced by a group of artisans working in London, there is reason to believe that they were not ignorant of French models.[48] Yet because the iconographic commonalities do not extend beyond this one miniature, it is clear that none of these three manuscripts served as the model for another, nor did any of them share some other manuscript as exemplar. So, in the final analysis, the illustration programs in these manuscripts are marked by considerable variety, resulting on the one hand from the text's rapid and wide diffusion, and, on the other, from the relative scarcity and diverse conditions of production of manuscripts with multiple illustrations.

---

[47] *DRP* 2.1.23–4.   [48] See below, pp. 56–60.

4 *The prince governing his family. Initial to Cambridge, University Library, MS Ff.3.3, fol. 67r*

CONTENTS

If the physical aspects of the *De regimine* manuscripts furnish several clues as to their production, dissemination, audience, and use, a great deal can also be gleaned from their contents. The term "contents" is here taken to mean both the matter and structure of each of the texts of *De regimine* as well as the overall contents of each manuscript, or what might otherwise be called *De regimine*'s codicological situation. Beginning with the first kind of contents, we find that the texts fall into the following categories and sub-categories:

5 *The prince governing his family and a servant. Baltimore, Walters Art Gallery,
MS W. 144, fol. 41v*

I. Latin
   A. full text (including imperfect copies and fragments)
   B. ancillary apparatus to *De regimine* (either attached or detached from full text)
      1. chapter lists
      2. alphabetical indexes
   C. abridgments and extracts
   D. alphabetical compilation
II. Translations
   A. Castilian translation and commentary of Juan Garcia de Castrojeriz (1340s)
   B. Catalan translation of Arnau Stanyol (s. xiv²)
   C. English translation of John Trevisa (*c.* 1400)
   D. Flemish abridged translation (s. xiv¹)
   E. French translations
      1. full text
         a. trans. of Henri de Gauchy (1282)
         b. trans. and commentary of Guillaume (1330)
         c. partial trans. of Giles Deschamps (1420)
         d. trans. of anonymous Dominican (1444)
      2. abridgments derived from Gauchy's translation
   F. German translations
      1. lower Rhenish trans. derived from French trans. of H. de Gauchy (*c.* 1400)
      2. Middle Low German adaptation of Johann von Brakel (before 1385)
      3. Middle High German complete translation, entitled *Das Puech von der Ordnung der Fursten* (before 1412)
      4. East Middle German adaptation by Johann von Vippach, entitled *Katherina divina* (s. xiv^ex)
      5. East Middle German abridgment, inc. "Welch furste. . ." (s. xiv/xv)
      6. West Middle German trans. of *DRP* 3.1–2 and commentary on Aristotle's *Politics*, entitled *Van der Regeronge der Stede* (after *c.* 1375)
   G. Hebrew translation of *DRP* 2.1 (s. xiv)
   H. Italian translations
      1. anonymous trans. derived from Gauchy's French trans. (1288)
      2. trans. of Giovanni di Nicola da Guando, derived from Gauchy's French trans. (s. xv?)
      3. anonymous trans. derived from the Latin (*c.* 1300)
      4. anonymous trans. derived from the Latin (s. xiv)
      5. lost trans. attributed to Giuliano Giraldi
      6. trans. of *DRP* 3
   I. Portuguese translation, now lost (before 1438)

It is quite clear from this list that during the later Middle Ages the original Latin text of *De regimine* experienced modifications of many and varied kinds, being either added to, subtracted from, translated, adapted, or commented upon, or some combination of two or more of these. By far the largest number of manuscripts contain the full Latin text, sometimes accompanied by chapter lists and/or alphabetical indexes (for the distribution of texts in manuscripts of the English Group, see table 5). And with the sole exception of Henry de Gauchy's French translation, which survives in thirty copies of either its complete text or some abridgment thereof, none of the variants, apparatus, or translations exists in more than a handful of copies. Although several of these mutations of and apparatus to the text will be discussed in much greater detail in later chapters, I would here like to stress a couple of points. First, it should be apparent that the astonishing diversity of forms created by the readers of *De regimine* is testimony to its heavy use in different political, linguistic, institutional, and vocational spheres, which often partially overlapped or interpenetrated one another. The second point, which follows from the first, is that the variety of forms which the text would take over the course of two centuries both resulted from and contributed to different ways of reading *De regimine*.

The makers of books in the later Middle Ages often put several works into a single volume. This was a fortunate habit in so far as modern-day scholars are concerned, since the differing composition of texts within manuscripts suggests how medieval readers would have classified and used the individual components therein. Caution must, however, be observed when using this technique. One must avoid anachronistic judgments based on volumes assembled later than one's period of study; after all, a miscellaneous book whose disparate elements were brought together in the eighteenth century will not tell us much about the intentions of fourteenth-century readers. But the contents of manuscripts that have been integral since the Middle Ages can also deceive. A reader might bind several works together simply in order to save money and keep handy a group of texts he or she found particularly useful. Sometimes, moreover, the items in a manuscript would have been brought together purely by accident, their proximity being the result merely of a medieval librarian's desire to tidy up and preserve some loose gatherings.[49] Finally, one must not forget that the contents of a book might have been determined solely by the contents of its exemplar.

All that having been said, however, the many composite *De regimine* manuscripts do, on the basis of their contents, suggest that medieval readers tended to approach the text either as a mirror of princes and book of knighthood, as an Aristotelian commentary or compendium, or as a pastoral and preaching aid (for the manuscripts of the English Group, see table 6). The first of these classifications really comprises two separate but, in terms of medieval usage, closely related

---

[49] G. S. Ivy, "The Bibliography of the Manuscript-Book," in *English Library before 1700*, ed. Wormald and Wright, p. 55.

genres.[50] The term "mirror of princes" has been variously defined. Wilhelm Berges in his book on *Fürstenspiegel* applied a broad definition which included any work of advice for princes, while more recently Jean-Philippe Genet has imposed a more precise taxonomy that limits the term to works that were written for the most part by mendicant friars, frequently borrowing heavily from Aristotle, which aimed at the moral, ethical, and political instruction of royal or noble patrons. *De regimine* fits either of these definitions perfectly (Genet, in fact, predicates his in large part on Giles's work) and occasionally the composite manuscripts couple it with other mirrors. Five of the thirty-four composite manuscripts in the English Group combine *De regimine* with other works of advice for princes, loosely defined, and an identical number of Latin manuscripts in Italian libraries have such groupings.[51] Of course, it could be argued, albeit in a circular fashion, that the much larger number of manuscripts in which *De regimine* is the sole text could also be used as evidence for reading it as a mirror of princes.

Books of knighthood comprised all those texts that treated of the conduct of knights and the art or laws of war. Works falling into this category that were particularly popular and influential in the later Middle Ages were Ramon Lull's *Libre del ordre de cavayleria*, the *De re militari* of the Roman Flavius Vegetius Renatus, and Honoré de Bouvet's *Tree of Battles*.[52] The *De regimine* would, it seems, be a particularly good candidate for coupling with Vegetius, since most of its tenth and last part is drawn from his treatise on the art of war. And this was indeed the case among English readers, as witnessed by the seven manuscripts in which *De regimine* and the *De re militari* (or in one case Christine de Pizan's adaptation of it), appear together. Yet this practice seems largely to have been confined to English readers, since the combination is absent in the Latin manuscripts of Italian origin, and is found in but one of the forty-four manuscripts I inspected in French libraries.[53] The rarity of this particular coupling in the French manuscripts is particularly

[50] On the close relationship of these genres in terms of the perceptions and uses of late medieval English readers see Keen, *Chivalry*, p. 16; A. K. Ferguson, *The Indian Summer of English Chivalry* (Durham, N.C., 1960), pp. 193–4; and D. Bornstein, *Mirrors of Courtesy* (New York, 1975), p. 62.

[51] Only one of the manuscripts of the English Group (Cambridge Univ. Libr. Ii.4.22) couples *De regimine* with another princely mirror, as Genet defines it, this being Aquinas's *De regimine principum*. In another four, however, *De regimine* is bound with works of advice for princes like the *Secretum secretorum* or the pseudo-Bernard's *De modo rei familiaris* (Canterbury Cath. Libr. B.11; Oxford Balliol Coll. 146a, Bodleian Bodl. 181 and Laud Misc. 645). For the five Italian manuscripts, three of which conform to Genet's definition, see Del Punta and Luna, *Catalogo*, pp. xxvii–xxviii.

[52] On the popularity of Lull's *Libre* see Ferguson, *Indian Summer*, p. 110. The diffusion of Vegetius is found in C. R. Shrader, "A Handlist of Extant Manuscripts Containing the *De re militari* of Vegetius Renatus," *Scriptorium* 33 (1979), pp. 280–305. The *Tree of Battles*, written in 1387, influenced the works of several fifteenth-century writers, including Christine de Pizan and the author (probably William of Worcester) of the *Boke of Noblesse*: Bouvet, *The Tree of Battles*, ed. Coopland, pp. 15–25.

[53] For the English manuscripts, see table 6, pp. 48–9. The one manuscript in France is BN lat. 6476, which contains an abridged Vegetius.

Table 5. *Matter and structure of* De regimine *in English groups MSS*

Manuscripts	Full text	Index	Ch. list	Abridg.	Fr. full	Fr. abridg.	English
Baltimore, Walters Art Gallery W. 144	*				*		
Bethesda, Nat. Libr. of Medicine 503	*						
Cambridge Univ. Libr. Dd.3.47		*					
Cambridge Univ. Libr. Ee.2.17						frag.	
Cambridge Univ. Libr. Ff.3.3	imp.	frag.					
Cambridge Univ. Libr. Ff.4.38		*					
Cambridge Univ. Libr. Ii.2.8	*	*					
Cambridge Univ. Libr. Ii.4.22	*	*					
Cambridge Univ. Libr. Ii.4.37	*						
Cambridge Univ. Libr. Kk.2.11	*						
Cambridge, Corpus Christi Coll. 283	*	*					
Cambridge, Gonville & Caius Coll. 113/182	*		*				
Cambridge, Gonville & Caius Coll. 508/387	*						
Cambridge, Jesus Coll. Q.B.9	*						
Cambridge, Pembroke Coll. 158	*						
Cambridge, Peterhouse 208	*	*					
Cambridge, Peterhouse 233	*						
Cambridge, St. John's Coll. A.12	*						
Cambridge, Trinity Coll. B.15.20	frag.						
Canterbury Cath. Libr. B.11	*						
Chicago, Univ. of Chic. Libr. 533–v		*					
Durham Cath. Libr. B.III.24	*						
Durham Cath. Libr. B.IV.31	*						
Durham Univ. Libr. Cos. V.I.9		*			*		
Edinburgh Univ. Libr. 106							
Glasgow Univ. Libr. Ham. 141	*		*				
Hereford Cath. Libr. P.V.7	*			*		*	
London, BL Ar. 384							
London, BL Roy. 4 D.iv	imp.						

Manuscript							
London, BL Roy. 5 C.iii		*	*	*			
London, BL Roy. 6 B.v			*	*			
London, BL Roy. 10 C.ix	*	*	*				
London, BL Roy. 12 B.xxi				imp.			
London, BL Roy. 15 E.vi						*	
London, Lambeth Pal. Libr. 150	*						
London, Lambeth Pal. Libr. 184	*						
London, Lambeth Pal. Libr. Arc. L.40.2/L.26	*	*					
New York, Pierpont Morgan Libr. M. 122					*		
Oxford, All Souls Coll. 92	*	*					
Oxford, Balliol Coll. 146a	*	*					
Oxford, Balliol Coll. 282	*	*					
Oxford, Bodleian Auct. F.3.2	imp.						
Oxford, Bodleian Auct. F.3.3	*						
Oxford, Bodleian Bodl. 181	*						
Oxford, Bodleian Bodl. 234	*						
Oxford, Bodleian Bodl. 544	*	*					
Oxford, Bodleian Bodl. 589	*	imp.					
Oxford, Bodleian Digby 233	*						
Oxford, Bodleian Hatton 15							*
Oxford, Bodleian Laud misc. 645				*			
Oxford, Bodleian Laud misc. 652	*						
Oxford, Bodleian Laud misc. 702	*			*			
Oxford, Jesus Coll. 12				*			
Oxford, Lincoln Coll. Lat. 69	*	*					
San Marino, Huntington Libr. EL 9.H.9	imp.	*					
Vatican, Bibl. Apost. Vat. Ottob. lat. 1102	*						
Vatican, Bibl. Apost. Vat. Ottob. lat. 1166			*				
Vatican, Bibl. Apost. Vat. Ottob. lat. 2071	*	*					
Verona, Bibl. Capitolare 234	imp.	*					
York Minster Libr. XVI.D.5	imp.	*					
NUMBER OF MSS	43	23	6	6	3	3	1

Table 6. Contents of English Group MSS

Manuscripts	DRP only	De re militari	Moral phil./politics	Moral instruction	Miscellaneous
Baltimore, Walters Art Gallery W. 144	*				
Bethesda, Nat. Libr. of Medicine 503	*				
Cambridge Univ. Libr. Dd.3.47				*	
Cambridge Univ. Libr. Ee.2.17		*			
Cambridge Univ. Libr. Ff.3.3	*				
Cambridge Univ. Libr. Ff.4.38					*
Cambridge Univ. Libr. Ii.2.8			*		
Cambridge Univ. Libr. Ii.4.22			*		
Cambridge Univ. Libr. Ii.4.37	*			*	
Cambridge Univ. Libr. Kk.2.11	*				
Cambridge, Corpus Christi Coll. 283	*				
Cambridge, Gonville and Caius Coll. 113/182	*				
Cambridge, Gonville and Caius Coll. 508/387			*		
Cambridge, Jesus Coll. Q.B.9	*				
Cambridge, Pembroke Coll. 158			*		
Cambridge, Peterhouse 208			*		
Cambridge, Peterhouse 233	*				
Cambridge, St. John's Coll. A.12	*				
Cambridge, Trinity Coll. B.15.20	*				
Canterbury Cath. Libr. B.11	*				
Chicago, Univ. of Chic. Libr. 533–v	*				
Durham Cath. Libr. B.III.24			*		*
Durham Cath. Libr. B.IV.31	*				
Durham Univ. Libr. Cos. V.I.9	*			*	
Edinburgh Univ. Libr. 106					
Glasgow Univ. Libr. Ham. 141	*				*
Hereford Cath. Libr. P.V.7	*				
London, BL Ar. 384				*	

Manuscript					
London, BL Roy. 4 D.iv				*	
London, BL Roy. 5 C.iii			*	*	
London, BL Roy. 6 B.v				*	
London, BL Roy. 10 C.ix			*	*	
London, BL Roy. 12 B.xxi		*			
London, BL Roy. 15 E.vi		*			
London, Lambeth Pal. Libr. 150				*	
London, Lambeth Pal. Libr. 184					*
London, Lambeth Pal. Libr. Arc. L.40.2/L.26	*				
New York, Pierpont Morgan Libr. M. 122	*				
Oxford, All Souls Coll. 92	*	*			
Oxford, Balliol Coll. 146a			*		
Oxford, Balliol Coll. 282			*		
Oxford, Bodleian Auct. F.3.2		*			
Oxford, Bodleian Auct. F.3.3		*	*		
Oxford, Bodleian Bodl. 181					*
Oxford, Bodleian Bodl. 234	*				
Oxford, Bodleian Bodl. 544	*				
Oxford, Bodleian Bodl. 589	*				
Oxford, Bodleian Digby 233		*	*		
Oxford, Bodleian Hatton 15			*		
Oxford, Bodleian Laud misc. 645				*	
Oxford, Bodleian Laud misc. 652				*	
Oxford, Bodleian Laud misc. 702	*				
Oxford, Jesus Coll. 12					*
Oxford, Lincoln Coll. Lat. 69					*
San Marino, Huntington Libr. EL 9.H.9					*
Vatican, Bibl. Apost. Vat. Ottob. lat. 1102	*				
Vatican, Bibl. Apost. Vat. Ottob. lat. 1166	*				
Vatican, Bibl. Apost. Vat. Ottob. lat. 2071	*			*	
Verona, Bibl. Capitolare 234	*				
York Minster Libr. XVI.D.5	*				
NUMBER OF MSS	25	7	13	12	9

interesting, since two of seven manuscripts in the English Group were made in France for English patrons.[54]

The *Ethics* and *Politics* were prescribed texts in the curriculum for the master of arts degree at medieval universities, and their study was marked by the production of a plethora of commentaries, *questiones*, digests, and indexes designed to help scholars access and understand their doctrine.[55] The frequent combination of *De regimine* with abridgments or extracts of the *Ethics* and *Politics* as well as with their ancillary texts strongly suggests that Giles's mirror was also used as a commentary on and compendium of Aristotle's moral philosophy.[56] Judging by the contents of composite manuscripts, the English again appear to have had a particular predilection for using *De regimine* in this way, since such combinations occur in twelve manuscripts of the English Group (table 6), but in only three of the Latin manuscripts in Italian libraries and one of the manuscripts I looked at in France.[57] One must, of course, bear in mind that the contents of composite manuscripts are but one gauge of a text's usage. Other kinds of evidence, like the several abridgments of *De regimine* produced in France and Italy that go by such titles as *Compendium moralis philosophie* or *Memoriale regiminis hominis secundum philosophiam moralem*, suggest that though *De regimine* may have experienced particularly heavy use among scholars at England's universities, it was by no means ignored by those in Italy and France.[58]

Arts graduates who moved on to the course in theology continued to study moral philosophy as part of their training in moral or practical theology.[59] And if the aim of their studies in the arts curriculum was to learn, understand, and correct the lore of the ancients, their goal as theologians was to apply what they had appropriated from these pagans to the care of Christian souls. More often than not *De regimine* is situated in manuscripts that contain a host of pastoral and preaching

[54] Cambridge Univ. Libr. Ee.2.17 and BL Roy. 15.E.vi. The reasons for this will be discussed below, pp. 65–6.

[55] Kretzmann, Kenny, and Pinborg (eds.), *Cambridge History of Later Medieval Philosophy*, pp. 657–72, 723–37. An exhaustive study of the commentaries and *quaestiones* on the *Politics* can be found in C. Flüeler, *Rezeption und Interpretation der Aristotelischen "Politica" im späten Mittelalter*, 2 vols. (Amsterdam and Philadelphia, 1992).

[56] The ancillary works in the *De regimine* manuscripts include commentaries on the *Ethics* by Thomas Aquinas and Peter of Corveheda, as well as extracts from John Buridan's *Questiones super Ethicam*; commentaries on the *Politics* by Raymond Acgerii and Walter Burley; and extracts, abridgments, or indexes of the *Ethics*, *Politics*, and *Economics*.

[57] Del Punta and Luna, *Catalogo*, p. xxviii. The French manuscript is BN lat. 12431.

[58] Del Punta and Luna, *Catalogo*, pp. xvi–xvii, list six abridgments in eight manuscripts. The manuscripts in French libraries are BN lat. 2191, lat. 6466, and lat. 12431; and Troyes Bibl. mun. 2137. An abridgment entitled "Succintus et utilis tractatus in genere morum" is also found in BN lat. 6697, a manuscript copied for the royal counsellor Jean Budé in 1487.

[59] J.-Ph. Genet, "La théorie politique en Angleterre au XIVe siècle: sa diffusion, son public," in *Das Publikum politischer Theorie im 14. Jahrhundert*, ed. J. Miethke (Munich, 1992), p. 272. The stress laid on practical theology at Oxford in the fifteenth century is discussed in J. I. Catto, "Theology after Wycliffism," in *History of the University of Oxford*, vol. ii, ed . Catto and Evans, pp. 263–80.

aids. Within the twelve manuscripts of this type in the English Group can be found such works as Thomas Aquinas's *De perfectione spiritualis vitae*;[60] Robert Holcot's *Moralitates in usum predicatorum*;[61] Francis de Maron's *De virtutibus moralibus* and *Questiones de virtutibus moralibus*;[62] Nicholas Trevet's *De officio missae*;[63] Roger of Waltham's *Compendium morale de virtuosis dictis et factis exemplaribus antiquorum*;[64] John of Wales's *Communiloquium*, *Forma predicandi*, *Tractatus de penitencia*, and *Tractatus de septem viciis*;[65] Giles's own *De peccato originali*; the anonymous *Lumen anime*;[66] the *Speculum consciencie*, variously attributed to St. Bernard and Hugh of St. Victor;[67] as well as collections of sermons and of moral exempla.[68] Works of a similar nature can be found in several manuscripts produced in Italy and France, though again less frequently – seven originated in Italy, three in France – than is the case with the manuscripts of the English Group.[69]

Several characteristics of these manuscripts of practical theology should be mentioned here. First, the form of *De regimine* in half of them is that of an abridgment or alphabetical index, which suggests they were designed for rapid reference. Second, seventeen out of twenty-two of these manuscripts can be assigned a date after 1375, and of the five bearing an earlier date, four are Italian, and the one English book dates to the second half of the fourteenth century. Third, four of the twelve English manuscripts also contain works of the Aristotelian commentary/compendium type. Thus it would appear that these manuscripts can be associated with the practical needs of priests trained at university, but that their use of *De regimine* as an aid to the care of souls is a phenomenon largely of the late fourteenth and fifteenth centuries, and not before. The reasons for this will be elaborated in chapters 5 and 6.

This chapter has taken the broad view in order to look for patterns in the production, reception, transmission, and use of *De regimine*. It has avoided reference to evidence outside the manuscripts in order to show how much can be gleaned from just the manuscripts alone, without recourse to textual explication or criticism, about the fortunes of a text that proliferated in a large number of copies. Briefly, this survey has revealed that *De regimine* was an exceedingly popular text in later medieval Europe, which proliferated early and rapidly in France and Italy, thanks

---

[60] Cambridge Univ. Libr. Kk.2.11.   [61] BL Ar. 384.   [62] Cambridge Univ. Libr. Dd.3.47.
[63] Lambeth Palace Libr. 150.   [64] Durham Cath. Libr. B.III.24.
[65] Cambridge Univ. Libr. Kk.2.11; BL Roy. 4.D.iv and Roy. 5.C.iii.
[66] Lambeth Palace Libr. 150.   [67] BL Roy. 6.B.v.
[68] BL Roy. 6.B.v; Bodleian Laud Misc. 652; Vat. Ottob. lat. 2071.
[69] Del Punta and Luna, *Catalogo*, pp. xxviii–xxix, list eight such manuscripts, seven of Italian and one of French origin. Some manuscripts of this type in French libraries are: BN lat. 6466 (a series of moral "exordia notanda de Cassiodori . . . excerpta"); BN lat. 12431 (Pierre d'Ailly's *Speculum consideracionis*). BN lat. 6482, which contains a Latin *De regimine* coupled with a moralized *Histoire d'Othea*, was made for the duke of Bourbon in the third quarter of the fifteenth century.

in large measure to the agency of the universities, but also to the Augustinian order and perhaps Giles himself, and then achieved considerable success in other parts of Europe, again thanks largely to the universities. It also circulated in several vernacular translations that, with the exception of Henri de Gauchy's French version, are each notable for being represented by one or just a few copies. This diversity and the variety in the choice of illustrations and illustration program shows that the text was disseminated from many different centers of patronage and production, despite its initial and continued association with the French monarchy. Nor was the diversity of forms limited to the vernacular translations, since the text's university-educated clerical readers frequently added to or changed it in order to facilitate its use, especially for the study of moral philosophy and practical theology at the universities, but also for the performance of their pastoral or administrative duties beyond the university.

3

A book of kings and knighthood

In that same 3ere Richard, the Kyngis brothir, weddid the lady Ysabelle, that was wyf to Gilbert Herl of Gloucester. That same Gilbert was ryth affectuous onto the Heremites of Seynt Austin; for, as it is seid, he was aqweyntid with Doctour Gilis in Frauns; and at his request Gylis was meved to make that bok of Governauns of Princes. But never the lasse he entitelid it to Philip, dauphin of Frauns.[1]

In this flight of anachronistic fancy, John Capgrave, prior of the Augustinian friary at Lynn and prior provincial of the English Augustinians from 1453 to 1457, credits the inspiration behind *De regimine* to the father of the founder of the order's first English convent, Richard of Clare; no matter that it was written a full half-century after Gilbert's death! This tradition of mistaken, even perhaps mendacious familial, institutional, and indeed national self-promotion, was also expressed *c.* 1450 by one of Capgrave's confreres at Earl Richard's foundation of Stoke Clare, who connected Giles's mirror with the founder himself, "which for a freris love that Giles hight / And his boke, clepid De Regimine Principum / Made first freres Augustynes to Ingelonde cum."[2] For although Earl Richard did indeed found the Augustinians' first house in England, he did so in 1248, only a few years after Giles's birth.[3] Despite the obvious falsity of their claims, Capgrave and his anonymous associate rightly identified a close relationship between *De regimine* and the English aristocracy. By the middle of the fifteenth century, several English aristocrats had come to own copies of the text. They desired it for several reasons, not the least of these being that it imparted to them some of the authority of kingship.

Capgrave's claims aside, Giles himself makes it clear that although nobles and even ordinary citizens can profit from his mirror, its primary audience is either kings or princes; and indeed, the history of *De regimine* and its lay audience in England almost certainly begins at the royal court itself; though exactly when is unclear. The earliest reference to what may have been lay ownership of *De regimine*

[1] John Capgrave, *The Chronicle of England*, ed. F. C. Hingeston (London, 1858), p. 152.
[2] From *The Dialogue between a Secular and a Friar*, quoted in C. Horstmann (ed.), *Osbert Bockenhams Legenden* (Heilbronn, 1883), p. 270.   [3] Gwynn, *English Austin Friars*, pp. 15–17.

in England is that of the "Liber de regimine regum" mentioned in the inventory of the Treasury of the Exchequer made in 1323 under the command of the treasurer, Walter de Stapeldon.[4] The problem with this entry is that it could refer to some other work, like, say, the *Secretum secretorum*, which sometimes goes by the same title as Giles's work in medieval catalogues and inventories.[5] And as for the likelihood that the king or anyone else in the royal household had read this book, whatever its contents, the books housed in the Treasury often came there by default, "so one would be hard pressed to demonstrate that the king, or indeed, any member of his *familia*, actually used them."[6]

While this entry represents the kinds of difficulties encountered by scholars who have tried and who continue to attempt to reconstruct the contents of medieval libraries, it is also particularly emblematic of the obstacles that stand in the way of a complete accounting of the books owned by medieval English kings and queens. In stark contrast with their Valois rivals across the Channel who, thanks to the bibliophilia of Charles V, had established a formal library in their palace of the Louvre by 1373, the English monarchy did not have anything even approaching such an institution until the time of Edward IV. And if, again owing to the precocity of Charles V, the French royal library was periodically inventoried beginning in 1373, the earliest known inventory of an English royal library dates to 1535; and even this is partial, accounting only for Henry VIII's books at Richmond.[7]

Of course, just because English monarchs did not have a formal library does not mean they did not keep, commission, receive, and read books. They did, though in a more modest, and usually less concerted and self-consciously political fashion than the monarchs of France. The problem lies, however, in determining what these books were, and what role the court played in circulating books and patronizing literary production. Royal books were dispersed in several locations, and were, moreover, under the guardianship of different branches of royal government. The king's personal collection of books would have been in the keeping of the Chamber and the Wardrobe. The Chamber would have been responsible for those books actively being used, while the remainder would have been cared for by the officers of the Wardrobe. Yet little survives of the accounts of the Chamber, while what can be gleaned of books from the Wardrobe accounts is never more than haphazard. Moreover, the books belonging to the queen were in the care of her own chamber and wardrobe, whose records are even less helpful in the matter of books.[8]

---

[4] F. Palgrave (ed.), *The Antient Kalendars and Inventories of the Treasury of His Majesty's Exchequer*, vol. I, Rolls Series (London, 1836), p. 106.   [5] See above, p. 8.

[6] S. H. Cavanaugh, "Royal Books: King John to Richard II," *The Library*, 5th ser., 10 (1988), p. 309.

[7] Delisle, *Recherches*, pt. I, pp. 1–9, 49–54; J. Backhouse, "Founders of the Royal Library: Edward IV and Henry VII as Collectors of Illuminated Manuscripts," in *England in the Fifteenth Century*, ed. D. Williams (Woodbridge, Suffolk, 1986), pp. 23–41; Green, *Poets and Princepleasers*, pp. 5–6; Cavanaugh, "Royal Books," p. 304.

[8] Green, *Poets and Princepleasers*, pp. 5–6; Cavanaugh, "Royal Books," pp. 304–10.

The English royal court's role as a center of literary patronage and of book pro-duction and dissemination remains a subject of some debate. Though I am inclined to agree with Richard Green that literary patronage in later medieval England was largely a royal and aristocratic affair, rather than the province of a new middle-class reading public, I also have to concur with J. W. Sherborne, V. J. Scattergood, and Ian Doyle that more often than not the role of the king himself in all this was limited.[9] Moreover, the court should be regarded less as a center of literary patron-age and book production than as an occasion when courtiers – here broadly defined to include anyone who attended parliament as well as those in regular attendance at court – transmitted and disseminated news about, as well as copies of, texts, and sometimes heard public readings of them. When it came to literary culture, then, the English monarch was no more than *primus inter pares* in relation to his mag-nates; and he, the magnates, and members of their respective affinities used the court and capital city "as a way station, one which joined otherwise unrelated courts, and courts which operated at a great distance from one another and from London."[10] In turn, the courts of these great men would themselves have func-tioned as centers of literary culture for the members of their extended families and affinities. However they may have been introduced to *De regimine*, several members of the later medieval English royalty, aristocracy, and middle classes had associations with this text, whether in its French, Latin, or English form.

Although nearly half a century divides the time of *De regimine*'s composition from its earliest recorded associations with English lay readers, it nevertheless was probably known, at least within the royal household, several years before this, given Edward I's marriage to Philip the Fair's half-sister, Marguerite, in 1299. Moreover, Edward probably knew of Giles well in advance of these nuptials, since Stephen de Maulay, to whom Giles dedicated his commentary on the *Posterior Analytics* in the mid 1280s, seems to have used his influence with the king to secure the foundation of several houses of Augustinian friars in England.[11] Edward II could have been exposed to *De regimine* through the agency of his wife, Isabella, who was Philip the Fair's daughter, or of ecclesiastics like the treasurer Walter de Stapeldon or Bishop Ralph de Baldock of London, both of whom had acquired copies of *De regimine* prior to the close of this king's disastrous reign.[12]

This period of uncertainty closes with Philippa of Hainault's gift to Edward III, either in late 1326 or early 1327, of a book (BN fr. 571) which originally contained

[9] Green, *Poets and Princepleasers*, pp. 9, 211; J. W. Sherborne, "Aspects of English Court Culture in the Later Fourteenth Century," in *English Court Culture*, ed. Scattergood and Sherborne, pp. 1–7; V. J. Scattergood, "Literary Culture at the Court of Richard II," pp. 29–41; A. I. Doyle, "English Books In and Out of Court from Edward III to Henry VII," in *English Court Culture*, ed. Scattergood and Sherborne, pp. 162–81.

[10] R. Hanna III, "Sir Thomas Berkeley and His Patronage," *Speculum* 64 (1989), p. 913.

[11] F. Lajard, "Gilles de Rome," in *Histoire littéraire de la France*, vol. xxx (Paris, 1888), p. 433.

[12] See below, p. 94.

among other items a copy of Henri de Gauchy's French translation, entitled in a contemporary list of contents *Le Gouvernement des Roys*.[13] There is some question as to whether this book was produced in Hainault or in England. It is also not clear if its patron was Philippa or Isabella. Philippa's family had long sponsored literary activities, though given Philippa's youth and Edward's mother's hand in arranging this marriage, as well as the latter's penchant for books, it is tempting to think Isabella was the guiding influence behind BN fr. 571.[14] This manuscript passed to Edward's trusted friend and counselor, Henry of Grosmont, first duke of Lancaster (d. 1361), and found its way into the library of Louis of Orleans by 1396. Sometime after its acquisition by Duke Louis, BN fr. 571 lost several of its constituent texts, including the *Gouvernement des Roys*.[15] Though there is no evidence that this copy of the French translation survives, some clues as to how it may have looked are found in the Gauchy translation in another manuscript, Baltimore, Walters Art Gallery W. 144.

Walters W. 144 is in its own right a fascinating yet frustrating manuscript. On the one hand, its workmanship is of the very highest quality and its extensive program of ten miniatures was executed by artists of the so-called Queen Mary group, a workshop responsible for some of the finest illuminated manuscripts produced in England during the first four decades of the fourteenth century.[16] On the other hand, this *de luxe*, lavishly illustrated book bears no evidence whatsoever of ownership prior to 1463, by which time it had come into the keeping of a "Monasterium Sancti Gualtheri."[17] Yet despite the lack of firm evidence of patronage or original intended ownership, Walters W. 144 has all the marks of a book destined for a king or, at the very least, a member of the upper aristocracy, at about the time of Edward III's succession. Although the manuscripts belonging to the Queen Mary group date from 1304 to shortly before 1340, the correspondence between certain features in Walters W. 144 and other manuscripts illuminated by Queen Mary group artists allows for a somewhat more exact dating. Its illumination is the work of two miniaturists and a decorator. One of the artists' work (fols. 10, 28v, 35v, 41v, 51v, 63v, 73v, and 92) is close to that in the portion of the *Liber legum antiquorum regum* now in Oxford, Oriel Coll. 46, a manuscript executed in 1321, while the decoration is rem-

---

[13] M. A. Michael, "A Manuscript Wedding Gift from Philippa of Hainault to Edward III," *The Burlington Magazine* 127 (1985), pp. 582–99; L. F. Sandler, *Gothic Manuscripts, 1285–1385*, A Survey of Manuscripts Illuminated in the British Isles, ed. J. J. G. Alexander, vol. II (London, 1986), pt. 2, pp. 103–5.

[14] The literary patronage of Philippa's family, the Avesnes, is discussed in J. Vale, *Edward III and Chivalry: Chivalric Society and Its Context, 1270–1350* (Woodbridge, Suffolk, 1982), pp. 42–4. Isabella's agency is supported by Michael, "Manuscript Wedding Gift," pp. 589–90. On Isabella and books, see Cavanaugh, "Royal Books," pp. 309–11.

[15] Michael, "Manuscript Wedding Gift," pp. 582–8.

[16] For a discussion of the history of this style, which derives its name from the Queen Mary Psalter (BL Roy. 2.B.vii), and of its characteristic features, see Sandler, *Gothic Manuscripts*, pt. 1, pp. 25, 30–2.

[17] Inscription on fol. 121.

iniscent of the roughly contemporary *Somme le roi* found in Cambridge, St. John's Coll. S. 30. Even more intriguing, the faces and hair painted by the other miniaturist, whose illustrations appear on folios 2, 3v, and 12, closely resemble those executed by one of the artists who worked on the manuscripts of the *Secretum secretorum* (BL Add. 47680) and the *De nobilitatibus, sapientiis, et prudentiis regum* (Oxford, Christ Church 92) commissioned, probably in 1326, by the royal clerk Walter de Milemete – who was also the author of the latter work – as gifts for Edward III on his coronation.[18] These stylistic similarities thus suggest the probability of Walters W. 144 having been executed in the 1320s.

The illustration program in Walters W. 144 is far more ambitious and elaborate than those found in any other *De regimine* manuscript of English origin. Indeed programs of equivalent quantity and quality survive in only a handful of other copies, and these are all of French origin and were produced at a much later date.[19] The program of illustrations in the Walters manuscript is as follows:

Prologue: historiated initial of kneeling author presenting book to seated prince (fol. 2).

1.1.1: initial inhabited by fantastic beast (fol. 2v).

1.1.3: miniature of seated prince conversing with three philosophers (or scholars) and two counselors (fol. 3v).

1.2.1: miniature of seated prince being instructed by philosopher holding a book (fol. 10).

1.3.1: historiated initial of seated prince being instructed by philosopher holding a book (fol. 28v).

1.4.1: miniature, only one-half column in width, of seated prince conversing with philosopher (fol. 35v).

2.1.1: miniature of seated prince admonishing his queen, two children (a boy and a girl), and a servant holding a rod (fol. 41v).

2.2.1: historiated initial of seated prince addressing two children (51v).

2.3.1: miniature of prince addressing his queen and two sons, one of whom is an adolescent, the other a child. It has been executed in the margin beneath the column, owing to the scribe having neglected to leave space for it in the column (fol. 63v).

3.1.1: miniature of prince and philosopher conversing atop the walls of a town (fol. 73v).

3.2.1: historiated initial of seated prince being addressed by standing philosopher (fol. 82).

3.3.1*: no miniature, nor was any space left for one.

[18] Sandler, *Gothic Manuscripts*, pt. 1, p. 79. Facsimiles and a discussion of the Milemete manuscripts are found in M. R. James (ed.), *The Treatise of Walter de Milemete De Nobilitatibus, Sapientiis, et Prudentiis Regum* (Oxford, 1913).   [19] These are discussed above, pp. 38–40.

One purpose of these illustrations was to mark major textual divisions and provide the reader with clues to the subjects treated in the portions of text being introduced. The program twice deviates from this, namely at 1.1.3 and 3.3.1. The first of these can be explained by medieval book designers' preference for loading up on illustrations in the early part of books and texts. As for the missing illustration at 3.3.1, it could well be that the team of artisans responsible for preparing this book was working on a tight schedule and simply ran out of time. Some aspects of the manuscript lend support to this idea. First, there is the design/scribal error at the beginning of 2.3.1, where no room was left for an illustration, thereby forcing the artist to make do by squeezing his miniature into the margin beneath the column. Likewise, although the writing in the manuscript is, on the whole, in the fine *textualis rotunda* of a very accomplished scribe, the entire penultimate gathering (fols. 107–114v) has been executed by two much inferior scribes, who abbreviated much more heavily than their more expert fellow, and worked with frayed quills and a thinner, lighter ink. Their handiwork, it should be mentioned, was not a later addition, since the painted initials, which were executed after the writing of the text, are most certainly the work of the artist responsible for decorating the rest of the manuscript.

The illustration program also authorized the text, in this case by investing it with the authority derived from the lore of ancient philosophers, particularly Aristotle. With the exception of the opening miniature, in which Giles presents his book to the prince, and the three illustrations accompanying the second book, the prince's association with the philosophers is made consistently throughout. These illustrations were meant, I think, to encourage the reader to identify the text, and indeed the practice of princely rule, with philosophy, and more especially with the wisdom of Aristotle, the prince of the philosophers. One reason for this was, of course, the debt which Giles's mirror owed to Aristotle and other philosophers. Another might well be the medieval attitude toward authorship, which vested more and more authority in a writer's works the longer he had been dead. As Walter Map once mused about one of his own works:

I know what will happen after I am gone. When I shall be decaying, then, for the first time, it shall be saluted; and every defect in it will be remedied by my decease, and in the most remote future its antiquity will cause the authorship to be credited to me, because, then as now, old copper will be preferred to new gold . . . In every century its own present has been unpopular, and each age from the beginning has preferred the past to itself.[20]

Similar views were expressed by Edward III's tutor and trusted counselor, Richard de Bury, who averred that:

[20] *De nugis curialium*, dist. iv, cap. 5, quoted in A. J. Minnis, *Medieval Theory of Authorship: Scholastic Literary Attitudes in the Later Middle Ages* (London, 1984), p. 12. In fact, as Minnis points out, the work to which Map was referring, his *Dissuasio Valerii ad Rufinum*, was credited by later medieval commentators to Valerius Maximus.

Though the novelties of the moderns have never been distasteful to us . . . yet with more reckless eagerness have we desired to search through the perfected labors of the ancients. For, whether they flourished by nature with a subtler kind of mind or chanced to indulge in more instant study, or whether they made their way supported by the help of both, this one thing we have found to be evident, that their successors scarce suffice to discuss the attainments of those that went before them or to receive even through a compend of their doctrine what the ancients produced by prolonged investigation.[21]

One imagines that, for Bury and most of his contemporaries, Aristotle would have been more the author of *De regimine* than the recently deceased Giles, who, in their minds, and in the illustration program of this manuscript, is relegated to the subsidiary role of a compiler "des dis de pluseurs philosophes."[22]

Yet despite this medieval attitude toward authorship, explicit pictorial association of the Philosopher with *De regimine* appears in but one other manuscript that I know of. This is the miniature in an early fourteenth-century copy (BN fr. 19920), likely produced at Paris, which depicts a philosopher presenting the book to the king, while a friar, who presumably represents Giles, stands in the background.[23] Yet if the idea expressed here appears to be very similar to that in Walters W. 144, there is little likelihood of any direct filiation between these manuscripts. The Gauchy translation in BN fr. 19920 is accompanied by only a single miniature, located at the beginning of I.I.I (fol. 2v), whose text, appropriately enough, begins "Li philosophes dit." Nor is the presentation scene in this manuscript anything like that found in Walters W. 144. Nevertheless, it is interesting to note that the miniatures that accompany the other texts in the Parisian manuscript repeatedly and consistently present the authority of philosophers.[24]

It has already been mentioned that there are stylistic affinities between some of the illuminations in the Walters *Gouvernement* and in the Milemete manuscripts. This is particularly apparent in the Milemete *Secretum secretorum*, whose Aristotle figure not only looks much like the philosopher in Walters W. 144, but also plays the same role as guide and companion of the prince – who in the case of the *Secretum* manuscript is ostensibly Alexander the Great. The message of the illustration programs in both manuscripts seems identical: that the prince should follow the example of Alexander the Great by paying heed to the wise counsel of the philosophers, and most especially of Aristotle. In Milemete's *Secretum* this message was meant for the young Edward III, who, it was hoped, would emulate Alexander,

---

[21] Richard de Bury, *The Philobiblon*, trans. A. Taylor (Berkeley, 1948), p. 57. Also discussed in Minnis, *Medieval Theory of Authorship*, p. 12.

[22] This sentiment is expressed in the title assigned to an abridgment of Gauchy's translation in BN fr. 573, fol. 195: "Le liure du gouuernement des Rois et des princes que freres Gilles de Romme de lordre de saint Augustin compila des dis de pluseurs philosophes."

[23] On this manuscript, see also above, p. 33.

[24] The accompanying texts are the *Lucidaire* (fols. 266–305v), attributed to St. Anselm, and *Les moralites des philosophes* (fols. 306–26v).

rather than the incompetent and impolitic Edward II. Could the new king also have been the intended recipient of the advice in the Walters *Gouvernement*? There are, after all, the stylistic and iconographic similarities between its illumination and those in the Milemete manuscripts. Moreover, both it and the Milemete manuscripts show signs of hurried execution. The mistakes in, and incomplete state of, the Milemete manuscripts have been ascribed to their having been rushed through production in order to be ready for the royal coronation.[25] Perhaps this too was the reason for the errors in the Walters manuscript.

Whoever the original intended owner of Walters W. 144 may have been, there is a strong likelihood that the person who commissioned it was at the time resident in England, and probably in or around London, the center of the Queen Mary group's activities. The preeminence accorded the Philosopher also suggests a patron famil-iar with the arts curriculum of the universities, perhaps a prelate. Someone like Richard de Bury comes to mind. Bury was an avid collector of books who appreci-ated the utility of enlisting Aristotle in the instruction of kings. He wrote in his *Philobiblon*, "We read that Philip [of Macedon] devoutly returned thanks to the gods because they had allowed Alexander to be born in the times of Aristotle, under whose instruction he was trained to become worthy of the rule of his father's kingdom."[26] He also had close ties to both Isabella and the young Edward, having become an official of the prince's household as well, probably, as his tutor in 1325. Moreover, he would have had occasion to become familiar with Gauchy's French translation during his sojourns in Paris and Hainault with Isabella and Edward in 1326.[27]

Leaving all speculation regarding Walters W. 144 aside, there is no doubt that the young Plantagenet at around the time of his royal accession was the recipient of several mirrors of princes, at least one of which was the French translation of *De regimine* that once was part of BN fr. 571. If Isabella was the patron of this manu-script, this suggests that in the weeks leading up to the royal coronation she wanted to prepare her son to rule well, whatever her and her lover Mortimer's subsequent goals may have been. Her choice to include the *Gouvernement* was natural, given that Giles had dedicated it to her father. Her son, in turn, was Philip's grandson, and it made sense that he should be instructed to rule like a Capetian monarch.

By the time of Edward III's own grandson's troubled reign, knowledge among the laity of *De regimine* had passed beyond the confines of the royal court to several members of the upper nobility. Henry of Grosmont's ownership of BN fr. 571 has already been mentioned. As for Richard II's contemporaries, the parliamentary peer William Lord Thorp of Northampton acquired a Latin copy (Bodleian Bodl. 234) sometime between *c.* 1380 and his death in 1390, while the inventory of move-

---

[25] J. J. G. Alexander, "Painting and Manuscript Illumination for Royal Patrons in the Later Middle Ages," in *English Court Culture*, ed. Scattergood and Sherborne, pp. 141–2.
 [26] Bury, *Philobiblon*, p. 78.   [27] Cavanaugh, "Royal Books," p. 311.

ables seized in 1397 after the murder of Richard's uncle and arch-nemesis Thomas of Woodstock, duke of Gloucester, lists "j veil livre appellez Egidius de regimine Principum."[28] Duke Thomas's taste for *De regimine* was shared by his wife, Eleanor de Bohun, who stipulated in her will, drawn up in August 1399, that her teenage son, Humphrey, should receive her "liure de Giles de regimine principum." It was said that Eleanor's grief over Humphrey's death but a few weeks after the drafting of her will was the cause of her own demise in late October of the same year.[29]

Gloucester's *De regimine* is, it seems to me, emblematic of one of the ways lay readers regarded this text. Giles takes pains in *De regimine* to remind the prince that he had best make a habit of seeking wise counsel, and that the wisest counsel of all will tend to come from members of the nobility.[30] Now, Duke Thomas could well have owned his copy thanks simply to his being a prince of the blood. Nevertheless, assuming he was actually familiar with its contents, it seems likely that he would have warmed particularly to Giles's insistence that the prince should regularly consult with wise and noble men of mature years.[31] Woodstock had chastised Richard in October of 1386 for adhering to unwise council rather than the advice of his magnates, and this would remain one of his and the other Appellants' chief complaints two years later.[32] Thomas Lord Berkeley was another of Richard's enemies who may have appreciated Giles's teaching regarding counsel. Certainly he was impressed enough by *De regimine* to commission John Trevisa to make a Middle English translation of it sometime in the later years of Richard's reign.[33]

But just as Richard's political opponents could have found much of value in *De regimine*, so too could the king and his supporters. Our knowledge of Richard's own books is so frustratingly incomplete that very little should be made of the fact that these spotty records do not record a copy of *De regimine*.[34] What is certain, however, is that Richard's tutor and trusted advisor Simon de Burley owned a French translation of it by the time of his demise at the hands of the Lords

[28] M. E. C. Walcott, "Medieval Libraries," *Transactions of the Royal Society of Literature*, 2nd ser., 9 (1870), p. 81. The duke's books are also described and discussed in H. A. Dillon and W. H. St. John Hope, "Inventory of the Goods and Chattels Belonging to Thomas, Duke of Gloucester," *Archaeological Journal* 54 (1897), pp. 275–308.

[29] N. H. Nicolas (ed.), *Testamenta Vetusta*, vol. 1 (London, 1826), p. 148; *DNB*, vol. XIX, p. 637.

[30] *DRP* 1.2.8, 1.4.5, 2.3.18, 3.2.4, 3.2.17–19.

[31] *DRP* 1.2.8, "Non enim decet regem in omnibus sequi caput suum, nec inniti semper solertiae propriae: sed oportet ipsum esse docilem, ut sit habilis ad capescendam doctrinam aliorum, acqui-escendo doctrinis et consiliis baronum seniorum sapientum et diligentium regnum." Though the counselors in this passage could also be construed as "barons, elders, wise men, and those loving the realm," John Trevisa's English rendering, "þe eldeste wise barons þat loueþ þe regne," probably reflects the way this passage would be read by an English nobleman: Trevisa, *Governance*, p. 53.

[32] A. Tuck, *Richard II and the English Nobility* (New York, 1974), pp. 103, 122–3.

[33] See below, chapter 4.

[34] E. Rickert, "King Richard II's Books," *The Library*, 4th ser., 13 (1933), pp. 144–7; R. F. Green, "King Richard II's Books Revisited," *The Library*, 5th ser., 31 (1976), pp. 235–39; G. Mathew, *The Court of Richard II* (London, 1968), pp. 22–3.

Appellant in 1388.[35] The historian Richard H. Jones seized upon this point in his study of Richard II's reign, going so far as to surmise that *De regimine* provided Burley and Richard with "a fully developed conception" of absolutist monarchy.[36] There was certainly plenty in *De regimine* that could have been used to justify absolutism. Giles advocates hereditary monarchy over all other forms of government, since rule by one is better than rule by many, and hereditary succession is more likely to guarantee peaceful succession as well as rulers who care for the welfare of their realms.[37] He also prefers the best king to the best law, on the grounds that the king, being a kind of animate law, is able in individual cases to judge equitably in accordance with reason and natural law, while positive law, being a kind of inanimate king, is in and of itself inherently inflexible and unresponsive to the needs of specific cases.[38] For Giles then, the just king, as the embodiment of the Aristotelian virtue of *epieikeia*, can dispense with positive law when he feels that it will render a judgment that is contrary to the general principles of natural law.[39] Giles's king is, in short, the archer who directs the arrow of his realm toward its goal, a ruler whose exemplary qualities make him a virtual half-god.[40]

Yet it should be borne in mind that though Jones may be right in his suspicions "that Richard II, like many another prince in his age, had been set to school to Giles of Rome and had learned his lessons well," the king's absolutist tendencies could nevertheless have found justification in a broad array of sources, including the writings of several scholastics, certain principles of Roman law, and the opinions of English jurists that find expression in Glanville and Bracton.[41] And if albeit Giles's lore could not be enlisted by advocates of constitutional monarchy, one suspects that men like Thomas of Woodstock and Thomas Lord Berkeley could have found much in Giles to recommend their cause against a king who they believed had become a tyrant. For by ruling according to passion rather than reason and by refusing to govern with proper counsel, he had become a tyrant, and according to Giles the reigns of tyrants tended in short order to be violently terminated.[42]

According to Thomas Hoccleve in his *Regement of Princes*, the eldest son of the agent of Richard's violent termination was already well acquainted with *De regimine* while he was still prince of Wales.[43] Although this could just have been a bit of flattery, one suspects that in this case Hoccleve knew whereof he wrote. The future King Henry V had received a fine education in his youth. Moreover he belonged to a family noted for its love of books. His mother, Mary de Bohun,

---

[35] V. J. Scattergood, "Two Medieval Book Lists," *The Library*, 5th ser., 23 (1968), p. 237.
[36] Jones, *Royal Policy*, p. 144.   [37] *DRP* 3.2.3–5.   [38] *DRP* 1.2.12, 3.2.29.
[39] *DRP* 3.2.23.   [40] *DRP* 1.1.5, 3.2.8, 3.2.15.
[41] Jones, *Royal Policy*, p. 161; Burns (ed.), *Cambridge History of Medieval Political Thought*, pp. 485–8.   [42] *DRP* 3.2.13–14.
[43] *Hoccleve's Works: The Regement of Princes*, ed. F. J. Furnivall, EETS, extra ser. 72 (1897), pp. 77–8.

descended from a long line of bibliophiles, and his brothers Humphrey and John would build up two of medieval England's largest private libraries. And though little evidence survives of Henry's own library, his appreciation for literature is demonstrated by his patronage of John Lydgate's *Life of Our Lady* and *Troy Book*. [44] It should also be recalled that his aunt, Eleanor de Bohun, the duchess of Gloucester, owned a copy of *De regimine*, as did her husband and Henry's uncle, Thomas of Woodstock.

In the period leading up to his succession, Henry, moreover, seems to have been keenly aware of the restorative and unifying role he would have to play as king. The English political community was, he knew, deeply disappointed with the governance of his father, Henry IV, as well as with that of Richard II. According to Gerald Harriss, Henry and the political nation understood that harmony would only return to England if all the estates did as they were supposed to, and that "regeneration must start from the head, from the king's example, exhortation, and authority. Henry V set himself to achieve this, to be the perfect king, the exemplar of kingship and the saviour of his realm and people." [45] Derek Pearsall has even argued that the *Regement of Princes* was "a calculated act of self-promotion by the prince," which, if true, lends greater significance to Hoccleve's inclusion of *De regimine* amongst the books read by Henry. [46]

Henry may well have been the most self-conscious of medieval English kings, and this quality was at least in part predicated upon the advice of men with university training, who would have fully appreciated the political utility of Giles's teaching that kings "ought to be rule and exemplar to others" (*ut sint aliorum data regula et exemplar*). [47] As rule and exemplar, Henry would thus function as what Giles calls a "figure" (*figura*), that is, a rhetorical convention that "moves and excites the feeling" (*moveant et inflamment affectum*) and thus fosters that "rectitude of the will" (*rectitudo voluntatis*) which is the precondition of good behavior. [48] This same self-consciousness is readily apparent both in Henry's decision to renew the Hundred Years War and in the way he subsequently prosecuted it. From the beginning of his reign in the spring of 1413, one of Henry's chief goals was "to make a reality of the terms of the 'great peace' of Brétigny of 1360." [49] The condi-

---

[44] On Henry's education, see K. B. McFarlane, "The Education of the Nobility in Later Medieval England," in *The Nobility of Later Medieval England* (Oxford, 1973), pp. 243–4. For manuscripts associated with the Bohuns, and Henry and his brothers, see Alexander, "Painting and Manuscript Illumination," pp. 148–9; Doyle, "English Books," pp. 172–74; M. J. Barber, "The Books and Patronage of Learning of a Fifteenth-Century Prince," *The Book Collector* 12 (1963), pp. 308–15.

[45] G. L. Harriss (ed.), *Henry V: The Practice of Kingship* (Oxford, 1985), p. 26.

[46] D. Pearsall, "Hoccleve's *Regement of Princes*: The Poetics of Royal Self-Representation," *Speculum* 69 (1994), p. 410.   [47] *DRP* 1.2.33.

[48] *DRP* 1.1.1. L. Scanlon, *Narrative, Authority, and Power: The Medieval Exemplum and the Chaucerian Tradition* (Cambridge, 1994), pp. 108–10.

[49] C. T. Allmand, *Henry V* (Berkeley, 1992), p. 66.

tions of this peace, never fully implemented, would have given the king of England the duchy of Aquitaine in full sovereignty and paid him King John the Good's substantial ransom. Though Henry first pursued diplomatic channels to effect this, he must also have been aware that he might have to resort to arms.[50] It was in this climate that an Epiphany sermon, entitled "Natus est rex," was preached before the king in 1414, which encouraged its audience of "kny3thes and oþur gentils" to diligently attend to the "many sotell questions and conclusions in mater of werre and armes, as þe Phylosofre declareþ, De Re Militari, and Gylus, De Regimine, parte vltima."[51] A significant body of evidence suggests that the message of this sermon fell on receptive ears, and that the king and his brothers would soon be applying the lessons of *De regimine* while waging the renewed war against France.

Two contemporary sources made explicit references to Henry's use of *De regimine* as a military manual. One of Henry's chaplains, the anonymous author of the *Gesta Henrici Quinti*, credited Giles as a source for Henry's tactics at the siege of Harfleur.[52] Moreover, the author of the *Gesta* refers to Giles twice more in his description of the siege.[53] Nor was the connection between Henry and *De regimine* limited to his immediate circle, for the prologue of an Oxford inception disputation of 1420 lauds the king for having "entirely laid waste all of France with his death-dealing archers, according to the most famous advice given in very many of the chapters in the last part of Giles's book On the Rule of Princes."[54] It is possible, of course, that Henry's use of Giles was a purely clerical confection, and that the king himself never drew these connections between his actions and Giles's military doctrine. Nevertheless, I am tempted to think these references were more than just instances of clerical wishful thinking. On the one hand, Henry's acquaintance with such literature should hardly surprise us, since there is plenty of evidence for the popularity of military literature among lay readers in the central and later Middle Ages.[55] On the other hand, however, such concrete contemporary connections between an English monarch and *De regimine* were both unprecedented and unre-

---

[50] On the negotiations, see *ibid.*, pp. 66–72.

[51] W. O. Ross (ed.), *Middle English Sermons Edited from British Museum MS. Royal 18.B.XXIII*, EETS, orig. ser. 209 (1960), xxxvi–xxxviii, p. 224.

[52] Quoted at the beginning of this study; see above, p. 1. The relevant passage in *De regimine* can be found in *DRP* 3.3.8.   [53] *Gesta Henrici Quinti*, ed. Taylor and Roskell, pp. 28–9, 40–1.

[54] "[Q]ui mortiferis nimis architenensium suorum totam Galliam precipitat in ruinam iuxta famosissimum consilium Egidii de regimine principum plerisque capitulis in ultima parte libri": Oxford, Magdalen Coll. 38, fol. 17v; quoted in D. R. Leader, *A History of the University of Cambridge*, vol. 1 (Cambridge, 1988), p. 165.

[55] P. Contamine, *War in the Middle Ages*, trans. M. Jones (Oxford, 1984), pp. 210–15; A. Murray, *Reason and Society in the Middle Ages* (Oxford, 1978), pp. 127–30. More recently, Michael Prestwich has written, rather curiously, that Vegetius' *De re militari* "was the only . . . treatise read in the medieval period that discussed military strategy": *Armies and Warfare in the Middle Ages: The English Experience* (New Haven, 1996), p. 186.

peated. Moreover, the Oxford disputant's intriguing characterization of Giles's military advice as "most famous" leads me to suspect that the cause of this notoriety went beyond a mere curricular familiarity with the text. Finally, there are the *De regimine* manuscripts themselves; and these bear witness not only to growth in aristocratic interest in the text, but also to a contemporary awareness, on the part of both the aristocracy and the clergy, of its utility as a military manual.

While Henry seems to have been the first English monarch for whom there is evidence of having used *De regimine* in this fashion, its utility as such had been recognized since at least the middle of the fourteenth century, when the French author of *L'estat et le gouvernement comme les princes et seigneurs se doivent gouverner*, advised readers who wanted to know more of the art of war, "voie le livre de Vegece sur le fait de chevalier, et le tiers livre du gouv. des princes et autres parlans de cest matiere."[56] Nor was he alone in using *De regimine* for militant ends, since King John I of Portugal is said to have referred to it during the siege of Ceuta.[57] Nevertheless, the manuscripts strongly suggest that *De regimine* gained a special preeminence in England, and that this liking on the part of lay readers began at about the time Henry became king. Fully seven manuscripts of the English Group contain copies of *De regimine* and Vegetius' *De re militari* (or, in one manuscript, Christine de Pizan's *Livre des fais d'armes et de chévalerie*, a work heavily indebted to Vegetius), whereas I have found this combination in but one manuscript of continental provenance (BN lat. 6476), and this contains only a very brief Vegetius abridgment. In four of the English Group manuscripts the two texts are unaccompanied by any other works, while in a fifth, containing several items executed in different hands, the *De regimine* and Vegetius are penned by the same hand. As for the dating of the manuscripts, five were produced at about the time Henry was king or within a generation thereafter. Of the two which clearly predate his reign, both are Latin copies, and probably university books, from the second half of the fourteenth century.

Three of the manuscripts can be identified with members of English royalty and aristocracy. The sole extant copy of John Trevisa's translation of *De regimine* (Bodleian Digby 233) is accompanied by the earliest English version of Vegetius, a work also translated at Berkeley's behest. Berkeley, who commissioned this book sometime between 1408 and his death in 1417, may have ordered the translation of Vegetius with the intention of its being a companion text for Trevisa's Giles. If so, Berkeley, whose precocity as a patron of English translation has been examined by Ralph Hanna III, may also have been the first English nobleman to appreciate the utility of combining *De regimine* and Vegetius.[58] Henry V's brother Humphrey, duke of Gloucester, owned two copies of *De regimine*, one of which is now found in

---

[56] Genet (ed.), *Four English Political Tracts*, p. 209. This same work was translated into English in the middle of the fifteenth century.   [57] Perez (ed.), *Glosa Castellana*, p. xxiv.
[58] On this, see below, p. 87.

Cambridge Univ. Libr. Ee.2.17, an early fifteenth-century manuscript of French origin containing a *Gouvernement* and a French translation of Vegetius.[59] This was a gift from his cousin and former ward, Sir Robert Roos, who probably obtained it during one of his several diplomatic missions to France.[60] An abridged *Gouvernement* and Christine de Pizan's *Livre des fais d'armes* make up part of BL Roy. 15.E.vi, an enormous *de luxe* book produced in Rouen for John Talbot, earl of Shrewsbury. Talbot presented this book as a gift to Margaret of Anjou shortly before her marriage in 1445 to Henry VI. Nevertheless it is possible that Talbot originally had intended the last four items of this manuscript – the *Gouvernement*, Alain Chartier's *Breviaire des nobles*, Honoré Bouvet's *Arbre des batailles*, and the *Livre des fais d'armes* – for his own use, and that "these 'masculine' texts . . . were being prepared for Talbot himself when news of the betrothal caused him to expand the collection in a way more appropriate to a young queen."[61] This may be why the *Gouvernement*, which is heavily abridged, nevertheless contains the full text of Giles's treatment of warfare.

Just as Henry V's example seems to have inspired the English nobility's interest in *De regimine* as a military manual, the English presence in France during his reign and that of his son furnished the English aristocracy with new opportunities to acquire the text. They could, like the earl of Shrewsbury, commission a new copy from French bookmakers, or they could do the same as Robert Roos, whose book appears to have been bought second-hand. It is well known that the English enriched themselves from the spoils of France during Henry's wars of conquest and his brother Bedford's regency. Bedford himself appropriated a large portion of the French royal library at the Louvre, including, perhaps, Cambridge, Jesus Coll. Q.B.9, a book that originally belonged to Charles V.[62] It could also be that Hotspur's son, Henry, fifth Lord Percy, obtained Bodleian Laud Misc. 702 during his time fighting with King Henry in France.[63] One other manuscript shows signs of having been brought from France to England in the fifteenth century. This is Univ. of Chicago Libr. 533–v, an early fourteenth-century *Gouvernement* decorated on the front flyleaf with a fifteenth-century rendering of the coat of arms of an English gentry family surnamed Garshall.[64]

[59] Duke Humphrey gave the other copy, a Latin *De regimine*, to Oxford University in 1443–4: H. Anstey (ed.), *Munimenta Academica, or Documents Illustrative of the Academical Life and Studies at Oxford*, Rolls Series (London, 1868), pt. 2, p. 772.

[60] E. Seaton, *Sir Richard Roos, c. 1410–1482, Lancastrian Poet* (London, 1961), pp. 42–7.

[61] C. Reynolds, "The Shrewsbury Book, British Library, Royal MS 15 E.VI," in *Medieval Art, Architecture and Archaeology at Rouen*, ed. J. Stratford (London, 1993), p. 111.

[62] L. Douët d'Arcq (ed.), *Inventaire de la bibliothèque du roi Charles VI fait au Louvre en 1423 par ordre du Régent duc de Bedford* (Paris, 1867), p. 176. I thank François Avril for bringing this account to my attention.

[63] This assumes Percy sailed to France in the summer of 1417. He commanded a contingent mustered for the king's expedition to France in July 1414, but was back in England in October to fight the Scots, *DNB*, vol. xv, p. 850.

[64] This information from the unpublished manuscript description was graciously provided by the staff of the Department of Special Collections, University of Chicago Library.

The Garshall ensign signals another fifteenth-century development regarding *De regimine*'s lay readership: its dissemination among the English gentry. Sir John Fortescue, Chief Justice of the King's Bench and late medieval England's most noteworthy political theorist, knew enough of *De regimine* to cite it on three occasions in his writings.[65] In 1467 Sir Peter Arderne, Chief Baron of the Exchequer, bequeathed his *Gouvernement* to his daughter Mary, wife of Sir John Bohun of Midhurst.[66] The names of two of Arderne's contemporaries, Sir Thomas Charlton and his cousin Henry Frowyck, show up in connection with "an engelische book calde Giles de regimine principum."[67] Both men were M.P.s for Middlesex, and Charlton served as Speaker of the House of Commons in 1454. Charlton was also a member of the royal household, and it may have been through his connections at court that he gained access to an English *De regimine* translation.[68] By the second half of the fifteenth century Humphrey of Gloucester's *Gouvernement* had passed to either the elder or younger Sir James Strangways; the elder Strangways was Speaker of the House of Commons in 1461–62.[69]

At the next rung down on the social ladder were the esquires John Broughton (active *c.* 1450) of Toddington, Bedfordshire, who owned the Latin *De regimine* in BL Roy. 6.B.v., and a member of the Pert family of Essex, possibly William Pert, who at the beginning of the sixteenth century came into possession of Jesus Coll. Q.B.9.[70] The latter manuscript, it will be recalled, is the same book that the duke of Bedford may have acquired from the Louvre, thus earning it the distinction not only of having crossed the Channel, but also of having made the journey from royal to noble to middle-class library over the course of about a century.[71] Only one manuscript can be associated with a non-armigerous owner, this being a very early copy of the *Gouvernement* (New York, Pierpont Morgan Libr. M. 122) which belonged to William Sonnyng, an alderman of English-occupied Calais, who was also the owner of a miscellany now in the Boston Public Library.[72] Interestingly, Sonnyng's is the only copy that shows signs of actually having been read by its lay owner. A late fifteenth-century English hand, probably Sonnyng's own, has made

---

[65] Once in the *Governance of England* (ch. 1), and twice in the *Opusculum de natura legis nature* (pt. I, chs. 16 and 24): Sir John Fortescue, *The Governance of England*, ed. C. Plummer (Oxford, 1885), pp. 109, 173–7.

[66] N. Orme, *From Childhood to Chivalry*, p. 96. G. E. Cokayne, *The Complete Peerage*, vol. II, rev'd. and ed. V. Gibbs (London, 1912), p. 201.

[67] Westminster Abbey Muniments, no. 6625, an inventory of Charlton's goods at his manor of Swalcliffe, Middlesex; see also McFarlane, "Education of the Nobility," pp. 237–8.

[68] J. S. Roskell, *The Commons and Their Speakers in English Parliaments, 1376–1523* (Manchester, 1965), p. 71.   [69] *DNB*, vol. XXIX, p. 21; C. E. Wright, *Fontes Harleiani* (London, 1972), p. 320.

[70] On Broughton, see *CCR* 1441–47, pp. 223, 267, 478; *CCR* 1447–54, p. 170; *CCR* 1454–61, p. 131. On William Pert, gentleman of "Alrechelay" in Essex, see *CCR* 1476–85, p. 16; *CCR* 1485–1500, p. 128.

[71] For more on this manuscript see Appendix D.

[72] Boston Public Libr. f. med 92: G. D. Painter, *William Caxton: A Quincentenary Biography of England's First Printer* (London, 1976), p. 161.

marginal and interlineal translations into English, Middle French, and Latin of more than one hundred words and phrases which the annotator found unfamiliar.[73] For instance, the text's *vergoigne* and *ramenez* have been translated into the English "shame" and "brought ayen"; *beus* and *odivete* to the more familiar French forms "biaulz" and "oyseusete"; and *soffretes* and *vesquist* to the Latin "inopia" and "vivat." These trilingual glosses are evidence of the familiarity with these languages which Tony Hunt and Serge Lusignan have suggested was a common result of late medieval English education.[74]

King Henry VI's education appears to have included some instruction in the doctrines of Giles. Sometime before 1450, and probably in the latter half of the 1430s, Henry was the recipient of a work heavily indebted to *De regimine*, entitled *Tractatus de regimine principum ad Regem Henricum Sextum*. Its anonymous author, who refers to himself as the king's "humilimus [*sic*] orator," reminds the young king of the military successes of his father, and recommends that he thoroughly acquaint himself with the section of *De regimine* on warfare, "so that with mighty hand your most royal highness may invade the lands of your enemies, and that either you or your commanders and lords may courageously subdue and overthrow those same lands."[75] Henry, of course, did no such thing; neither was this achieved by his uncles, the dukes of Bedford and Gloucester, nor other nobles, like Sir Robert Roos and the earl of Shrewsbury, who had also read their Giles.

Given the late medieval English aristocracy's fondness for Giles, it is hardly a surprise to find a copy of it in the possession of Henry's archrival, Richard, duke of York. Duke Richard's *De regimine* (Lambeth Palace Libr. Arc.L.40.2/L.26) seems to have been designed to function as a testimony to his power and learning. His power is symbolized in the illumination program of fifteen coats of arms identifying the manuscript with the House of York and its affinity (plate 6). The opening page is particularly impressive in this regard. It depicts the arms of Richard II and the old House of Lancaster, signifying the duke's royal lineage, as well as three shields that appear to express the support of families active in the Yorkist service.[76] The duke's

---

[73] Glosses listed in Molenaer (ed.), *Li Livres du Gouvernement*, pp. 458–60.

[74] T. Hunt, *Teaching and Learning Latin in Thirteenth-Century England*, 3 vols. (Cambridge, 1991), vol. I, pp. 433–7; S. Lusignan, *Parler vulgairement: Les intellectuels et la langue française aux XIIIe et XIVe siècles* (Montreal, 1987), pp. 91–127.

[75] "Hec, enim, prestantissime Rex et princeps, bello seu tempore belli congruencia recitat venerabilis Egidius De Regimine Principum libro tercio ac eiusdem voluminis tercia parte in quo prout veraciter considero, sufficiens exemplificacio spiritualis inseritur, ut vester regalissimus principatus terras inimicorum manu valida invadat et easdem terras per vos seu vobis subiectos regentes et dominos expugnet viriliter ac prosternat": Genet (ed.), *Four English Political Tracts*, p. 85. About Henry V, the author writes that he "vestre corone victoriosius cumulavit," and that he and his royal predecessors "invaserunt et manu belligera devastarunt" France: Genet (ed.), *Four English Political Tracts*, pp. 54, 78.

[76] The coats of arms in Lambeth Palace Libr. Arc.L.40.2/L.26, as identified by Sir Anthony Wagner, are on fol. I Richard II (Edward the Confessor impaling France Modern and England with the royal crest over), the old House of Lancaster, and the three shields probably belonging to families active in

6 Arms of St. Edmund. London, Lambeth Palace Library, MS Arc.L.40.2/L.26, fol. 84r

De regimine is also accompanied by an alphabetical index, a feature common enough in copies produced for the text's university-educated audience, but found in no other copy destined for the laity. Although the inclusion of this index may have been fortuitous, the result of having been unthinkingly copied from this manuscript's exemplar, it should nevertheless be noted that it occupies several folios, and therefore would have added to the production time and cost of the book. I am thus inclined to think that the index's presence here was the result of a conscious decision on the part of those responsible for the book's design. York, according to the chronicler John Hardyng, prided himself on his latinity, and such a distinctively clerical trapping could well have been meant to pay homage to the duke's learning.

One, and perhaps both, of Richard of York's royal sons possessed copies of *De regimine*. The duke's own copy passed to Richard, duke of Gloucester and the future King Richard III, as witnessed by the inscription on folio 1, "Liber illustrissimus Principis Ducis gloucestr'." The last three words of this inscription are now only visible under ultraviolet light, owing to their having been erased, a common fate of inscriptions in books formerly belonging to England's most vilified medieval king.[77] More ambiguous is the evidence for Edward IV, whose Wardrobe accounts for the year 1480 record payment "for binding gilding and dressing of a book called Le Gouvernement of Kinges and Princes," a book which the accounts later call "the Gouvernal of Kinges and Princes."[78] This title is so generic that it could refer to *De regimine* in its French or Middle English translations, or to some other similarly titled work, like Lydgate and Burgh's *Secrets of Old Philosophers*.[79] Nevertheless, the wording of the first entry may refer to a French translation of *De regimine*. It does appear, after all, that the Wardrobe clerk was making a deliberate effort to Anglicize French titles, and thus may have erred in copying the title of a French Giles, leaving the French article "le." Edward's ownership of a *Gouvernement* is certainly in keeping with what is known of his preference for works in French imported from the Low Countries.[80]

Since at least the twelfth century, the royalty and nobility of Europe had been aware of the connection between chivalry and learning.[81] Yet whereas the learning, or

Yorkist service; the king of the Romans (fol. 6v); Durham Cathedral Priory (fol. 22); The Ferrers family (fol. 27v); St. George (fol. 32); Richard of York with Mortimer in pretence (fol. 42); Henry Percy, earl of Northumberland, impaling his wife Eleanor Neville (fol. 51); the city of London (fol. 60); unidentified [argent, five lions or, on a cross gules] (fol. 68); St. Edmund (fol. 84); perhaps Bury St. Edmunds [azur, three crowns or] (fol. 84v): P. Tudor-Craig, *Richard III*, 2nd edn. (Ipswich, 1977), p. 65.   [77] Tudor-Craig, *Richard III*, p. 65.
[78] N. H. Nicolas, *Privy Purse Expenses of Elizabeth of York: Wardrobe Accounts of Edward the Fourth* (London, 1830), pp. 126, 152.   [79] On this problem, see above, p. 8.
[80] Backhouse, "Founders of the Royal Library," pp. 23–30.
[81] In his *Cligès*, Chrétien de Troyes remarked, "Our books have informed us that the pre-eminence in chivalry and learning once belonged to Greece. Then chivalry passed to Rome, together with that

clergie, of the upper stratum of the laity in 1200 had little of the bookishness that one associates with clerical learning, it had become fairly literary and even, in some ways, clerical, by the later Middle Ages.[82] Much of this was owing to the efforts of clerics like Giles of Rome, who had transferred to their lay audience aspects of that learning formerly reserved to clerical circles. In this chapter the focus has been on this audience's use of a single work. Yet it is important to remember that Giles's mirror was but one representative of an ever-expanding body of literature, in Latin and the vernacular, either originally destined for, or consequently appropriated by, a lay audience that was itself expanding and would come by the end of the Middle Ages to include not just royalty and aristocracy, but also representatives of the rural and urban middle classes.[83] The libraries of these literate lay people usually included many works besides *De regimine*, two of the most popular of these being the pseudo-Aristotelian *Secretum secretorum* and Vegetius' *De re militari*.[84] Both of these were closely associated with *De regimine* in the minds of their medieval readers, the *Secretum* as a book of princely instruction and the *De re militari* as a military manual, or book of knighthood.[85]

As this chapter has tried to show, the lay audience of *De regimine* used it for several different reasons, which varied depending on the current preoccupations and needs of the readers. All their uses were consonant with the subject matter of the text itself. And yet while the text remained largely static (with some variation owing to translation and abridgment, of course) the portions of the text read, as well as the interpretations of them, would vary in accordance with the needs and agendas of different readers. Those responsible for the instruction of Edward III may have been interested primarily in the formation of a responsible ruler. Richard II and his supporters may have fastened their attention especially on the portions of the text that lent legitimacy to a policy of absolutist rule, while Richard's opponents may have been particularly struck by Giles's insistence that the prince rule in accordance with the needs of his people and with the council of his magnates. Henry V

---

highest learning which now has come to France": quoted in J. Le Goff, *Medieval Civilization*, trans. J. Barrow (Oxford, 1988), pp. 171–2.

[82] G. Duby, *The Three Orders: Feudal Society Imagined*, trans. A. Goldhammer (Chicago, 1980), pp. 306–7; N. Orme, "The Education of the Courtier," in *English Court Culture*, ed. Scattergood and Sherborne, pp. 70–85; McFarlane, "Education of the Nobility," pp. 228–47.

[83] M. B. Parkes, "The Literacy of the Laity," in *Literature and Western Civilization: The Medieval World*, ed. D. Daiches and A. Thorlby (London, 1973), pp. 555–77.

[84] On the manuscripts and use of the *Secretum*, see Manzalaoui (ed.), *Secretum Secretorum*, pp. xxii–xlvi; A. H. Gilbert, "Notes on the Influence of the *Secretum Secretorum*," *Speculum* 3 (1928), pp. 84–98. On the manuscripts and use of Vegetius, see Shrader, "Handlist," *Scriptorium* 33 (1979), pp. 280–305; D. Bornstein, "Military Manuals in Fifteenth-Century England," *Mediaeval Studies* 37 (1975), pp. 467–77; J. A. Wisman, "L'*Epitoma rei militaris* de Végèce et sa fortune au Moyen Age," *Le Moyen Age* 85 (1979), pp. 13–31.

[85] The genres of mirrors of princes, books of knighthood, and courtesy books were closely related in the minds of their lay audience: Keen, *Chivalry*, p. 16; Ferguson, *Indian Summer*, pp. 193–4; Bornstein, *Mirrors of Courtesy*, p. 62.

and his nobles recognized *De regimine*'s utility as a military manual along the lines of Vegetius' *De re militari.* They may even have thought it a bit more useful than its late antique model, thanks to its user-friendly organization and more up-to-date material on siegecraft.[86] After the great warrior king's death, there would have been those like the clerical author of the *Tractatus de regimine principum ad Regem Henricum Sextum*, as well perhaps as nobles like Humphrey of Gloucester and John Talbot, who must have hoped that Henry V's less illustrious son would also ingest and put to use the valuable lessons of Master Giles. Proud and power-hungry men like Thomas of Woodstock, Richard of York, and perhaps Richard III, may have believed that their possession of and familiarity with the lore found in texts like the *De regimine* added legitimacy to their pretensions to the royal throne, while lesser or less ambitious men probably appreciated the fact that ownership of *De regimine* was an attribute of princes.

All these uses and perceptions of *De regimine* were grounded in the recognition of the importance of learning, and thus of education, the path to learning. Of course, the *De regimine* is in essence a book of instruction, and this instruction extended to children and youths, as well as adults. Giles not only dedicated an entire part of *De regimine* to the subject of child-rearing and education, all of his mirror's first book focuses on the elementary ethical formation of the individual. Personal ethics were a constant subject of medieval discourse, whether in the literary genres of mirrors of princes, books of courtesy, and devotional texts, or in words spoken from the pulpit and in the confessional. Children were expected to learn their morals, and I presume that many children of royal and aristocratic households were exposed to at least some of Giles's teaching on this subject.[87] One manuscript in particular may have been used for precisely this purpose. Durham Univ. Libr. Cosin V.I.9, a French-language Giles executed in England *c.* 1400, bears several features that suggest it may have been intended to serve as a child's schoolbook. It contains only the first book of the *Gouvernement*, and thus its text is limited to the material that would have been most appropriate for the instruction of a child or youth. Moreover, it is written in an exceptionally large Anglicana script: so large, in fact, that while the page size of this manuscript measures a not ungenerous 290 x 185 mm, the text space is limited to a single block of only eighteen lines, this, despite the manuscript consisting entirely of paper, an exceedingly rare commodity in late fourteenth- and early fifteenth-century England.[88] The choice to write so large on such a rare support has led me to think that whoever commissioned this book never intended to have the entire text of Giles, for if he or she had, the scribe would

---

[86] F. H. Sherwood, "Studies in Medieval Uses of Vegetius' *Epitoma rei militaris*," Ph.D. dissertation, University of California at Los Angeles, 1980, pp. 229–49.

[87] On this, see also Orme, *From Childhood to Chivalry*, pp. 92–7.

[88] R. J. Lyall, "Materials: The Paper Revolution," in *Book Production*, ed. Griffiths and Pearsall, pp. 11–12. N. R. Ker in *MLGB* lists only three paper manuscripts from the early fifteenth century.

almost certainly have been asked to write in a script of standard dimensions, and this would easily have allowed for the inclusion of all three books. But the material of the first book, written so large, would have been well suited to the purpose of educating a child, who would at the same time have been able to improve his or her command of written French.[89]

---

[89] Ian Doyle first suggested to me the notion that this manuscript may have been intended for a child. Another manuscript containing only the first book of *De regimine* is BN lat. 12431.

4

From Latin into English

Philosophers saw that no vulgar idiom was complete and perfect enough to express perfectly ... things that they wished to dispute about. So they fashioned for themselves a sort of idiom appropriate for these ends, that is called Latin ... which they made so large and copious that with it they could sufficiently express everything they thought of. Wherefore if Latin is a complete language, and we cannot properly and distinctly speak other languages lest we have been habituated to them from childhood, for the sake of eloquence – that is, so that we may speak Latin properly and distinctly – if we wish to learn letters, we should set to this task from very childhood.[1]

If Giles's advice here had been followed, there would have been little need to translate *De regimine* or any other learned Latin works, since the latinity of princes and nobles would have been beyond reproach. Yet although some later medieval rulers and aristocrats attained fluency in reading Latin, the vast majority of non-clerical readers during this time would have had trouble understanding unaided the learned Latin of texts like *De regimine*. Still, from the latter part of the thirteenth century there was a growing hunger on the part of the laity for the lore contained in just these sorts of texts. This desire, matched by a willingness on the part of many clerics to make this literature available to their lay patrons, was the cause of one of the most striking intellectual movements of the later Middle Ages: the vernacularization of a great body of learned Latin works.

The first wave of this movement began in the latter part of the thirteenth century in France.[2] At its heart lay the "problématique médiévale du rapport entre le

---

[1] "Videntes enim philosophi nullum idioma vulgare esse completum et perfectum, per quod perfecte exprimere possent naturas rerum, et mores hominum, et cursus astrorum, et alia de quibus disputare volebant; invenerunt sibi quasi proprium idioma, quod dicitur latinum, vel idioma literale: quod constituerunt adeo latum et copiosum, ut per ipsum possent omnes suos conceptus sufficienter exprimere. Quare si hoc idioma est completum et alia idiomata non possumus recte et distincte loqui, nisi ab ipsa infantia assuescamus ad illa: ex parte eloquentiae, videlicet ut recte et disincte loquamur idioma latinum, si volumus literas discere, debemus ab ipsa infantia literis insudare": *DRP* 2.2.7.

[2] J. Monfrin, "Les traducteurs et leur public en France au Moyen Age," *Journal des savants* (1964), pp. 5–20; P. F. Dembowski, "Learned Latin Treatises in French: Inspiration, Plagiarism, and Translation," *Viator* 17 (1986), pp. 256–69.

pouvoir politique et le savoir," as conceived by the later Capetian and early Valois kings.[3] Those who gave expression to this same problematic and who attempted to provide the monarchy with the means to address and exploit it were the translators, most of whom had been educated at the University of Paris. Under Charles V the connection between learning, translation, and royal power would attain its ripest expression in the prologue of Nicole Oresme's translation of Aristotle's *Ethics* and *Politics*. In contrast to Giles, Oresme did not believe that Latin was inherently superior to the vernacular, for he reckoned that when the learning of the Greeks arrived in Rome, the Romans' vernacular, that is Latin, had been no more able adequately to express learned concepts than was the French of his own day. Latin had to be made into a learned language, and so would French. Once this had been effected, French would replace Latin as the language of learned discourse: "par mon labeur pourra estre mieulx entendue ceste noble science et ou temps avenir estre bailliee par autres en françois plus clerement et plus complectement."[4]

Produced in 1282, Henri de Gauchy's French translation of *De regimine*, entitled *Li livres du gouvernement des roys et des princes*, was one of the very earliest of these vernacular prose translations prepared under the auspices of the French royal family. What Gauchy and the other translators shared was a desire to faithfully render the form and content of the translated text, and thus, in effect, to serve the source text and its audience.[5] Gauchy's "service translation" of *De regimine* became the standard French-language version, as the thirty surviving copies of its full text or abridgments attest. Nevertheless, during the fourteenth and fifteenth centuries three independent French translations of *De regimine* would be produced. The motivation of these translators and their patrons may have been to prepare fuller and more accurate renderings of Giles's Latin original. For, if one examines Gauchy's *Gouvernement* closely, it becomes apparent that his translation is not as faithful as it might have been. It is, to begin with, slightly shorter than the Latin original, thanks to Gauchy's skillful removal of some repetitious material and his more compressed phrasing. He also made some structural modifications, for although he honored the book and part divisions of the original, he consolidated some chapters and completely excised a few others, thereby reducing 209 chapters to only 193. Though most of these excisions were made in order to streamline Giles's often ponderous arguments, in one case Gauchy removed a chapter whose subject matter he thought too complicated for a lay reader. Chapter 26 of the second part of book 3 of the Latin original delves into Roman law theory and discusses the differences between the law of peoples, the law of animals, and natural law. In Gauchy's version, however, this chapter (bk. 3, pt. ii, ch. 23 of the *Gouvernement*)

---

[3] S. Lusignan, "La topique de la *translatio studii* et les traductions françaises de textes savants au XIVe siècle," in *Traduction et traducteurs au Moyen Age*, ed. G. Contamine (Paris, 1989), p. 306.

[4] Quoted in Lusignan, "Topique de la *translatio*," p. 312.

[5] Dembowski, "Learned Latin Treatises," pp. 256–61.

consists only of this heading: "Le xxiij chapitre enseigne comment droit de nature de gent et droit de bestes sont diverses de droit de nature et propres ans clers et ou ne les puet parler entendiblement et le puet hom savoir par le latin a dire a clerc."[6]

Gauchy abridged slightly in the interest of informing an audience that was accustomed neither to the meticulous and repetitious discourse of the university classroom, nor to the highly technical material treated therein. The later French translators seem to have taken a somewhat different view of the needs of their readers. Rather than shortening Giles's text and sending the reader to a clerk in order to gain an understanding of the contents of particularly difficult portions of the text, they prepared versions that adhered very closely to the original.[7] The translator of the earliest independent version, now uniquely preserved in Bibl. de l'Arsenal 2690, even added a substantial commentary. In one of the glosses he informed his patron, a bourgeois of Orleans named Guillaume de Beles Voies, that his job as translator was to understand completely the meaning of the Latin text so that he might properly translate it into French.[8] His patron, however, was expected to attain a full understanding of Giles's *sentence* in French, and to help him achieve that the translator prepared the commentary, which draws heavily from Scripture and the works of Thomas Aquinas.

The six French translations in the English Group are without exception copies of Gauchy's version. With the exception of Walters Art Gallery W. 144, none appears to have been produced or to have arrived in England prior to the end of the fourteenth century. Only three copies, two of which originated in France, contain the full text. The remaining three copies are abridgments and, of these, two are French products. All these copies of the *Gouvernement*, as well as the lost copy prepared for King Edward III and later owned by Henry of Grosmont, another in the possession of Sir Peter Arderne, and possibly one other in the library of King Edward IV, belonged to lay readers. Several other English lay readers were familiar with the Latin original; these included William Lord Thorp of Northampton, Thomas of Woodstock and his wife, Eleanor de Bohun (though hers may possibly have been in French), Humphrey, duke of Gloucester, Henry Lord Percy, Richard, duke of York, and his son King Richard III, John Broughton of Toddington, and a member of the gentry family of Pert, as well, presumably, as King Henry V and John, duke of Bedford.[9]

Among lay readers, then, *De regimine* achieved an admirable popularity. Common sense would seem to dictate that the presence of such a substantial audi-

[6] This is quoted from Walters Art Gallery W. 144, fols. 96v–97; also printed in Molenaer (ed.), *Li Livres du Gouvernement*, p. 347. [7] See above, pp. 16–17.

[8] Arsenal 2690, fols. 6–6v: "Si com se ie uous doi enseigner ce que est contenu en cest liure que ie translate a uostre requeste de latin en francois par ma translacion presuppose chose est de part moi que ie aie entendement de la sentence entierement la quelle est contenue en cest liure en latin et que ie fache le francois ou quel le latin doit estre transmuhe . . ."

[9] See above, table 5 and chapter 3.

ence receptive to this text, in what for them amounted at best to a second language, would have provided fertile ground for an even larger lay readership for the text in their mother tongue, English. This was to be the case, after all, with the *Secretum secretorum* and Vegetius' *De re militari*, Latin works closely related to *De regimine* in the minds of their medieval readers. Thus when, at around the turn of the fifteenth century, John Trevisa prepared his translation of the *De regimine* for his patron, the powerful West Country nobleman, Thomas Lord Berkeley, both translator and patron may well have expected that this translation would eventually become the standard vehicle through which the English laity would learn Giles's lore on the rule of princes.

Trevisa probably became inspired to translate Latin works into English while a scholar at Queen's College, Oxford during the 1370s, where with fellow residents John Wyclif and Nicholas Hereford, he may well have participated in the translation of the Bible into English.[10] Whether or not he cut his teeth as a translator on the English Bible project, by 1385–7, the years during which he translated Ranulf Higden's *Polychronicon* for Lord Berkeley, he had formulated the theoretical justification and framework for the translation project that he was to pursue for the remainder of his life. Trevisa reveals his views about the usefulness and worthiness of English translations of Latin works in his *Dialogue between a Lord and a Clerk upon Translation*, a work which he prefixed to the *Polychronicon* translation, and in a gloss which he inserted in the *Polychronicon* itself. In the *Dialogue* he makes it quite clear that English stands with Hebrew, Greek, Latin, and French as a worthy vehicle for the accurate transmission of information, whether sacred or profane:

Aristoteles bokes and oþere bokes also of logyk and of philosophy were translated out of Gru into Latyn. Also, atte prayng of Kyng Charles [the Bald], Iohn Scot translated Seint Denys hys bokes out of Gru ynto Latyn. Also holy wriyt was translated out of Hebrew ynto Gry and out of Gru into Latyn and þanne out of Latyn ynto Frensch. þanne what haþ Englysch trespased þat hyt myȝt noȝt be translated into Englysch?[11]

For Trevisa, matter was committed to writing in order to transmit and retain meaning. For those who "konneþ Englysch and no Latyn" the meaning contained in Latin must "be told an Englysch" and to do this "hit nedeþ to haue an Englysch translacion." But mere spoken translation from a Latin text, in the manner frequently employed by preachers, was insufficient "for to kepe hyt in muynde þat hyt be noȝt vorȝut hyt ys betre þat such a translacion be ymad and ywryte þan yseyde and noȝt ywryte."[12]

[10] D. C. Fowler, *The Life and Times of John Trevisa, Medieval Scholar* (Seattle, 1995), pp. 225–31, and "John Trevisa and the English Bible," *Modern Philology* 58 (1960), pp. 81–98; S. L. Fristedt, *The Wycliffe Bible: Part III* (Stockholm, 1973), pp. 8–58. See also A. Hudson, *The Premature Reformation: Wycliffite Texts and Lollard History* (Oxford, 1988), pp. 394–7.

[11] R. A. Waldron, "Trevisa's Original Prefaces on Translation: A Critical Edition," in *Medieval English Studies Presented to George Kane*, ed. E. D. Kennedy, R. Waldron, and J. S. Wittig (Wolfeboro, N.H., 1988), p. 292.   [12] Waldron, "Trevisa's Original Prefaces," p. 292.

Yet if Trevisa's impetus for making English translations may have sprung from an egalitarianism that arose in part from attitudes expressed at Queen's College by his Wycliffite colleagues, why did Thomas Berkeley promote vernacular translation? Ralph Hanna has argued that Berkeley's patronage of Trevisa's translations was to some extent a manifestation of his desire to exercise lordship; thus it was a unique expression of an utterly conventional desire.[13] As for why he embarked upon this particular course, Hanna turns to the words of the Lord in the *Dialogue between a Lord and Clerk* (a character whom Trevisa clearly identified with Berkeley himself), who recommends the translation of the *Polychronicon* because it contains "noble and gret informacion and lore." Of course, for a layman like Berkeley not learned in the Latin of the schools, translation played a crucial role in all of this, because it removed "any Latin linguistic screen between the lay reader and authoritative materials" thereby allowing him "to operate on the text without a clerical intermediary." This "informacion and lore" would come to include "a complete analysis of the created world, which placed man among all 'things'" ([Bartholomaeus Anglicus's] *Properties*); a complete depiction of human activity (in Higden's universal history); and a model for the exercise of control over the world (*De regimine*)."[14]

Missing from Hanna's consideration is the fact that when Trevisa made his translations, two of those works, *De regimine* and Bartholomaeus's *De proprietatibus rerum*, had already been translated into French.[15] Trevisa, however, in a gloss to the *Polychronicon* translation gives a neat answer to this *desideratum*, wherein he claims that Higden's statement that children in England learn to construe Latin through the medium of French is out of date, for though "this manner was much used before the first Death [of 1348–49] . . . John Cornwall, a master of grammar, changed the lore in grammar school and construction of French into English" so that "now children of grammar school know no more French than their left heel," and moreover, "gentlemen have now much left off teaching their children French."[16] Trevisa's assessment of the decline of French in late fourteenth-century England seems to be confirmed by the flourishing of Middle English literature at this time, as well as by the gradual shift, beginning in the reign of Edward III, from French to English as a language for official government business.[17] As for the Berkeley household itself, David Fowler has surmised that though Sir Thomas may

---

[13] Hanna, "Sir Thomas Berkeley," pp. 885, 914–16.   [14] *Ibid.*, p. 898.

[15] Jean Corbechon translated Bartholomaeus for Charles V in 1372, which translation was certainly circulating in England by the fifteenth century: Sherman, *Imaging Aristotle*, p. 8; Green, *Poets and Princepleasers*, p. 153.

[16] Quoted, with modernized spelling, in Fowler, *Life and Times*, pp. 183–4.

[17] A statute of 1362 ordered (albeit with little success) the use of English in the law courts, and in the following year parliament was first opened in English. From 1417 Henry V consistently used English as the language of his signet letters drafted to English speakers: M. McKisack, *The Fourteenth Century, 1307–1399* (Oxford, 1959), pp. 197, 524; Allmand, *Henry V*, pp. 421–2.

well have been schooled in French, this familiarity may not have extended to the younger members of his family.[18] Moreover, since Berkeley undoubtedly had nothing like native fluency in French, he would probably have preferred reading a text in English over French, given the choice.[19]

It is worth remembering that quite possibly neither Trevisa nor Berkeley had access to the French translation of *De regimine*, and that they were probably unaware of the French *Propriétés des choses*, since very few copies of the former circulated in England prior to 1400 and Jean Corbechon had only recently translated the latter for Charles V.[20] Consequently, what appears to have been a preference for Middle English over French on Berkeley's part, may to some extent have been a preference for an easily comprehended text in the absence of French translations. If, on the other hand, he and Trevisa were acquainted with Gauchy's translation of *De regimine*, there is some reason to believe that Trevisa might have eschewed using it for the same reasons as the later French translators thought they could improve upon it, that is that it was not sufficiently "trysty and truwe" to its Latin source. Trevisa, to a much greater extent than Gauchy, made a translation that serves its source text. To begin with, he neither removes matter nor modifies the textual divisions of his source. But beyond this, he also takes great care to preserve the scholastic flavor of Giles's Latin discourse, even importing Giles's Latin citations of authorities and a good bit of Latin technical vocabulary;[21] in doing so, however, he still manages to respect the syntax and vocabulary of his native tongue, using native words (frequently in the form of doublets) and syntax when he can. He also makes a point of expanding upon and commenting on words or passages that he thinks his audience might find particularly difficult to understand. The end result is a translation that is intelligible and accurate, yet suitably idiomatic.[22] Some examples will serve to demonstrate his method. I have italicized the several instances where Trevisa has inserted explanatory words or phrases, and I have put in small capitals his use of Latin or latinate words or citations of authorities.

---

[18] Fowler, *Life and Times*, p. 184.   [19] Green, *Poets and Princepleasers*, p. 153.

[20] See above, p. 76.

[21] Compare, for example, the Latin and English passages from *DRP* 1.2.22 given below with Gauchy's rendering, which is more compressed and avoids direct borrowing of Latin words and phrases: Molenaer (ed.), *Li Livres du Gouvernement*, pp. 71–2.

[22] On these qualities in Trevisa's translations, see T. Lawler, "On the Properties of John Trevisa's Major Translations," *Viator* 14 (1983), pp. 267–88; R. A. Waldron, "John Trevisa and the Use of English," *Proceedings of the British Academy* 74 (1988), pp. 177–201.

Latin

In magnis autem honoribus tripliciter quis se habere potest, nam quidam in talibus deficiunt ut pusillanimes, quidam vero superhabundant ut presumptuosi, quidam autem se habent ut decet ut magnanimi. Videmus enim aliquos de se aptos ad magna potentes magna et ardua exercere quadam tamen pusillanimitate ducti retrahunt se ab huiusmodi magnis. Tales igitur in talibus deficiunt sed quidam econverso superhabundant in gerentes se ad aliqua que conplere digne non possunt quos philosophus vocat cahymos, id est fumosos et ventosos, nos autem eos presumptuosos vocare possumus.

Magnanimus igitur medius est inter pusillanimum et presumptuosum. Non enim se retrahit ab arduis operibus que potest digne agere, ut pusillanimus, nec se ingerit ad ea que digne complere non potest, ut presumptuosus. Quare manifeste patet quid sit magnanimus. Nam sicut liberalitas, quia est media inter avaricias et prodigalitates, ideo est virtus quedam reprimens avaricias et moderans prodigalitates, sic magnanimitas que est media inter pusillanimitatem et presumpcionem est virtus quedam reprimens pusillanimitates et moderans presumpciones (*DRP*, 1.2.22).

English

[A man may haue hymself] in gret honour and worschep in þre maner wise, for som hauen defaute and failen þerinne and is icleped PUSILLANIMUS, þat is <unherty> – <modeles>; and som passen and is icleped PRESUMPTUOSUS, *proude*; and som hath hymself wel and as he scholde and is icleped MAGNANIMUS. For we seeth þat som is of hymsilf able to grete dedes and may do grete dedes and vse grete dedes and is som what vnherty and coward and wiþdraweth hymself fro suche grete dedes, þanne suche oon hath defaute and failleth. And somme aȝenward passen and putteþ hemself to som dedes þe whiche he may not worthilich do at þe folle; and þe philosofer clepeth suche on KA(U)NUS, ID EST, FUMOSUS ET VENTOSUS (*smeche and fol of wynd*), and we may clepe suche oon PRESUMPTUOSUS.

þanne MAGNANIMUS is mene bytwene PUSILLANIMUS and PRESUMPTUOSUS, for he withdraweth hym nouȝt fro grete dedes þat he may worthilich do atte þe fulle as PUSILLANIMUS doþ, noþer taketh more vppon hym þan he may worthilich do at þe folle as PRESUMPTUOS dooþ. And so it is declared what is MAGNANIMITAS: for as LIBERALITAS is mene bitwene AUARICIA (*scarsete and chincherie*) and PRODEGALITAS (*passynge and vnwys spendyng*), and is þerfore a certyn vertue abatyng AUARICIA and moderatyng PRODEGALITAS, so, for MAGNANIMITAS is mene bytwene PUSILLANIMITAS and PRESUMPCIOUN, it is a vertue abatynge PUSILLANIMITAS and moderatyng PRESUMCIOUN (*Governance*, pp. 85, line 39–86, line 17).

Viso ergo quid est magnanimitas et qualiter se habet ad virtutes alias, de levi patet qualis sit illa virtus de qua nunc intendimus, que dicitur honoris amativa. Nam sicut eadem opera possunt esse aliarum virtutum, et magnanimitatis sic eadem esse possunt aliarum virtutum et honoris amative. Opera enim aliarum

For it is declared what is MAGNANIMITAS and how it hath itsilf to oþere vertues, it is sone iknowe which is þe vertue of þe whiche now we schal trete: þat vertue hatte HONORIS AMATIUA. For as þe same workes may be þe workis of oþer vertuis and of MAGNANIMITATE, so þe same workis may be þe workis of oþer vertuis and of þe vertue

virtutum ut sunt magno honore digna pertinent ad magnanimitatem. Sed ut sunt proportionata nobis et ut ordinantur ad mediocres honores, pertinent ad virtutem, que dicitur honoris amativa (*DRP*, 1.2.24).	þat hatte HONORIS AMATIUA *by þe whiche vertue we louen honour and worschep.* And workes of oþere vertues bien worthi greet honour and worschep þat perteyneth to MAGNANIMITE; but as þei bien PROPORCIONATE to vs and to mene honour and worschip, he perteyneth to þe vertue þat hatte HONORIS AMATIUA, *as it were loue and desire of worschep* (*Governance*, p. 90, lines 25–34).

Trevisa's explanations and expansions of the Latin are usually quite brief, as can be observed in the above passages. Occasionally, however, he includes rather more lengthy comments, three of which he signs "Trevisa."[23] These longer explanatory passages seem designed to clarify concepts that may not have been readily comprehensible to his intended lay audience. Yet, as Fiona Somerset has recently observed, the location in the text of several of these signed and unsigned Trevisan notes suggests a particular concern on Trevisa's part, and perhaps on Lord Berkeley's as well, to explain thoroughly that portion of Giles's text that treats specifically of tyrannical government and of counsel, two problems that loomed large in the charged political atmosphere of Richard II's reign.[24] A similar preoccupation may have lain behind a pair of interpolations that occur in the last four lines of each of the columns on folio 48 in the Digby manuscript, and in a chapter (1.3.5) which discusses "how kynges and princes schulde haue hem in trist and hope, in wanhope and dispeir." Neither interpolation finds any precedent in extant Latin copies of *De regimine*, and both have been crossed out by the same person responsible for crossing out several other passages in the manuscript. The interpolations (in italics) and text immediately surrounding them are given below:

And by twey weyes we may preue þat kynges and *princes shulde auenture hemself as in goodnesse schewyng to alle oþer sogettes, for foly hardynesse of hem my3t destrue manye //* princes sholde not auentre in doyng þat passeth here owne my3t and strength, noþer hath more hope þan he scholde.

3if it is inconuenient to pute al þe men and al þe regne *in subieccioun and peril and þerfore it is semelich þat euery astat take hede þerof for it is nedfol þat kynges and princes put hem in strengþe //* to peril kynges and princes schulde wiþ longe counseille and with greet besinesse and auysement bythenke in what doyng he schulde auenture.[25]

The source of these interpolations cannot be determined with certainty, though I would be surprised if they originated with the Digby scribe. What seems more

---

[23] Trevisa, *Governance*, pp. 335, 352, 354.
[24] From a chapter on Trevisa which Dr. Somerset graciously shared with me from her forthcoming contribution to Cambridge Studies in Medieval Literature, provisionally entitled *Clerical Discourse and Lay Audience in Late Medieval England.*   [25] Trevisa, *Governance*, p. 124.

likely, given the state of the text in Digby (a subject to which I will turn shortly), is that either Trevisa himself, or a reader of the Trevisan autograph which served as the exemplar of Digby, penned these remarks, and that the scribe unthinkingly incorporated them into the text: a "mistake" later discovered and crossed out. Nor is their meaning very clear. According to David Fowler, the interpolations "seem to offer refinements or qualifications" of Giles's warning that rulers ought to avoid foolhardiness. The first interpolation "suggests that kings and princes should be bold in doing good," while from the tenor of the second, "it sounds as if, at the time these lines were written, English society was beginning to feel like an armed camp."[26]

Whatever the motivations behind this translation may have been, whatever the sentiments expressed in the additions to its text, and however useful Trevisa and Sir Thomas may have felt it was, one thing is certain: the text did not proliferate.[27] The only copy of the English translation of *De regimine* that survives is the one found in Bodleian Digby 233. Moreover, there is precious little evidence of lost copies. What little there is, the "engelisce booke calde Giles de regimine principum" in the inventory of Sir Thomas Charlton's goods, though it may have been a second copy of Trevisa's translation, could also have been an independent translation, now lost (though I think this is unlikely), or the result of mistaken labeling of an English *Secretum secretorum* or Hoccleve's *Regement of Princes*, two popular works that frequently went by the title *De regimine principum*, and that contemporaries sometimes confused with Giles's mirror.[28]

Trevisa's version's failure to multiply can be explained, at least in part, with reference to both general and specific causes. As far as the general causes are concerned, there was the ambiguous status of the English language itself. In France, the promotion of French played an important role in the political and ideological program of the Capetian and Valois monarchs, as well as of some of the great ducal houses in the fifteenth century.[29] In England, on the contrary, prior to the middle of the fifteenth century the status of the mother tongue was hampered by two factors. One of these was of long standing, that is the preeminence of French since the time of the Conquest as the language of courtly culture, the courts of law, and parliament. Thus, while the French monarchy could make a relatively straightforward correlation between the promotion of vernacular translation and the *pouvoir royal,* English kings of the late thirteenth to the fourteenth century could make no such connection between their interests and the promotion of English as a language of learning. And yet at the same time as they discredited the worthiness of their own

[26] Fowler, *Life and Times,* p. 198.

[27] For photographs and a somewhat more detailed discussion of this manuscript, see C. F. Briggs, "MS Digby 233 and the Patronage of John Trevisa's, *De regimine principum,*" *English Manuscript Studies, 1100–1700* (1998, forthcoming).   [28] See above, p. 8.

[29] Lusignan, *Parler vulgairement,* pp. 133–40.

mother tongue for such pursuits, the status of their cultivated tongue, French, was also ambiguous, since on the one hand it could not be regarded as the language of the English, while on the other it could be construed as the language of England's enemy in the Hundred Years War. This was hardly the recipe for an aggressively pursued policy of vernacular translation, whether into English or French, and so far as translations of learned Latin works were concerned, the English royal court was relegated to the status of consumer of translations made for its rival across the Channel. It is little wonder, then, that the center of England's earliest and most prolific program of vernacular translation was not in the capital but rather in the household of a provincial nobleman.

Of much more recent advent was the association of English with Lollardy and sedition. The latter probably had very little impact on the fate of the English *De regimine*, since Archbishop Arundel's prohibition of 1409 against the use of English was aimed at texts with a religious content.[30] Nevertheless, as Anne Hudson has pointed out, it may have helped create a climate of fear that "the expression of ideas gained from Latin books and expressed in English" might be taken as "*ipso facto* evidence of heresy." Moreover, Arundel's prohibition promoted and was in turn supported by reactionary sentiments against English like those expressed in the Oxford *determinatio* (*c.* 1401–7) of Thomas Palmer, who characterized English as a "barbarous tongue . . . grammatically and rhetorically inadequate as a vehicle for truth."[31] Thus the climate of fear in the aftermath of Arundel's Constitutions against heresy and the fostering of prejudice within the academic community against English may together have helped ensure that quite some time would pass before the ambitious translation project begun by Trevisa would be taken up again.

These observations on the ambiguous and contested status of English help account for why the enterprise of producing translations of learned Latin works never flourished in late medieval England to the same extent that it did in France and Italy. They do not explain, however, why the fate of Trevisa's *De regimine* was so at odds with the success of his versions of the *Polychronicon* and *De proprietatibus rerum*. Fourteen copies of the former survive, while the latter is extant in eleven manuscripts;[32] and their circulation was not limited to manuscripts, as Caxton printed them both. He did not print the *De regimine*, however; nor, for that matter, was he even aware that Trevisa had ever translated it.[33] Attempts have been made to

---

[30] N. Watson, "Censorship and Cultural Change in Late-Medieval England: Vernacular Theology, the Oxford Translation Debate, and Arundel's Constitutions of 1409," *Speculum* 70 (1995), pp. 828–9.

[31] *Ibid.*, pp. 829, 842–3.

[32] R. A. Waldron, "The Manuscripts of Trevisa's Translation of the *Polychronicon*: Towards a New Edition," *Modern Language Quarterly* 51 (1990), pp. 281–317; M. C. Seymour *et al.* (eds.), *On the Properties of Things: John Trevisa's Translation of Bartholomeus Anglicus, De Proprietatibus Rerum*, vol. III (Oxford, 1988), pp. 12–26.

[33] A. S. G. Edwards, "John Trevisa," in *Middle English Prose: A Critical Guide to Major Authors and Genres*, ed. A. S. G. Edwards (New Brunswick, N.J., 1984) pp. 137–8.

explain the peculiar conditions that militated against the English *De regimine*'s successful proliferation. There are those who have argued that Lord Berkeley himself constricted its circulation. According to David Fowler, who thinks Trevisa translated *De regimine* for Berkeley in 1388–92, the period falling between his two other major translation campaigns, Sir Thomas may have confined Trevisa's translation strictly to personal use during the 1390s.[34] Fowler has suggested to me that Berkeley's impetus for this could have ranged from a desire to keep such useful information to himself and his closest associates as they thought about ways to control the damage arising from Richard II's misrule, to fear that active dissemination of such a text might have smacked of treason to King Richard and his supporters. Fiona Somerset has entertained the notion that Berkeley may have decided an English *De regimine* was too politically efficacious to fall into the hands of lesser people, who might enlist its information for subversive ends.[35] Others have approached the problem from the direction of audience demand. For Richard Green, the availability of French translations of *De regimine* would have undercut the English version's audience, while Ralph Hanna has credited the same effect to the publication, beginning in 1411, of Hoccleve's *Regement of Princes*.[36]

Fowler's suspicions about Berkeley's concerns may be plausible enough, but what about the years between Richard's deposition in 1399 and Lord Berkeley's death in 1417? Somerset's hypothesis, of course, moves the *terminus ante quem* right up to the time of Berkeley's decease. Yet I am inclined to think that such apprehensions were far more likely in the context of scriptural or Lollard texts than in that of princely mirrors. Such a fate did not await other mirrors or the English version of Vegetius' *De re militari*, a work also translated at Berkeley's bidding. Green's and Hanna's arguments both seem to me to have considerable merit for the years after around 1415; for by that time copies of the *Regement* had begun to circulate, and within a few years English involvement in France would lead to the importation of copies of Gauchy's *Gouvernement* as well as of some Latin *De regimine* manuscripts of French origin. Moreover, the appetite of the English aristocracy for the French translation may have been whetted by renewed English efforts at schooling in French. Henry V, after all, claimed France as its rightful king, and there is evidence that the English nobility began to study the French of Paris in order to serve more effectively as soldiers and diplomats, and as administrators in English-held parts of France.[37] Neither Hanna nor Green, however, accounts for the period between *c.* 1390 and *c.* 1415.

Physical and textual evidence in the sole surviving copy of Trevisa's English *De regimine*, however, seems to provide a plausible solution to the problem of this text's failure to achieve much of an audience. Digby 233 is a very large (460 × 325

[34] Fowler, *Life and Times*, pp. 189–90.   [35] Somerset, *Clerical Discourse*.
[36] Green, *Poets and Princepleasers*, pp. 153–4; Hanna, "Sir Thomas Berkeley," p. 913.
[37] Lusignan, *Parler vulgairement*, pp. 101–18.

mm), elegant, illuminated book, that pairs Trevisa's *De regimine* with the earliest known copy of the Middle English translation of Vegetius' *De re militari*. Though the manuscript contains very little in the way of the kinds of evidence usually relied upon to establish date of execution and patronage or intended original ownership, a number of features in the manuscript, when considered *in toto*, firmly establish its credentials as a book produced by a local group of artisans for the Berkeley household between the years 1408 and *c.* 1417. Most obviously, both of the translations in Digby 233 are closely associated with Berkeley patronage. The *De regimine* translation is clearly the work of Trevisa, who from the 1380s until his death in 1402 was Sir Thomas Berkeley's chaplain and in-house translator; its companion text concludes with a translator's colophon (fol. 227) that explicitly states it was made for Lord Berkeley by the "worschepful   toun" (variously identified as John Walton or William Clifton) and completed on All-Hallows Eve in 1408.[38] Moreover, a tiny swan badge located at the bottom of the intercolumnar space on the verso of folio 199 could very well signify Richard Beauchamp, earl of Warwick, the husband of Sir Thomas's only child, Elizabeth.

Turning now to the book's conditions of production, the dialect of Digby's scribe is southwestern, with features localizable to the region around Berkeley castle, while the script itself is a fine rounded Anglicana Formata of the early fifteenth century. The firmest proof of Digby's Berkeley origins, however, comes from a comparison of certain of its features with those in Bodleian Bodl. 953, a copy of Richard Rolle's glossed prose English Psalter, the one manuscript we know was locally produced for Thomas Berkeley.[39] The same artist executed the decorated borders in both manuscripts;[40] even more interesting is the presence of the same spidery corrector's hand in the margins of both books. These corrections, it should be pointed out, were completed while the manuscripts were still "in the workshop," since they were done prior to either book's having been illuminated.

Digby 233 reveals its intimacy with the Berkeley household in another way as well, in that the manuscript bears several traits that tie its English *De regimine* (hereafter called the *Governance*) directly to Trevisa's autograph. Yet these same marks are also evidence of a relationship between exemplar and copy that was problematized considerably by the condition of the exemplar. For, it appears, Trevisa had left to posterity not a completed fair copy of the *Governance*, but rather an unfinished working version, loaded with obscure, variant, and interpolated passages, and very likely in a highly abbreviated and current script. The most striking sign of this is the unusually extensive corrections written over erasures that litter the *Governance* (but not the Vegetius) portion of Digby 233. These corrections were first noted by Ralph Hanna, who mistakenly suspected they resulted in part from a

[38] Fowler, *Life and Times*, pp. 84–117.
[39] Doyle, "English Books," p. 173; Hanna, "Sir Thomas Berkeley," pp. 883–5.
[40] My thanks to Kathleen Scott for verifying this.

discontinuous method of copying.[41] Careful inspection of the Digby manuscript with an ultraviolet lamp has revealed that these corrections are far more extensive than Hanna realized, for erasures and overwrites of at least two or three lines, but very often of several lines, occur on virtually every page. The overwrites are mostly in the hand of the text scribe. Occasionally, however, these were executed in a more angular, though contemporary, script.

The ultraviolet lamp also shows that the immediate sources for the text of these overwrites were marginal corrections, written in the same hand responsible for the marginal corrections in Berkeley's copy of Rolle's prose Psalter. Hanna and others had missed these because they were thoroughly erased subsequent to their having been incorporated in the text space. Indeed the method of correction is identical in the Digby and Bodley manuscripts. What is not the same is the extent of correction, which is quite modest in Rolle's Psalter, but so heavy in the Digby *Governance* that it often required the corrector to cram his changes into the side, top, and bottom margins in order to locate them as closely as possible to the portions of text they were meant to correct, while at the same time he marked the boundaries of the text to be replaced with either carets or Xs. Very often the script of these overwrites is more compressed than that of the neighboring text, suggesting that the scribe had originally failed to incorporate material. While eye-skip could have accounted for some of these instances, the frequency and length of these corrections may very well also be evidence that the scribe often either misconstrued material from his exemplar, or made wrong choices between variant renderings therein.[42] Unfortunately, the erasure of the marginal corrections is so thorough that I have been unable to reconstruct their content and thus firmly determine their purpose. Mistakes also arose owing to scribal dittography, but instead of erasing the redundant passages in these cases, the corrector simply crossed them out.

Two conspicuous absences from the Digby *Governance* appear to support my suspicions regarding its exemplar. Trevisa provided colophons to his two other major translations, giving his name, the name of his patron, and the date of completion, yet one looks in vain for a translator's colophon at the conclusion of the *Governance*. Had Trevisa completed a fair copy of this translation, he likely would have penned a colophon; and had there been a colophon in the scribe's exemplar, he almost certainly would have copied it, as he copied the colophon of the Vegetius. Chapter headings also fail to appear in the *Governance*. This is highly uncharacteristic at several levels. To begin with, Trevisa's Latin exemplar probably had chapter headings, since I know of but one surviving Latin manuscript lacking them, and this could not have been Trevisa's exemplar.[43] Moreover, chapter head-

---

[41] Hanna, "Sir Thomas Berkeley," p. 897; Fowler, *Life and Times*, p. 192.
[42] Compare the strategies employed in Italian autographs and "author's books" in A. Petrucci, *Writers and Readers in Medieval Italy: Studies in the History of Western Culture*, ed. and trans. C. M. Radding (New Haven, 1995), pp. 145–68.   [43] Cambridge Univ. Libr. Ii.4.22.

ings do appear in Bodleian Hatton 15, the surviving Latin copy whose text most closely resembles that found in Digby 233. Assuming then that the Latin text from which Trevisa made his translation had chapter headings, it is fair to assume that he would have included them in his fair copy, as he made sure to do in his other translations.

Therefore, either the scribal team or their exemplar was responsible for the missing rubrics in the Digby *Governance*. The makers of Digby 233 can quickly be exonerated on the ground that they left no spaces between chapters for the subsequent inscription of headings – something they surely would have done had there been chapter headings in the exemplar. Spaces were, however, provided for this purpose in the Vegetius. Curiously, the spaces in the Vegetius are blank for the first couple of chapters, but then have been completed in black ink throughout its remainder. The decision to use black ink, rather than the red ink more usually employed for this purpose, may have resulted from an editorial decision on the part of the scribal team to maintain an even aesthetic of the page throughout the book.[44] Thus the exemplar appears to have been the culprit responsible for the missing chapter headings. Perhaps Trevisa, working in the same manner as a scribe making a copy, first translated the text only, anticipating, but never achieving, the later inclusion of chapter headings.

When considered together, the several anomalies in Digby 233 lend considerable weight to the idea that its makers worked not from a fair copy, but rather from Trevisa's own working copy. This also helps explain why the English *De regimine* never proliferated. Hanna has presented a strong argument for Berkeley's having avidly promoted his other Trevisan translations, either via local artisans or the London book trade, up until 1405.[45] If, as has been previously supposed, Trevisa completed this translation during the years 1388–92, it seems most unlikely that Berkeley would have avoided doing the same with the *De regimine*, if not before Richard II's deposition in 1399, then during the six years following. Yet the first and only surviving witness to this text was not begun until after All-Hallows Eve 1408, the date when another Berkeley translator completed the *De re militari* translation. Perhaps Berkeley even intended the Vegetius translation to serve as a companion text to the *De regimine*, given the propensity of the English to couple together these two works.[46] This is not to say that the *De regimine* was the last started of Trevisa's translations, since he could have worked on it during the period 1388–92. Yet it was certainly the last finished, or rather not even finished by Trevisa himself but by

[44] The editor of this English translation of Vegetius, who has mistakenly assumed that the copy in Digby was executed in the middle of the fifteenth century, misinterprets the absence of Latin headings in Digby as the result of scribal error. In fact, the Latin headings were a later addition, resulting perhaps from later copyists having assumed that the English headings were the initial sentences of the chapters they introduce: G. A. Lester (ed.), *The Earliest English Translation of Vegetius' "De re militari"* (Heidelberg, 1988), p. 34.　　[45] Hanna, "Sir Thomas Berkeley," pp. 909–13.

[46] See above, pp. 45–6.

Digby's scribes and corrector. It was they who were saddled with the difficult task of not only reconstructing the text in accordance with what they could surmise was Trevisa's final intention, but of doing so on the same parchment leaves that were destined to be bound into their patron's elegant book of politics and war. I am tempted to think that most of the success in this venture is owed to the corrector. He had, after all, also worked on Berkeley's copy of Rolle's Prose Psalter, a manuscript probably produced before Trevisa's death. Thus he may have been personally acquainted with Trevisa and his working methods, and was thereby able in large measure, and perhaps with the assistance of Lord Berkeley himself, to sort out the hash that the Digby scribe had understandably made of Trevisa's, and Giles's, *sentence*. In this sense, then, the Digby *Governance* was the product of a team effort, but of a team assembled expressly because its star player was missing. Quite possibly, then, Digby 233's scribes, corrector, and artists did not complete their labors until after the appearance in 1411 of Hoccleve's *Regement of Princes*, whose popularity, as Hanna has postulated, may have attenuated the potential demand for the English *De regimine*. Indeed the opportunities for Trevisa's translation to reach its potential audience could well have remained tightly constricted by hesitation on the part of Sir Thomas and its subsequent owners to part even temporarily with a book whose English *De regimine* was, after all, the only fair copy. Here it is instructive to compare the English *De regimine*'s failure to proliferate with the success of its companion text, the *De re militari*, whose exemplar, a separate fair copy, would then have served as the exemplar for other copies.[47]

After Berkeley's death, Digby 233 may have passed to his only child, Elizabeth, and her husband Richard Beauchamp, earl of Warwick. The swan badge inserted into the base of the partial border on folio 199 verso was probably meant to signify the Beauchamp connection.[48] Moreover, it may be Beauchamp's sentiment that lies behind a comment in a fifteenth-century hand – which is other than that of the scribes and corrector – found in the margin besides an injunction that rulers be open in their dealings. Here is the text with the addition in italics: "Also þei schulde be oponliche iknowe wheþer þey loue oþer hate, *and rese opon no man vnwarned nor sodaynly, nor with feyned sembland of luf,* so þat þei hate opunlich vices and pursewe euel doers and sufre not passyng euel doers alyue." The earl's father, Thomas Beauchamp, had been one of the Lords Appellant condemned by Richard II during the parliament of 1397. Though the elder Beauchamp survived, he did so at the cost of his honor, having been forced to make a degrading and humiliating public confession of treason, upon which he forfeited his lands and titles, and went

---

[47] There are eleven extant manuscripts: Lester (ed.), *Earliest English Translation*, pp. 17–23.

[48] For the use of the swan badge by the Beauchamps and by Henry V's mother's family, the Bohuns, see A. R. Wagner, "The Swan Badge and the Swan Knight," *Archaeologia* 97 (1959), pp. 127–38. Doyle, "English Books," p. 173, entertains the possibility that the swan in Digby may therefore signify Henry V.

into exile. One can well imagine that this marginal addition reflects the younger Beauchamp's anger and resentment toward a Richard II who had indeed showed false friendship for Earl Thomas, while all the while planning his revenge against him.

The lengths to which Berkeley and his Bristol book artisans went is proof of their desire to produce an accurate rendering of Trevisa's text (an effort for which Trevisa undoubtedly would have been grateful), and to present it in an aesthetically pleasing form. An important component of this aesthetic, the figural illustrations, may shed some light, albeit ambiguously, on the attitudes and intentions of this late medieval English aristocrat. The first two miniatures survive of the three that originally would have introduced each of the text's three books.[49] Both of the extant miniatures are in the form of long horizontal strips at the top of the page. In the first (fol. 1) a king, who occupies the center of the frame, sits upon an elaborate, rather architectonic throne. Immediately to his left, Giles, wearing the black cassock of his order, kneels and presents his open book to the sovereign. This standard presentation scene occurs in a courtly setting, for flanking the principals stand five lay and clerical courtiers, one of them bearing the ceremonial sword of state. Several courtiers accompany the king in the second miniature as well. Here, however, the crowd of courtiers, who stand to the right of the king, is counterbalanced on his left by a kneeling Giles, who directs the king's attention to a structure, meant to represent either the royal palace or the city, and who is himself immediately flanked on his left by a crowd of people, signifying either the household or the populace, and on his right by a figure bearing the sword of state.

Some aspects in these surviving illustrations invite comparison with miniatures found in other manuscripts. The king accompanied by courtiers was a common enough motif in a large number of English manuscripts of several unrelated texts.[50] And though the same motif is not found in other *De regimine* manuscripts of English origin, representations of the king, either with or without Giles, in a courtly setting appear in a few French manuscripts.[51] Depictions of a structure signifying the household or the city are also common enough in *De regimine* manuscripts, and the scene in the second Digby miniature puts one particularly in mind of the miniature that introduces *De regimine*'s third book in Cambridge Univ. Libr. Ff.3.3 (fol. 119v).[52] Yet if individual elements in the illustrations in Digby 233 are unremarkable in and of themselves, their message when combined together seems to accord well with what one suspects were Lord Berkeley's own preoccupations and aspirations regarding governance. The courtiers who accompany the prince were probably included in order to signify the ruler's duty to seek out the advice of

[49] Reproduced in Trevisa, *Governance*, pp. 2, 158.
[50] Scott, "*Caveat Lector*," pp. 32–4, 58. The resemblance is particularly striking in a miniature in Sir William Herbert's copy of Lydgate's *Troy Book* (BL Roy. 18.D.ii, fol. 6): Lawton, "Illustration," pp. 66–7.   [51] BL Harley 4385, fol. 1; BN fr. 213, fol. 3; BN fr. 1202, fol. 1.   [52] See above, p. 39.

his "natural councillors," the peers and prelates of the realm, while the kneeling Giles may have put Berkeley in mind of Trevisa's vernacular translations of learned literature, for these translations, though they gave the prince (or nobleman) direct access to the learning of scholars and the ancients, were nevertheless subservient to him, in that he was free to use their advice as best he saw fit.[53]

Mary Lady Hastings and Hungerford (d. 1533) is the only person besides Sir Thomas Berkeley whose association with Digby 233 prior to the modern era is beyond the realm of conjecture. Her inscription appears at the bottom of folio 288: "loyallte me ley / Mary Hastyngs Hungreford / bottreaux mollens and Mulles / god help me / Mhh m b / MH." The manuscript may have come into her possession by way of inheritance, since she was a descendant of Walter Lord Hungerford of Heytesbury, who had had business dealings with Thomas Berkeley and married one of his relatives, or she may have received it by way of her father-in-law, William Lord Hastings, Edward IV's chamberlain and a victim of Richard III's coup in 1483.[54] For whatever reasons, Lady Mary belonged to a group of readers, never amounting in total to more than a handful, who experienced the kind of direct access to Giles's lore that Trevisa and Lord Berkeley had envisioned. Nevertheless, as was made abundantly clear in the preceding chapter, the *De regimine* in Latin and French, as full text, abridgment, or adaptation, was well known among the English upper classes of the later Middle Ages. Unlike Trevisa and his patron, the majority of English lay readers were not purists but pragmatists when it came to picking and digesting the fruits of Giles's learned discourse. Moreover, thanks to the kind of education many English aristocrats were receiving by the latter part of the fourteenth century, Gauchy's French, though a trifle outdated, was on the whole readily comprehensible to them, while some, like Richard of York or the sons of Henry IV, were competent in Latin. As for those whose Latin was not up to the standards of a Humphrey, duke of Gloucester, they were probably not averse to calling on the services of a clerk, so that the *sentia* of the Latin text might be "reported in the common idiom," as Giles himself had recommended.[55]

---

[53] My analysis and interpretation of the miniatures differs somewhat from Hanna, "Sir Thomas Berkeley," p. 898. Somerset gives a very different interpretation in her forthcoming book.

[54] Doyle, "English Books," p. 173; Hanna, "Sir Thomas Berkeley," p. 897.

[55] *DRP* 2.3.20: quoted above, p. 1.

5

A university textbook

Here begins the Compendium of Moral Philosophy. This book contains some things drawn (according to sense, rather than word-for-word, to avoid prolixity) from a book which is called "On the Rule of Princes." Nevertheless, since certain things have been added from the sayings of others (and have been placed to one side in the manner of glosses) this book shall be called the "Compendium of Moral Philosophy" and will be divided into ten parts, as will be apparent in what follows.[1]

Although Giles of Rome ostensibly wrote his mirror primarily for the benefit of the future king of France, and secondarily for the instruction of the lay upper classes, the ranks of its clerical readership far outnumbered those of its lay audience. It is not hard to understand why. For rather than making concessions to the literary aesthetic of his stated audience in the manner of Guillaume de Lorris's and Jean de Meun's *Roman de la rose* or Brunetto Latini's *Livre du tresor*, Giles composed a quintessentially *scholastic*, and thus clerical, text on all points, be that language, style, content, or organization. Nevertheless, though *De regimine*'s adherence to the discursive norms of the schools was doubtless an advantageous precondition for its popularity with university-educated clerics, that alone would scarcely have guaranteed its success. Clerical readers sought out *De regimine* because they thought it to be both authoritative and useful, for Giles, in producing the first exhaustive systematic treatment of Aristotle's moral philosophy designed for practical political ends, had also made his source's doctrines more comprehensible and accessible to his contemporaries, both clerical and lay. The introduction to a glossed abridgment of *De regimine* by the Dominican Bartolomeo da San Concordio (1262–1347), with which this chapter opens, succinctly expresses some of the key roles played by Giles

---

[1] "Incipit compendium moralis philosophie. Libellus iste continet quedam que assumpta sunt de quodam libro qui dicitur de regimine principum, magis quid secundum sentenciam quam secundum verba, propter prolixitatem vitandam. Additis nichilominus quibusdam aliorum dictis, que quasi loco glosarum separati sunt posita. Appellatur autem liber iste compendium moralis philosophie, et dividitur in decem partes ut in processu patebit": Paris, BN lat. 6466, fol. 1.

of Rome's mirror of princes among its clerical audience.[2] Most telling of all, he has chosen the title *Compendium moralis philosophiae*. Up to a point this seems perfectly natural, since in terms of the medieval division of the sciences, *De regimine* belonged essentially to the general category of moral philosophy, which in turn became one of the subject areas of the university arts curriculum. Yet *De regimine* also constituted a specific species of moral philosophical text, whose goal was to instruct the ruling classes. Bartolomeo, however, in clothing Giles's mirror in an academic guise, expresses what by his time had become a well-established practice in the medieval schools, that is the use of *De regimine* as a textbook of moral philosophy.

Bartolomeo clearly believed that *De regimine* was a most useful moral philosophical treatise, since he made his abridgment of it the base text of his *Compendium*, and even went so far as to preserve his source's ten-part structure. Yet he also judged it insufficient in and of itself to express fully the depth and breadth of the field of moral philosophy; thus the glosses are drawn from a wide array of classical, biblical, patristic, and scholastic authorities, in order to create a work which, it seems to me, reflects the way moral philosophy was studied and taught in the medieval universities. His own impressive academic credentials include having studied law and theology at Bologna and Paris, and having taught logic, philosophy, and canon law at several Italian *studia* of the Dominican order. He was reckoned to be a superb teacher by his contemporaries, a quality reflected in his writings, all of which are characterized by a "notevole capacità di assimilazione."[3] It seems reasonable to assume then that the *Compendium* was a teaching text, designed to assist young Dominican scholars in their study of moral philosophy. Thus it is interesting to observe Bartolomeo's choice of the *De regimine* over its principal sources the *Ethics* and *Politics*, that is those very works which constituted the set texts of the moral philosophy portion of the arts curriculum in the medieval universities. Of course, although Aristotle provided the authority underlying the moral philosophy component of the curriculum, his goal in preparing those works had not been to teach medieval university students. Hence the commentaries of medieval scholars who tried to make sense of the teaching of the Stagirite, while at the same time appropriating his doctrine for the purposes of a Christian and clerical audience.[4] Hence also the attraction for Bartolomeo and other medieval clerics of Giles of Rome's digested, modified, reorganized, amplified, and Christianized version of Aristotle's moral philosophy. Bartolomeo, however, also had the reputation for being a tal-

---

[2] All the biographical information here is taken from the entry devoted to Bartolomeo in the *Dizionario biografico degli italiani*, vol. VI, pp. 768–70. The entry incorrectly identifies the *Compendium moralis philosophiae* as an abridgment of the *De regno* of Thomas Aquinas.

[3] *Ibid.*, p. 768.

[4] Kretzmann, Kenny, and Pinborg (eds.), *Cambridge History of Later Medieval Philosophy*, pp. 657–72, 723–37.

ented preacher. Moreover, since he was a Dominican, the primary goal of his peda-gogy, one suspects, would have been the formation of preachers and confessors. He was, after all, the author of several sermons, as well as a much consulted penitential manual, the *Summa de casibus conscientiae*, or *Pisanella*, and a florilegium, the *Documenta antiquorum*, which Bartolomeo himself translated into Italian under the title *Ammaestramenti degli antichi*. Thus his homiletic and pastoral preoccupa-tions may have prompted the frequent citations of scriptural and patristic author-ities in the *Compendium*'s glosses.

Although no single English cleric has left such an extensive attestation of his uses of *De regimine*, the combined evidence of the ownership and contents of their manu-scripts, along with the glosses and apparatus they composed to accompany the text, shows that they approached it in much the same way as Bartolomeo. And, as Bartolomeo's students likely did, they received their first considerable exposure to *De regimine* while studying moral philosophy either for the master of arts degree at university or, if they were mendicants, in the arts course taught at the *studia* of their orders.[5] Often, indeed, the size and makeup of this clerical audience can be gleaned from the number of individuals and institutions that left some record of their association with the text prior to the Dissolution of the monasteries in the 1530s. Thirty-six individuals (not including scribes) owned or cited *De regimine*; of these, twenty were seculars, ten Benedictine monks, four Augustinian friars, one a Franciscan, and one a Dominican. All the secular clerks were university alumni, as were most of the religious. As for institutional libraries, twenty-six possessed copies of *De regimine*. The incipient university libraries of Oxford and Cambridge each had copies, as did three secular colleges and one monastic college at Oxford, and three colleges at Cambridge. Beyond the universities, the Benedictines took pride of place, with eight monasteries or monastic cathedral priories owning copies; it was also in the keeping of two secular cathedrals and a collegiate church, and of a single foundation of each of the following monastic or mendicant orders: the Augustinian friars, Augustinian canons, Franciscans, Boni Homines, and Gilbertines.[6] It should

---

[5] This practice is reflected in the placement of *De regimine* manuscripts among the books of moral philosophy in the bookpresses of medieval libraries: M. R. James, *A Descriptive Catalogue of the Manuscripts in the Library of Peterhouse* (Cambridge, 1899), p. 14; N. R. Ker, *Records of All Souls College Library, 1437–1600*, Oxford Bibliographical Society Publications, new ser. 16 (1971), pp. 38–9; H. Bradshaw, "Two Lists of Books in the University of Cambridge Library," in chapter *Collected Papers* (Cambridge, 1889), pp. 27, 39; R. Weiss, "The Earliest Catalogues of the Library of Lincoln College," *Bodleian Quarterly Record* 8 (1937), pp. 350, 353.

[6] These manuscripts and owners will be mentioned in the course of this and the following chapter. The only exception is the collegiate church of St. George's, Windsor, which owned Bodleian Bodl. 544. Although the earliest record of ownership in this case comes from an early seventeenth-century catalogue, most of St. George's manuscripts came there during the later fifteenth and early sixteenth centuries: M. R. James, "The Manuscripts of St. George's Chapel, Windsor," *The Library*, 4th ser., 13 (1932), p. 66.

be remembered, however, that several of the copies kept in monastic or cathedral libraries had come there by way of gifts of university alumni, who very likely obtained their copies of *De regimine* while at university, either through purchase or gift, or by copying them themselves. This is borne out by the fact that almost all the Latin copies of English origin manifest signs of having been products of the university book trade.

Widespread use of *De regimine* by English scholars seems not to have occurred until several decades after the text's dissemination among their counterparts in France and northern Italy.[7] Once English scholars began to apply *De regimine* to their studies, however, they appear to have devoted considerable attention to it. The first mention of *De regimine* in English sources comes from a bequest, dated 1313, of the books of Ralph de Baldock, bishop of London, to the cathedral chapter of St. Paul's.[8] Baldock was both learned and politically active. After attending Oxford, he continued avidly to study and patronize learning while dean and later bishop at St. Paul's. In 1308 he initiated a practice of appointing Mertonian theologians as chancellors of the cathedral with the attendant duty of overseeing the cathedral school, and his collection of 126 *libri scholastici* would form much of the core of St. Paul's library of theology and canon law texts.[9] Baldock's political activities included serving as royal chancellor in the last months of Edward I's reign in 1307 and joining the Lords Ordainers, who sided against Edward II in 1311. Baldock's episcopal colleague, Walter de Stapeldon of Exeter, left behind two copies of *De regimine* at the time of his murder in 1336 by a London mob angered by his loyal service as treasurer to Edward II. Stapeldon, like Baldock, was a man of learning and a notable collector of books.[10] He had received his doctorate in canon and civil law by 1306 and his interest in the patronage of young scholars from his diocese was so great as to lead him to found Exeter College at Oxford in 1316.[11] Just as it is likely that the Capetian Isabella was responsible for bringing the French *Gouvernement* to England, so too it is probable that scholarly prelates like Baldock and Stapeldon introduced the Latin *De regimine*. Their duties as royal councilors and administrators, as well as their diocesan responsibilities, would have provided ample motivation for acquiring the text, and their continental connections would have furnished the opportunity. Stapeldon, for instance, went overseas on at least five occasions, while we know from the example of Richard de Bury of Durham

---

[7] See above, pp. 13–16.

[8] A "Postille super Cantica et Apocalipsim et Egidius de regimine principum et de corpore Christi": for this and Baldock's biography, see *BRUO* Appendix, pp. 2147–9.

[9] W. J. Courtenay, *Schools and Scholars in Fourteenth-Century England* (Princeton, 1987), pp. 89, 101.

[10] The scholarly attributes of both men are discussed in K. Edwards, "Bishops and Learning in the Reign of Edward II," *Church Quarterly Review* 138 (1944), pp. 57–86.

[11] F. C. Hingeston-Randolph (ed.), *The Register of Walter de Stapeldon, Bishop of Exeter (A.D. 1307–1326)* (London, 1892), pp. 563–5; *BRUO* 3, pp. 1764–5.

that book-loving bishops could harvest recently composed works from France and Italy through intermediaries.[12]

Early copies probably also entered England by way of members of the religious orders, especially the Augustinians, whose reverence for Giles as doctor of their order prompted them to promote the study of his works. The English Augustinians could have obtained copies while attending meetings of the general chapter of the order, from members of the order who were sent to study at Paris, or from foreign confreres visiting England. The Benedictines may have provided another early avenue of textual transmission. In his bequest of 1331 to the monks of Christ Church, Canterbury, Henry of Eastry, who had been prior there since 1285, left a "liber de regimine principis" among his books of civil law.[13] This could well have been a copy of *De regimine*; and although its characterization as a book of civil law may appear a bit odd, it is not entirely out of keeping with the ways in which the text could be used, as it was cited by the great Italian jurist Bartolus of Sassoferrato in his *De regimine civitatis*, and "acquiert, dans le courant du siècle et notamment chez les juristes, un statut d'auctoritas qui le rapproche des textes universitaires."[14] Prior Eastry, like Bishops Baldock and Stapeldon, had a keen interest in matters of governance, which in Eastry's case would have specifically entailed providing the enlightened, disciplined, and efficient rule over the priory and its lands for which he was remembered; a bent also reflected in the very practical and legal subject matter of the books in his personal library.[15] Though not a university alumnus, Eastry may have acquired books from any number of places, given Christ Church's importance as a pilgrimage site and its connections with Oxford and London.[16] He also may have obtained it from overseas, thanks to his associations with "a group of young clerics connected in one way or another with Canterbury to whom he acted as patron in their university careers at Orléans, Bologna and elsewhere."[17]

Although copies of the Latin *De regimine* were in England by the early 1300s, the text does not appear to have been read in association with the university curriculum until the middle years of the century. Of the six Latin *De regimine* copies of the English Group whose date of execution can be assigned to the period prior to 1350, four were imported from abroad, and only one English copy seems to have been produced before *c.* 1325.[18] But by the third quarter of the century English scholars began to study *De regimine* in connection with the university curriculum, a fact attested by the nine surviving copies of English origin which date from this period or a few years earlier, and to the survival of the earliest English alphabetical index (in

---

[12] Stapeldon went overseas in 1306, 1315, 1319, 1320, and 1325. The last four trips were certainly to France. On Bury, see above, p. 60.

[13] M. R. James, *The Ancient Libraries of Canterbury and Dover* (Cambridge, 1903), p. 145.

[14] Walther, "Legistische und aristotelische Herrschaftstheorie," p. 119; J.-Ph. Genet, "Théorie politique," p. 272.   [15] James, *Ancient Libraries*, pp. 143–5.

[16] D. Knowles, *The Religious Orders in England*, vol. 1 (Cambridge, 1948), pp. 49–54.

[17] *Ibid.*, p. 53.   [18] See above, table 2, pp. 23–4.

Balliol Coll. 282), composed in the mid 1300s, probably at Balliol College, Oxford. In the remainder of this chapter I would like to examine the membership of the English clerical audience, beginning with seculars and turning then to the religious.

In 1361 John Lecche left his library of fifty-seven volumes to the Augustinian Canons of Lanthony Priory near Gloucester. Among his books was a copy of *De regimine* which survives today in London, Lambeth Palace Libr. 150. Lecche's academic career began in 1321, when he was granted license to study at Oxford. There he received doctorates in canon and civil law and served as chancellor of the university in 1338. Away from university, he held the post of official of the court of Canterbury and was employed as king's clerk between 1347 and 1353.[19] His manuscript of *De regimine*, which also contains Giles's *De peccato originali* and Nicholas Trevet's *De officio missae*, is written in the informal Anglicana often found in university books produced in the middle of the fourteenth century. Judging from Lambeth Palace Libr. 150's script and Lecche's long association with Oxford, it is likely that at some time during his residence at university he became acquainted with the text and acquired this manuscript. Lecche does not seem to have had attachments to any college or hall during his time at Oxford, which would explain why he left his books to a priory of canons regular rather than to one of the handful of secular colleges that had been founded at the university by the time of his demise. He may have chosen the canons of Lanthony as the beneficiaries of his largesse in return for their promise to pray and perform masses for the welfare of his soul.

Secular owners of *De regimine* manuscripts tended to donate their books to the colleges with which they had been affiliated. The catalogue compiled in 1474 of the library of Lincoln College, Oxford lists an "Egidius de regimine principum cum aliis ex dono magistri Iohannis Marchall." John Marshall, M.A., B.Th., who had been a fellow of Lincoln College, as well as of University and Queen's Colleges, was a prebendary of Lincoln Cathedral who served as king's clerk in 1407. Marshall's copy was kept in the library for the common use of the fellows, while a companion copy is mentioned in the 1476 list of "Libri qui . . . sunt in communi eleccione sociorum."[20] This second copy would have circulated among the fellows according to the practice of *electio*, whereby books were distributed to the fellows at yearly or longer intervals.[21] Similarly, at Corpus Christi College, Cambridge, one of the fellows, Thomas Markaunt, stipulated in 1439 that his considerable book collection, among which was a copy of *De regimine*, be made available on loan to the fellows, rather than being put in the library.[22] Other seculars who left their copies

---

[19] *BRUO* 2, pp. 1118–19.

[20] *Ibid.*, pp. 1227–8; Weiss, "Earliest Catalogues," p. 350, 353.

[21] Ker, "Oxford College Libraries before 1500," in *The Universities in the Late Middle Ages*, ed. J. Ijsewijn and J. Paquet, Mediaevalia Lovaniensia, ser. 1, studia 6 (1973), p. 294.

[22] C. R. Cheney, "A Register of MSS Borrowed from a College Library, 1440–1517," *Transactions of the Cambridge Bibliographical Society* 9 (1987), pp. 103–29, esp. 114; *BRUC*, p. 390.

of *De regimine* to their colleges were Bishop Roger Whelpdale of Carlisle, D.Th. (to Balliol College, Oxford, in 1423), Thomas Lay, M.A. (All Souls Coll. 92, to All Souls College, Oxford, *c.* 1450), John Newton, D.C.L. (perhaps Peterhouse 233, to Peterhouse, Cambridge, in 1417), John Clenche, D.Th. (to Pembroke College, Cambridge, *c.* 1430), and Thomas Lavenham (Pembroke Coll. 158, to Pembroke College, in 1435).[23]

Books belonging to college fellows did not, however, always find their way into the collections of their colleges. Although Thomas Alne gave several books to his college, Peterhouse, at his death in 1440, his copy of *De regimine* was not among them.[24] He left this instead to York Minster where he had been priest of the altar of St. Nicholas and had held the post of examiner general in the ecclesiastical court of York; he made this gift on condition that it first be reserved for the use of Robert Semer, rector of St. Martin's in "Conyngstrete," for the term of his life.[25] Christopher Forster, a fellow of University College, Oxford who incepted for the M.A. in 1483 and died in 1496, deposited Glasgow Univ. Libr. Hamilton 141 in the Guildford loan-chest *c.* 1481, but presumably never retrieved it.[26] Later it came into the possession of someone surnamed Clayton, possibly William Clayton, who was at Oxford *c.* 1505–1515 and served as a chaplain to Henry VIII.[27] Loan-chests played a vital role at both English universities. Books, after all, were valuable portable assets, and scholars would often pledge their own books as securities in return for ready cash or loans of other books.[28] Proof that a book had been pledged was entered on the pastedown of the book in the form of a *caucio*. Two other copies besides Forster's contain *cauciones*. Bodleian Hatton 15 was deposited at Oxford in the Thecheley chest in 1461, and in the Warwick chest in 1463 and 1465, while York Minster Libr. XVI.D.5 shows signs of having been twice deposited in loan-chests, either at Oxford or Cambridge.[29]

Most of the *De regimine* manuscripts belonging to seculars were probably obtained by them, through gift or purchase, new or second-hand, while at university; and these books would travel with them during the course of their careers

---

[23] *DNB*, vol. xx, p. 1358 (Whelpdale). Mynors, *Catalogue*, p. xix. *BRUO* 2, p. 1114 (Lay); Ker, *Records of All Souls*, p. 124, misidentified the owner as one of two Oxford scholars surnamed Lee. *BRUC*, pp. 421–2; S. H. Cavanaugh, "A Study of Books Privately Owned in England, 1300–1450," Ph.D. dissertation, University of Pennsylvania, 1980, p. 613 (Newton). James, *Cat. Peterhouse*, p. 4. *BRUC*, p. 137; Cavanaugh, "Study," pp. 193–4 (Clenche). *BRUC*, p. 356 (Lavenham).

[24] *BRUC*, pp. 10–11; J. C. T. Oates, *Cambridge University Library, a History: From the Beginnings to the Copyright Act of Queen Anne* (Cambridge, 1986), pp. 9, 11.

[25] "Domino Roberto Semer, rectori ecclesie Sancti Martini in Conyngstrete, usum Egidii de regimine principum, ad terminum vite sue, et post ejus mortem volo quod remaneat librarie Ecclesie Cathedralis": Cavanaugh, "Study," p. 46. This book should probably not be identified with York Minster Libr. XVI.D.5, since the dates of the latter's *cauciones* appear to come after the period of Alne's residence at Cambridge.   [26] *BRUO* 2, p. 707.   [27] *BRUO 1501–40*, p. 121.

[28] On the use of loan-chests at Oxford see Parkes, "Provision of Books," pp. 409–12.

[29] The *cauciones* in Hatton 15 appear on fol. 3v; those in York Minster Libr. XVI.D.5 are on fol. 95 v.

after they had graduated. Those graduates who did not have college affiliations usually left their books in the keeping of an ecclesiastical foundation with which they had been associated. We have already seen this in the case of John Lecche, who bequeathed his books to Lanthony. Owen Lloyd, at his death in 1478, gave Hereford Cath. Libr. P.V.7 to the chapter of Hereford Cathedral. Lloyd had had a lengthy association with Oxford University from some time before he became a fellow of Paul Hall *c.* 1446 until he received his doctorate in civil law in 1458. Though Lloyd held several rectories as prebendary and canon of Exeter during the course of his career, he was first and foremost an administrator, occupying the posts of archdeacon of Totnes and Barnstaple, and vicar general of the bishop of Exeter.[30] It is not clear why Lloyd decided to leave his copy of *De regimine* as well as several other books to Hereford, since there is no record of his ever having had anything to do with the chapter or diocese. Nevertheless, he was a Welshman, and probably also an absentee canon of the cathedral, and thus may have donated his rich trove of books because he was "burdened by the consciousness of how little he had done for Hereford," hence the request in the *ex dono* inscriptions of all his books left to Hereford: "Orate pro eo."[31] Another Welshman, David Rice, B.Th., probably acquired Oxford, Jesus Coll. 12 while a student at Oxford. Like William Clayton, Rice was one of Henry VIII's chaplains. He was also rector of Llandettye in his native Wales, and very likely took his *De regimine* with him there, from whence it would return to Oxford by way of Sir John Prise's posthumous donation of manuscripts to Jesus College.[32] Bodleian Laud Misc. 652 was brought to the church of Stoke in Rutland by its prebendary, Hugh Tapton, a Cambridge B.Th. who died in 1481. Tapton probably acquired this manuscript while a student at Cambridge during the 1440s, and according to an inscription on an end flyleaf (fol. 223) it was still at Stoke in the sixteenth century.[33]

BL Roy. 5.C.iii, a miscellany containing an abridgment, chapter list, and alphabetical index of *De regimine*, along with several pastoral and preaching texts, provides the one clear exception to the rule of book acquisition while at university. Thomas Eborall, an Oxford D.Th. and Master of Whittington College in London in the mid fifteenth century, purchased this book from John Pye, a London stationer who seems to have specialized in the second-hand academic book trade.[34] Eborall, who preached before King Edward IV on Passion Sunday, 1465, went to some pains to work out the inheritance of this book, desiring first that it pass after

---

[30] *BRUO* 2, pp. 1153–4.

[31] R. A. B. Mynors and R. M. Thomson, *Catalogue of the Manuscripts of Hereford Cathedral Library* (Cambridge, 1993), p. xxiv.

[32] *BRUO 1501–40*, p. 121; although Ker lists Rice's *De regimine* among the manuscripts in the "not found" category of Prise's books, Jesus Coll. 12 can almost certainly be identified with this manuscript: N. R. Ker, "Sir John Prise," *The Library*, 5th ser., 10 (1955), p. 13.   [33] *BRUC*, p. 576.

[34] On Pye, see C. P. Christianson, *A Directory of London Stationers and Book Artisans, 1300–1500* (New York, 1990), pp. 145–8.

his death to a former student at Whittington, Henry Mosie, "if he should attain the priesthood"; failing this, it was to be "the book of John Sory, priest, so that it be not sold but rather pass among my relations, if any can be found, and if not, then from one priest to another."[35]

The potential audience of *De regimine* at the universities was, of course, considerably larger than the group of clerks whose names appear in *ex libris* inscriptions, *cauciones*, and library catalogues. College fellows had access to the copies in their libraries and others could have purchased copies or borrowed them from stationers, loan-chests, or fellow scholars.[36] John Trevisa furnishes a good example of a scholar whose name appears in no surviving Latin copy but who may first have come into contact with the text while a student at Exeter College, which may have had a *De regimine,* thanks to the beneficence of its founder Walter de Stapeldon. Nevertheless, later he almost certainly must have had his own copy, probably purchased with money provided by his patron Lord Berkeley, in order to make his translation. Moreover, there were the copies preserved in the incipient university libraries. The earliest extant catalogue of Cambridge University library, compiled in 1424, records a *De regimine* of Thomas Paxton, M.A., D.C.L., a fellow of King's Hall, Cambridge who died in 1371.[37] Presumably his copy was available at the fledgling University Library from the time of his death. By 1473, the date of the library's next earliest catalogue, Paxton's gift had been complemented by another *De regimine*, and at the end of the fifteenth century Thomas Rotheram, the politically influential archbishop of York and chancellor of England during the reign of Edward IV, added Cambridge Univ. Libr. Ff.4., a manuscript containing an alphabetical index of *De regimine*.[38] The index in this manuscript would have been a useful tool for scholars wishing to look up subjects quickly in either of the library's two copies of *De regimine*. Oxford University had practically nothing in the way of a library before the 1430s, at which time it became the recipient of the generous book donations of Humphrey, duke of Gloucester. Among the gift of 135 books which the duke made in 1443–44 was an "Aegidium de regimine principum."[39] Prior to the opening of Duke Humphrey's library in 1488, this copy of *De regimine* would have been available to scholars willing to brave the library's cramped quarters in the upper room of the congregation house of St. Mary's church, though they may also have been able to take it out on loan.[40]

---

[35] *BRUO* I, pp. 622–3. The inscription, which is now lost, was recorded in the first half of the eighteenth century: "Liber T. Eyburhale, emptus a Iohanne Pye pro 27s. 6d. Do Henrico Mosie, quondam scolari meo, si contingat eum presbyterari; aliter erit liber Domini Iohannis Sory, sic quod non vendatur, sed transeat inter cognatos meos, si fuerint aliqui inventi, sin autem, ab uno presbytero ad alium": G. F. Warner and J. P. Gilson, *Catalogue of the Old Royal and King's Collection in the British Museum* (London, 1921), pp. xxx, 105–6.   [36] Parkes, "Provision of Books," pp. 407–24.

[37] *BRUC*, p. 445; Bradshaw, "Two Lists of Books," p. 37.

[38] Bradshaw, "Two Lists of Books," pp. 39–40; Oates, *Cambridge University Library*, pp. 37–52.

[39] Anstey (ed.), *Munimenta Academica*, p. 772.   [40] Parkes, "Provision of Books," pp. 470–4.

The two universities also played an important role in the dissemination of *De regimine* among English religious. Copies of the text acquired by monks and friars who studied at the universities often returned with them to their respective houses; once there, the books became the common property of the house and were kept for consultation in the communal library or were distributed according to the practice of *electio*. Books could also travel with the monks from their houses to the universities. English religious, then, could acquaint themselves with a text like *De regimine* either at university or in the libraries of their own houses and *studia*. Yet while most of the religious orders sent their members to study at the universities, only the Augustinian friars and Benedictines seem to have made a habit of using *De regimine*. The proof of this should only partly be sought in extant manuscripts and medieval library catalogues, given the frustratingly uneven patterns of survival of these kinds of sources.[41] A better gauge is the several names of Augustinians and Benedictines associated with the alphabetical indexes of *De regimine*. The Augustinian interest in *De regimine* is, of course, hardly surprising, but the Benedictines' use of it is less easily explained. It could simply have been the result of their having been more free to pick and choose among authoritative texts, owing to their being less strictly bound by a particular set of doctrines or a strong tradition of recent intellectual achievements by members of their order. Thus they adopted *De regimine* because it was in common use among secular scholars and the Augustinians by the latter part of the fourteenth century, and they chose to use it for the same reasons that secular clerks did.

This is not to say, however, that *De regimine* was entirely ignored by members of other religious orders in England. The Dominican William of Norham, D.Th., obtained Bodleian Laud Misc. 702 from Henry Lord Percy in 1419.[42] BL Roy. 4.D.iv belonged to the London Franciscans, and the Minorite John Lathbury (d. 1362) cited the work in his Commentary on Lamentations. Likewise, a sermon in a manuscript that appears to have been linked to the Franciscans, twice quotes from *De regimine*.[43] Some copies were also the property of houses of canons regular. It has already been mentioned that from 1361 Lambeth Palace Libr. 150 belonged to the Augustinian canons of Lanthony, and by the time of the Dissolution copies

[41] See above, pp. 7–8.

[42] B. Smalley, *English Friars and Antiquity in the Early Fourteenth Century* (Oxford, 1960), pp. 222, 353. *BRUO* Appendix, p. 2201.

[43] "Genera vero bellorum secundum Egidium de regimine principum, tractatu 10°, capitulo 10° [*sic* for *DRP* 3.3.16], sunt quatuor, scilicet campestre, obsessivum, defensivum, et navale"; and "quia sic per paludis sordes et cor[ruptionem] metallorum inficitur aqua, ut patet per Egidium de regimine principum, tractatu 7°, capitulo 3° [*sic* for *DRP* 2.3.4], et in de secretis secretorum": Balliol Coll. 149, fols. 55 and 57v; sermon on "Cum fortis armatus custodit atrium suum in pace sunt omnia que possidet" (Luke 11:21). My thanks to Siegfried Wenzel for providing me with this quotation. On the manuscript, see S. Wenzel, *Macaronic Sermons: Bilingualism and Preaching in Late-Medieval England* (Ann Arbor, 1994), pp. 43–4, 60, 179.

were also to be found at the house of Bonshommes at Ashridge in Hertfordshire (Huntington Libr. EL 9.H.9) and at the Gilbertine priory of Bullington in Lincolnshire.[44] Nevertheless these few examples pale in comparison with the large number of surviving and lost copies owned by the Augustinian friars and Black Monks, and the several indexes which they compiled and copied.

Although it is quite likely that the English Augustinian friars had access to copies of *De regimine* by the early fourteenth century, the earliest recorded copy associated with the order in England dates from an entry made in the 1370s in the catalogue of the library of the York convent. A second copy may later have been added, as an entry in the margin of the catalogue mentions a miscellany containing a *De regimine*; this entry, however, is crossed out.[45] Evidence that the English Augustinians actively studied the princely mirror of their order's *Doctor Fundatissimus* comes from an entry of *c.* 1435 in the same catalogue. One of the convent's brethren, John Bukwode (alias Birkwood), donated a book containing the works of John Kervyle (alias Karvilem), who had been the Augustinians' regent master of theology at Oxford in 1388.[46] The catalogue lists the book's contents as follows:

Item Kervyle super libros politicorum Aristotelis cum duabus tabulis
Egidii de regimine principum;
tabula Johannis Crisostomi;
abbreviatio prefati magistri Kervyle super libros politicorum sancti Thome;
et tabula super problemata Aristotelis.[47]

On the basis of the commentaries attributed to him in this entry, neither of which is known to have survived, Kervyle seems to have taken a keen interest in moral philosophy.[48] Moreover, the wording of the first item suggests that he may have been the compiler of the "du[e] tabul[e] Egidii" attached to his commentary on the *Politics. Tabula* was the standard medieval Latin term for index, and could designate either a table of chapters or an alphabetical index. Though it is possible Kervyle was not the author of the two *tabulae* to *De regimine*, he certainly had an

[44] D. N. Bell, *The Libraries of the Cistercians, Gilbertines and Premonstratensians*, Corpus of British Medieval Library Catalogues 3 (London, 1992), p. 153; J. R. Liddell, "'Leland's' Lists of Manuscripts in Lincolnshire Monasteries," *English Historical Review* 54 (1939), p. 92; J. P. Carley, "John Leland and the Contents of English Pre-Dissolution Libraries: Lincolnshire," *Transactions of the Cambridge Bibliographical Society* 9 (1989), pp. 330–57.

[45] K. W. Humphreys, *The Friars' Libraries*, Corpus of British Medieval Library Catalogues 1 (London, 1990), pp. 69, 72. The York catalogue was also edited by M. R. James, "The Catalogue of the Library of the Augustinian Friars at York," in *Fasciculus Ioanni Willis Clark Dicatus* (Cambridge, 1909).   [46] Humphreys, *Friars' Libraries*, pp. xxviii–xxix; *BRUO* 2, p. 1027.

[47] Humphreys, *Friars' Libraries*, p. 82. Humphreys has mistakenly assumed the book contained the full text of *De regimine*.

[48] Genet, "Théorie politique," pp. 271–2, includes Kervyle among the English authors of political "textes virtuels."

interest in compiling such apparatus, as is proved by the ascription to him in the explicit of a *tabula* of 1379 on Augustine's *De trinitate* in Pembroke Coll. 242.[49] Certainly Kervyle was active during the very period when two of the five versions of alphabetical indexes to *De regimine* appear to have been compiled. The earliest extant copy of one of these, an alphabetical index beginning with an entry for *Abstinentia* and ending with the entry *Zelotipus* (in Cambridge Univ. Libr. Ii.4.22), is accompanied by something that its compiler calls a "contratabula," and that exists uniquely in this manuscript. It could well be that this alphabetical index with its *contratabula* is the same combination referred to in the catalogue description of Bukwode's book. If so, this makes it quite likely that Kervyle was the compiler of the *Abstinentia* index version.

Whether or not Kervyle himself compiled this index, however, there is ample evidence to suggest that it was the Augustinian friars' standard index to *De regimine.* Two copies of this index that are of slightly later date than Cambridge Univ. Libr. Ii.4.22 conclude with the colophon: "Explicit tabula venerabilis egidii de regimine principum edita a fratre Galfrido Horsford ordinis fratrum heremitarum sancti augustini sacre theologie lectore."[50] Horsford may in fact have been the compiler of the *Abstinentia* version, though the lack of such an ascription in the earliest copy suggests that he was responsible for copying (a common contemporary usage of the Latin *editus*), rather than for compiling this index. Neil Ker, moreover, has shown on the basis of its pressmark that one of these copies, Bibl. Apost. Vat. Ottob. lat. 2071, very probably belonged to the Augustinian convent at Cambridge.[51] Yet if this version originated with the Augustinians and circulated among them, their associations with the universities guaranteed that it would not long remain their exclusive preserve. Four copies are in manuscripts with no ostensible connection to the Augustinians. Two of these, Cambridge, Peterhouse 208 and Oxford, Lincoln Coll. Lat. 69, are miscellanies dating from the fifteenth century, whose handwriting and contents point to their having been produced at the universities. Another, in Lambeth Palace Libr. Arc.L.40.2/L.26, was made in the second quarter of the fifteenth century for Richard, duke of York, a book whose script and illumination suggest that it may have been produced elsewhere in England than at the universities, though some university scribes could write in

---

[49] F. Roth, *The English Austin Friars, 1249–1538* (New York, 1966), p. 554.

[50] Bethesda, Nat. Libr. of Medicine 503, fol. 155v; Bibl. Apost. Vat. Ottob. lat. 2071, fol. 69v. Although Horsford identifies himself as a teacher of theology, no references can be found to him in Roth, *English Austin Friars, BRUO*, or *BRUC.* He may have studied at one of the Augustinian *studia* on the continent.

[51] N. R. Ker, "Cardinal Cervini's Manuscripts from the Cambridge Friars," in *Xenia Medii Aevi Historiam Illustrantia Oblata Thomae Kaeppeli, O.P.,* ed. R. Creytens and P. Künzle (Rome, 1978), pp. 57, 69. One of the other alphabetical indexes, a *Tabula super Augustini De civitate Dei*, was written "per stowyxlaye," who may well be synonymous with the apostate friar Robert Stokesley of York, who in 1387 was accused of Lollardy for having preached against the friars: Gwynn, *English Austin Friars*, pp. 273–6.

scripts not normally used for a university audience.[52] This version could have disseminated to a wider public through several channels, one of them being university loan-chests. As Neil Ker observed, several books of the Augustinians found their way into Cambridge loan-chests, where they could be borrowed or, if forfeited, purchased by anyone who wanted them.[53] One copy of *c.* 1400 is in a manuscript (York Minster Libr. XVI.D.5) that was deposited in loan-chests on at least two occasions.

Conversely, although the *Abstinentia* version amounted to a kind of Augustinian "house" index, it should not be assumed to have been the only one they relied upon to search the text of *De regimine*. In the colophons of two copies of the version beginning with the entry *Abhominacio* and ending *Zelotipia zelotipus* there appears the name of the Augustinian friar Thomas Abendon.[54] This was presumably the Friar Thomas of the Bristol convent who incepted in theology at Oxford by 1443, and who two years later was granted license to preach in the diocese of Bath and Wells while also receiving dispensation to become rector of a parish in the same diocese.[55] The John Drayton who was responsible for the copy of this same version in Cambridge Univ. Libr. Ff.4.38 may also have been an Augustinian, though more probably he was the synonymous Benedictine monk of Abingdon who was at Oxford in 1445. Drayton the friar was ordained a subdeacon in 1381, which means he would have been in his seventies at least by the 1436 date given in this copy's colophon.[56] Indeed this index version is particularly closely tied to the Benedictines, who, perhaps to an even greater extent than the Augustinians, expended considerable effort in the compilation and revision of *De regimine* indexes.

The Black Monks associated with *De regimine* tended to be those who studied at Oxford or belonged to houses that regularly sent their members there to study. This was particularly the case with the monks of Christ Church, Canterbury and of Durham Priory, as both of these houses had founded colleges at Oxford, though monks from houses affiliated with Gloucester College, Oxford also had access to copies of *De regimine*. Cambridge University, on the contrary, played a negligible role in the dissemination of the text among the Benedictines, since they established no colleges there.[57] It has already been mentioned that one of the earliest recorded English owners of Giles's mirror was the prior of Christ Church, Henry of Eastry, who donated his copy to the priory in 1331. Christ Church would inherit another copy, in Canterbury Cathedral Libr. B.11, from one of its monks, John Kyngton, in

---

[52] Parkes, "Provision of Books," pp. 413–14; G. Pollard, "The University and the Book Trade in Medieval Oxford," in *Beiträge zum Berufsbewusstsein des mittelalterlichen Menschen*, ed. P. Wilpert, Miscellanea Mediaevalia 3 (Berlin, 1964), p. 337.   [53] Ker, "Cardinal Cervini's Manuscripts," p. 58.
[54] Oxford, All Souls Coll. 92 and Bodleian Auct. F.3.2.   [55] *BRUO* 1, p. 3; *BRUO* 2, p. ix.
[56] Roth, *English Austin Friars*, p. 532; *BRUO* 1, p. 593.
[57] D. Knowles, *Religious Orders*, vol. 1, pp. 14–28.

1416. Kyngton may well have acquired his copy during an active life as a secular clerk before becoming a monk in 1410. He obtained degrees in arts and law at Oxford and held several benefices, including prebends in the cathedral chapters of Shrewsbury, London, and Lincoln. He also entered royal service shortly after Henry IV's accession, serving as a clerk of chancery, a royal envoy to the Baltic countries, and chancellor of Queen Joan.[58]

Not too many years after Kyngton's *De regime* was deposited in the library of Christ Church, a copy of the *Abhominacio* version was appended to it. This copy is attributed to "J.S.," initials which are probably those of John Sarysbury, a monk of Christ Church. Sarysbury had had a long association with Oxford. He was a fellow of Canterbury College in 1414, and became warden there in 1428, at which time he also incepted for the doctorate in theology. After his tenure at Oxford, Sarysbury returned to Christ Church, where he became prior in 1438.[59] I suspect that when Sarysbury was at Canterbury College he would have had access to a copy of *De regime* in the College's library. Certainly two copies were there by 1501, including probably Bodleian Auct. F.3.2., one of the manuscripts that contained a copy of the *Abhominacio* version attributed to the Augustinian Thomas Abendon.[60] The third extant copy of this version with a demonstrable Benedictine provenance is found in Edinburgh Univ. Libr. 106, a tabulary (i.e. miscellany of indexes), likely of Oxford origin, that by 1395 had entered the library of the monks of Durham Cathedral Priory, where it was kept in the "communi almariolo noviciorum."[61] This copy is also the version's earliest surviving representative, having been produced *c.* 1390, and thus some three decades before the next oldest copy. According to the 1395 catalogue of the priory's library, the index had been prepared "per R. Masham," this being the Robert Masham who was professed a monk at Durham *c.* 1383 and who later held the post of bursar at Durham College from 1395 until at least 1397.[62] On the grounds of this copy's early date, then, it could well be that Masham compiled, rather than copied, this index.

Yet Masham's index is actually only a revision of a preexisting and much longer index uniquely surviving in the rather late copy found in BL Roy. 10.C.ix. While at Oxford, Masham compiled several indexes and concordances, and it seems likely that he also made his revision of the long *Abhominacio* index there.[63] This was then

---

[58] *BRUO* 2, pp. 1075–6.

[59] He also attended the Council of Basel in 1432–3: W. A. Pantin, *Canterbury College Oxford*, vol. I, Oxford Historical Society, new ser. 6 (1947), pp. 226, 229; *BRUO* 3, pp. 1631–2.

[60] *BRUO* 3, pp. 1631–2; Pantin, *Canterbury College*, p. 26.

[61] B. Botfield (ed.), *Catalogi veteres librorum ecclesiae cathedralis Dunelm*, Surtees Society, vol. VII (1838), p. 83; *MLGB* Supplement, p. 29.

[62] *BRUO* 2, p. 1240; W. A. Pantin (ed.), *Documents Illustrating the Activities of the General and Provincial Chapters of the English Black Monks, 1215–1540*, vol. II, Camden Third Series 47 (1933), p. xii.

[63] Masham's indexes and concordances survive in Durham Cath. Libr. B.IV.31 and B.IV.43; and BL Harley 3858: R. B. Dobson, *Durham Priory, 1400–1450* (Cambridge, 1973), p. 377.

delivered to Durham in order to satisfy the monks' collection of reference materials: a collection which grew rapidly during the years surrounding 1400, thanks to the concerted efforts of the priory's monks who busied themselves with compiling, copying, and purchasing these materials while studying at Oxford.[64] At Durham, Masham's index would have been used in conjunction with the priory's copy of *De regimine*, now Durham Cath. Libr. B.III.24, a book probably also produced at Oxford, and which contains marginal notes by Masham himself.[65] It could even be that the Durham monk who, sometime between 1389 and 1430, twice quoted *De regimine* in a sermon preserved in Cambridge, Jesus Coll. 13, art. vi (fol. 79v), derived his quotations by means of this index, since both passages are referred to therein.[66]

Yet the long *Abhominacio* index in BL Roy. 10.C.ix is itself but an extensively reorganized version of an index surviving in three manuscripts, one of which (Cambridge, Corpus Christi Coll. 283) likely belonged to the Benedictines of Norwich Cathedral Priory. The entries in this index, which begins with *Avarus*, and ends *Uncis ferreis*, have been alphabetized by first letter only, whereas those in BL Roy. 10.C.ix, and its shorter revision are alphabetized through the word. Yet the overall contents of the *Avarus* index and of the long *Abhominacio* index are identical, and since alphabetization through the word is a marked improvement over alphabetization by first letter only, it is clear that the *Avarus* index provided the raw material for the reworked version in Roy. 10.C.ix, rather than the other way around.[67] The *Avarus* and long *Abhominacio* indexes could themselves have originated in a Benedictine milieu. In the 1389 catalogue of the library of Dover Priory, a dependency of Christ Church, is listed a copy of *De regimine*, now lost, accompanied by a "tabula J. Whit' super eodem." This "J. Whit'" was John Whytefeld, the priory's precentor and an avid collector of books.[68] Given the date of the Dover catalogue, Whytefeld could not have made his index after 1389, and may well have done so several years earlier; thus Whytefeld may have been the compiler, rather

<hr/>

[64] Dobson, *Durham Priory*, pp. 370–75. Books also traveled in the other direction, from Durham to Oxford: A. J. Piper, "The Libraries of the Monks of Durham," in *Medieval Scribes, Manuscripts and Libraries: Essays Presented to N. R. Ker*, ed. M. B. Parkes and A. G. Watson (London, 1978), p. 246.

[65] In the 1392 catalogue it was listed among the "libri de novo adquisiti ad communem armariolum, in recompensationem librorum oxoniam missorum": Botfield (ed.), *Catalogi veteres*, p. 43. The notes in Durham Cath. Libr. B.III.24 have been identified as Masham's by Alan Piper. This manuscript's Oxford origin was noted by Ker in the annotated Borland catalogue in Edinburgh University Library's department of special collections.

[66] "Reverendi mei, dicit Egidius De regimine principum, libro 3, parte prima, capitulo 2, quod civitas materialis constituta est propter tria, videlicet propter vivere, sufficienter viv[er]e, virtuose vivere. Sed principaliter propter bene et feliciter vivere. Et patet ibidem libro 3, parte 2ª, capitulo 32." Sermon preached on the theme "Ingredere civitatum" (Acts 9:7), on the occasion of an English woman named Alice Huntingfield entering a religious order: S. Wenzel, "The Classics in Late-Medieval Preaching," in *Mediaeval Antiquity*, ed. A. Welkenhuysen, H. Braet, and W. Verbeke (Louvain, 1995), pp. 135–40. [67] See below, pp. 135–8.

[68] James, *Ancient Libraries*, pp. xci, 463.

than merely the copyist of this lost index. In turn, this index could very well correspond either to the *Avarus* or to the long *Abhominacio* version. Certainly Whytefeld's index could have found its way to the Benedictines at Oxford since Dover regularly sent a few of its members to study at Canterbury College. Further work on the index would then have been carried out at Oxford, where it is likely that Robert Masham redacted the shorter, and what from now on will be designated "common" *Abhominacio* recension, owing to its subsequent popularity. This recension quickly made its way to Durham Priory and eventually came to Christ Church via Oxford, thanks to John Sarysbury. At Oxford, Masham's index seems eventually to have disseminated among secular scholars as well as Augustinian friars; and from Oxford it seems eventually to have migrated to Cambridge and London.[69]

De regimine's Benedictine readership was not limited to the monks of Christ Church and Durham, however. The monks of Norwich Cathedral Priory probably owned Cambridge, Corpus Christi Coll. 283, while Cambridge Univ. Libr. Ii.4.37 bears the inscriptions (fols. 3, 146v) of John Molet, prior of Norwich from 1453 to 1471, and Robert Catton, who was a monk there by 1492.[70] In 1376 the monks of Westminster were due to receive the books of their former abbot, Simon Langham, whose bequest included a copy of *De regimine*. Langham had left Westminster to become bishop of Ely, after which he assumed the archiepiscopal see of Canterbury, and finally a cardinal's hat. He and his books went to Avignon, where he died a few years later. It is not known if his copy of *De regimine* ever arrived at its intended destination.[71] Westminster had, however, acquired the copy in Lambeth Palace Libr. 184 by the second half of the fifteenth century. As for other monasteries, in 1392 Evesham obtained a *De regimine* from its prior Nicholas of Hereford (not to be confused with the notorious Wycliffite), while Cambridge, Gonville and Caius Coll. 113 belonged to John Cranewys, who was subprior and sacrist of Bury St. Edmunds in the 1420s. Reading and Worcester also appear to have been associated respectively with Bodleian Auct. F.3.2 and Bodleian Hatton 15.[72] With these houses as well, it is likely that Oxford University provided the setting wherein their monks gained familiarity with *De regimine* and obtained copies for their houses, since they all maintained their ties with the university through their affiliation with

---

[69] Oxford, All Souls Coll. 92 (Thomas Lay, Oxford); BL Roy. 15.C.iii (Thomas Eborall, London); Cambridge Univ. Libr. Ff.4.38 (Thomas Rotherham, Cambridge).

[70] *MLGB*, p. 137; N. R. Ker, "Medieval Manuscripts from Norwich Cathedral Priory," *Transactions of the Cambridge Bibliographical Society* 1 (1949), p. 18. *BRUC*, p. 126.

[71] R. Sharpe *et al.*, *English Benedictine Libraries: The Shorter Catalogues*, Corpus of British Medieval Library Catalogues 4 (London, 1996), p. 620; J. A. Robinson and M. R. James, *The Manuscripts of Westminster Abbey* (Cambridge, 1909), p. 5.

[72] Sharpe *et al.*, *English Benedictine Libraries*, p. 141; W. Dugdale, *Monasticon Anglicanum*, vol. II, ed. J. Caley, H. Ellis, and B. Bandinel (London, 1846), p. 7; Cavanaugh, "Study," p. 424. *MLGB*, pp. 17, 156; *BRUO* I, p. 510.

Gloucester College. This was especially true of Westminster, Norwich, Bury, and Worcester, all of which kept monks in nearly continuous residence at the college throughout the fourteenth and fifteenth centuries.[73] That these monks, like their confreres at Durham Priory and Durham College, drew material from the text for their preaching, is revealed in the quotations of it in two sermons found in a manuscript which was associated with Worcester Cathedral Priory during the middle years of the fifteenth century.[74]

This chapter has demonstrated the importance of the universities as sites for the dissemination of *De regimine* among its clerical readers. It has further been argued that the production of these copies and the apparatus that came to accompany them arose on the one hand from these readers' need to come to grips with the demands of the curriculum, especially in moral philosophy, but also in practical theology and even law, and, on the other hand, from the practical professional duties which these segments of the curriculum were supposed to prepare the student to perform; these included service in ecclesiastical or royal government, and the pastoral duties of the preacher and confessor. How exactly the members of this audience went about using *De regimine* for these ends is the subject of the next and final chapter.

---

[73] Knowles, *Religious Orders*, pp. 18–19; B. Harvey, "The Monks of Westminster and the University of Oxford," in *The Reign of Richard II: Essays in Honour of May McKisack*, ed. F. R. H. Du Boulay and C. M. Barron (London, 1971), pp. 112–13.

[74] "Egidius de Regimine principum, libro 3°, parte 3ª, capitulo 18 [*sic* for *DRP* 3.2.18], ostendit quod consiliarius debet habere istas tres condiciones: quod sit bonus, sapiens, et amicus"; and "docet enim Egidius de regimine principum, libro 2°, parte 3ª, capitulo 4°, quod aqua que transit per venas metallinas attrahit iinfeccionem ex ipsis nec civitati est salubris ad potandum; immo secundum quod dicit Palladius de agricultura": Worcester Cath. Libr. F. 10, fol. 177 and 249v; sermons on "Veritatem dico vobis, quare non creditis?" (John 8:45), and "In civitate sanctificata requievi" (Sir 24:15). My thanks to Siegfried Wenzel for giving me these quotations. On the manuscript, see Wenzel, *Macaronic Sermons*, pp. 55–8, 192, 194, 198.

6

Improving access and removing the chaff

Here ends Brother Giles's book On the Rule of Princes, clearer and briefer than its exemplar, but in no way mutilated. Herein are the chapters and all the arguments, with not a little of the chaff removed.[1]

Iacobinus, the scribe, and perhaps compiler, of the abridgment of *De regimine* whose colophon is quoted above, betrays a rather ambivalent attitude towards his source text.[2] On the one hand he regards it as useful enough to be worth the bother of abbreviating, while on the other, he seems to think his abridged version – it occupies only twenty-seven leaves in a manuscript of average dimensions – has greater utility, owing to its being able to deliver the full import of Giles's text, but more comprehensibly and efficiently. The desire to render authoritative texts and the subjects they contained more accessible – whether that meant finding, understanding, or retaining material – and useful provided one of the chief impetuses for the scholarly activity of the medieval universities. I have argued here that *De regimine* was itself a result of this preoccupation, and that it attained its popularity among clerical and lay readers thanks largely to its utility. Nevertheless, its very comprehensiveness could make it unwieldy for the scholar wanting a cheaply and/or quickly produced copy of the "essential" elements of the text, or seeking to cull some citations rapidly from this lengthy work, hence Iacobinus' boast that his distillation was somehow better than its source, a sentiment less forcefully expressed but still detectable in abridgments of English and French origin as well.[3]

---

[1] "Explicit liber de Regimine principum fratris Egidii, in nullo decurtatus sed exemplari lucidior et brevior. Sunt hic capitula et omnes rationes paleis abiectis non paucis": Venice, Bibl. Naz. Marc. Lat. VI, 13, fol. 55.

[2] The Italian scribe of this manuscript identifies himself in the colophon as "Iacobinus" and explains that he completed the manuscript at Chioggia in March 1403. Another somewhat modified copy of this abridgment exists in the diminutive (152 x 102 mm) Modena, Bibl. Estense Gamma. H. 7. 43, fols. 1–113v.

[3] The abridgment in BL lat. 6697 is entitled "Succinctus et utilis tractatus in genere morum excerptus ab Egidio de Roma in de regimine principum." The English abridgment is discussed below, pp. 119–21.

These wants thus led to a boiling down of the text in the form of abridgments or analytical tables of contents, the inclusion of glosses and schematic summaries in the margins, and the compilation of alphabetical indexes and compilations. This chapter is devoted to analyzing these derivative, ancillary, and often anonymous products of late medieval scholarship, since they reveal the working methods of these clerical readers and better illuminate their interests in and attitudes toward *De regimine* specifically, and moral philosophy more generally.

MARGINALIA

The very earliest copies of *De regimine* were already equipped with the finding aids that had become standard fare in books produced for academic readers. Their readers were guided by the headings, often rubricated and numbered, at the beginning of each chapter; and these headings could be found, in turn, in the chapter lists that preceded each book or part. There was also the hierarchy of initials, often illuminated, at the beginnings of books, parts, and chapters, and in the chapters themselves capitals and colored paraph marks. Usually the book and part numbers were written at the top of each double-page opening, though these sometimes had to be added by later readers. These devices alone seem to have sufficed for lay readers, in whose Latin and vernacular copies they appear. But learned clerical readers often found themselves looking for ways to improve the text's utility. The easiest and most immediate means of doing so was by the addition of marginalia. These could take the form of brief notes – opinions of the reader or citations of other authorities, but more often just key words pulled from the text – schematic summaries, or the more generalized *nota bene* marks and pointing hands.

The most extensive marginal material in the manuscripts of the English Group appears in Lambeth Palace Libr. 150, the manuscript given by John Lecche to Lanthony priory in 1361.[4] Lecche's *De regimine* is equipped throughout with an impressive array of marginal notes, schematic summaries, and pen and ink sketches; the vast majority of these marginalia are in the hand of the text scribe, though two other hands also wrote extensive notes. Overall, the marginalia executed by the scribe perform two functions. The first is to draw the reader's attention to particularly important portions of the text, chiefly through the use of key words underlined in red and contained within rectangular or triangular frames, and of *notae* and pointing hands. More rare, though most striking, are the lively sketches, either of figures that Giles singles out for scorn, like the tyrant, the flatterer, or the arrogant despiser, or of more worthy characters, including an old man, a father, a

---

[4] See above, p. 96.

king, and the head of a knight wearing a helmet bearing the English royal crest.[5] The last of these is particularly interesting, for it appears beside a discussion of the physical attributes to look for in a good soldier. Here Giles compares the body of the best warrior to the body of the lion, the very same animal that appears on the royal crest.[6] Marginalia could also be employed to summarize subject matter in a schematic form; these were usually written in the margin below the relevant contents, though they were occasionally inserted on the side. Most of the schematic summaries are found in the first book, though they continue to appear throughout. An example of one of these is at the foot of the page on folio 65, below the discussion in *DRP* 2.1.10 on the preferability of monogamous marriages:

una mulier viri viro nubat propter $\left\{\begin{array}{l}\text{nature ordinem}\\\text{amicicie pacem}\\\\\text{prolis propagationem}\\\text{prolis educationem}\end{array}\right.$

Here the scribe has reduced the text of this chapter to Giles's four principal *rationes*, or arguments. Schematic summaries like this were meant both to catch the eye of a reader searching through the text and to cue the memory of someone already familiar with the summarized material.

The most elaborate schematic summaries, however, have been executed on the recto and verso of the leaf immediately following the explicit. The first of these is a summary of topics treated in each of the major divisions of the text. This is followed by a schematic display of the twelve moral virtues and the twelve passions, which are the principal subjects respectively of the first book's second and third parts. It seems, however, that this summary's description of the passions was not thought to be sufficiently detailed, thus calling for another, more articulated one. From this it seems somewhat likely that the intended original owner of this manuscript had a particular interest in the virtues and passions. The same preoccupation lies behind the schematic summaries that have been added to the verso of the flyleaf facing the incipit of *De regimine* in Bodleian Auct. F.3.3 (plate 7). Here are the first two schematic summaries of Lecche's manuscript, and in a contemporary hand using the same grade of Anglicana script. There are enough differences in the two hands to make it unlikely that they were the work of the same scribe, but the fact that they were executed at about the same time and contain virtually the same text strongly points to some sort of affiliation between them.

I have found similar summaries of major textual divisions in two other English

---

[5] *Rex tyrannus*, fol. 40 (1.3.3); *adulator*, fol. 52v (1.4.5); *iactator et despector*, fol. 53 (1.4.6); *senex*, fol. 74v (2.1.22); *pater*, fol. 77v (2.1.4); *rex*, fol. 125 (3.2.4); helmet bearing royal crest, fol. 157v (3.3.3).

[6] "Signa vero conformantia nos animalibus bellicosis sunt magnitudo extremitatum et latitudo pectoris. Videmus enim leones, animalium fortissimos, habere magna brachia et latum pectus": *DRP*, 3.3.3.

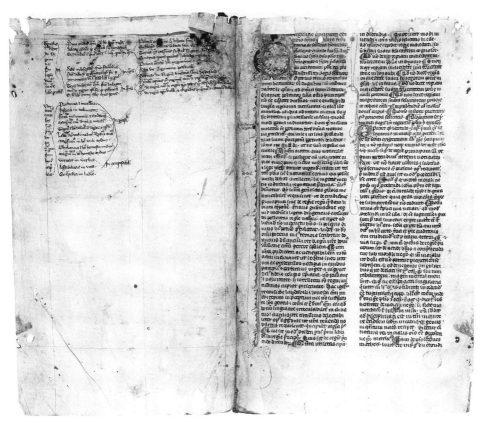

*7 Schematic contents summary. Oxford, Bodleian Library, MS Auct. F.3.3,
flyleaf and fol. 1r*

manuscripts, one of which, Bodleian Laud Misc. 702, is actually an early Parisian
pecia copy that had made its way to England by 1419, the year Henry Lord Percy
gave it to his confessor, the Dominican theologian William of Norham.[7] Brother
William, it seems, took his reading of *De regimine* seriously, as notes in an English
hand contemporary with Norham frequently punctuate the text. This same reader
also penned a schematic summary of the subjects of each book and each part on the
book's front flyleaf (plate 8). A more thorough summary of subject matter treated
in the major textual divisions precedes the *De regimine* in Hereford Cath. Libr.
P.V.7. This copy, which was produced *c.* 1400, was given by the Oxford graduate
Owen Lloyd to Hereford in the latter part of the fifteenth century. The summary, in
a mid fifteenth-century hand that does not appear to be Lloyd's, is bipartite, the
second part being a more condensed and schematized version of the first.[8] Thus the
first part summarizes the first book as follows:

[7] See above, p. 66.
[8] For an example of Lloyd's glossing hand, see Mynors and Thomson, *Catalogue*, pl. 59.

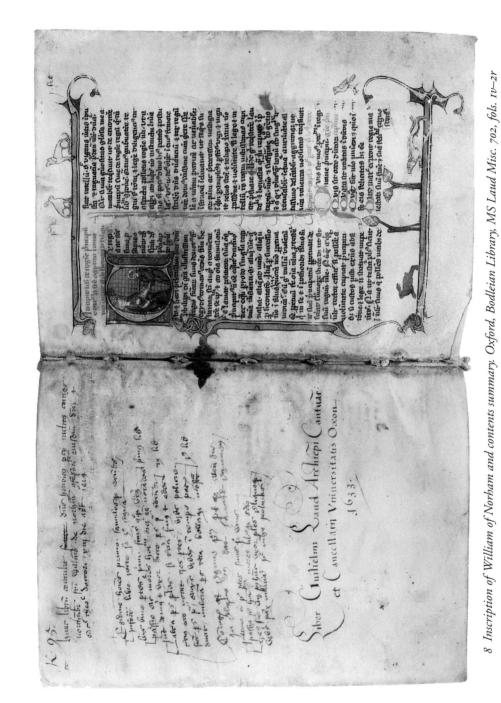

Primus liber tractat de regimine principis in seipso
prima pars huius libri docet quod felicitas principis est solum ponenda in statu virtutis
2ᵃ pars est de sufficienti virtutum distinctione et quibus virtutibus principes debent pollere
3ᵃ pars est de diversis passionibus et motibus animi et de earum moderatione
4ᵃ pars de laudabilibus et vituperabilibus moribus diversorum statuum

While the second renders it thus:

primo raptus ad statum proprium $\left\{\begin{array}{l}\text{prima docet viri felicitas}\\\text{post virtutum magna varietas}\\\text{passionum frenatur feritas}\\\text{post ad mores status diversitas}\end{array}\right\}$ partes primi libri

The same hand also penned the fairly heavy marginal notes that occur in the first several leaves of the text. Interestingly, the most extensive display (fol. 30) accompanies the first two chapters of book 1, part 3, whose subject matter is the twelve passions (plate 9). Thus nearly a century after the writing of the marginalia of Lambeth Palace Libr. 150 and Bodleian Auct. F.3.3, the same preoccupations with the text are in evidence.[9]

Marginalia and summaries are in many ways our most direct evidence of how these medieval clerical readers used *De regimine*. Though I have not done a detailed study of all the marginalia in all the manuscripts, I have observed some generalized patterns of use. First, these readers seem to have taken a particular, though by no means exclusive, interest in the subject matter of the first book, and most especially the contents of the first three parts, which treat in turn the proper and improper ends of human life, the virtues, and the passions.[10] It could be that they did so owing simply to a lack of diligence, that they tired of reading and/or annotating as they progressed through the text. I think, however, that this pattern of glossing more often reflects the relative importance of ethics in the university curriculum; for although the statutes of Oxford appear to give equal weight to the study of ethics, economics, and politics in their prescription that those studying for the master of arts degree were required to attend three terms' lectures on any one of the three subjects, surviving copies of Aristotle's *Ethics* outnumber those of the *Politics*

---

[9] A keen interest in the passions is also evinced in the schematic summary in BN lat. 6476, fol. 29, a manuscript that belonged in the fifteenth century to a French physician name Alain Blanchet. The summary appears to be in Blanchet's hand.

[10] For example, Cambridge Univ. Libr. Dd.3.47; Peterhouse 233; Glasgow Univ. Libr. Hamilton 141; Hereford Cath. Libr. P.V.7; BL Roy. 4.D.iv and Roy. 6.B.v; Bodleian Bodl. 589; Bodleian Hatton 15 and Laud Misc. 652. Manuscripts with a French provenance show the same pattern. See, for example, BN lat. 6475, lat. 6476, lat. 10208, lat. 16123, and lat. 18428. Some manuscripts that do not conform to this pattern, either because the marginalia are consistent throughout, or even heavier in other portions of the text are: Bodleian Laud Misc. 645 and Laud Misc. 702; and BN lat. 15449 and lat. 16124. The owner of the last of these, the Parisian scholar Peter of Limoges (d. 1306), seems to have been particularly interested in Giles's discussions of the just war and the poor in *DRP* 2.3.5–6. On Peter of Limoges, see M. Mabille, "Pierre de Limoges et ses méthodes de travail," in *Hommages à André Boutemy*, ed. G. Cambier (Brussels, 1976), pp. 244–51.

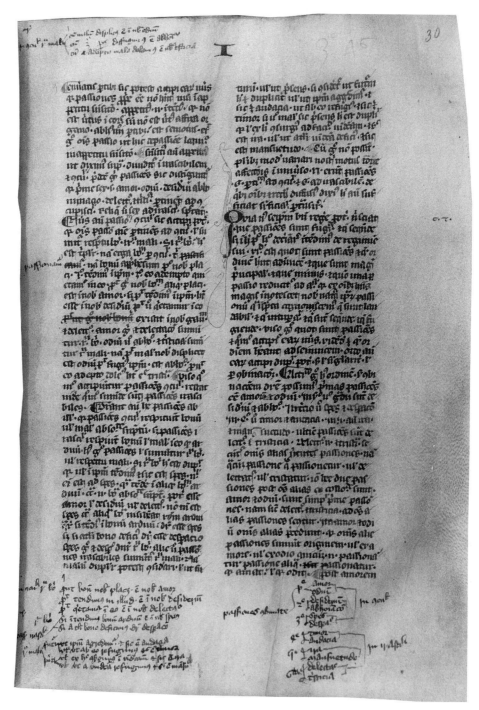

9 *Schematic summaries of the passions. Hereford, Cathedral Library, MS P.V.7,*
fol. 30r

by a ratio of three to one.[11] The relative importance of the *Ethics* is more clearly expressed in the statutes of the University of Paris, where in 1366 completion of a course of lectures on the *Ethics* became a requirement for the M.A., whereas lectures on the *Politics* or *Economics* remained optional.[12] I have noticed the same trend in the two medieval university manuscripts I have looked at that contain copies of both the *Ethics* and *Politics*, wherein the glosses on the *Ethics* are substantially heavier than those accompanying the *Politics*.[13]

De regimine's clerical readers also habitually participated in the standard scholastic practice of *divisio*, whereby all discourse proceeded according to a rigorous pattern of hierarchical topical division and subdivision, hence the frequent recourse to the schematic summaries which these scholars had become accustomed to using in the classroom, either for the purpose of taking notes from someone else's lecture or when preparing the notes for their own lectures.[14] Of course Giles's narrative already lent itself to such treatment, since it proceeded in the fashion of a university lecture, according to the principle of *divisio*; a fifteenth-century reader of Bodleian Bodl. 589 even went so far as to stress these *divisiones* by numbering Giles's *rationes* in the margins. Finally, both the scribes and the readers of these manuscripts frequently made a point of noting the several *exempla* and *similitudines* that adorn the text.[15] The volume in the *Typologie des sources* series devoted to the medieval exemplum defines it as, "un récit bref donné comme véridique et destiné à être inséré dans un discours (en général un sermon) pour convaincre un auditoire par une leçon salutaire."[16] Exempla can be further subdivided into the two types known variously as the "sermon" or "morality" exemplum and the "classical," "profane," or "public," exemplum.[17] It is this latter type which Giles utilizes in *De*

---

[11] Surviving copies of the *Ethics* (all versions) in the *Aristoteles Latinus* catalogue total 367, versus 110 copies of the *Politics*. A comparison of the number of copies just of William of Moerbeke's *Ethics* and *Politics* translations yields a ratio of 246 to 107: Kretzmann, Kenny, and Pinborg (eds.), *Cambridge History of Later Medieval Philosophy*, pp. 77–8. On the curriculum at Oxford, see Courtenay, *Schools and Scholars*, pp. 32, 56–77; G. Leff, *Paris and Oxford Universities in the Thirteenth and Fourteenth Centuries: An Institutional and Intellectual History* (New York, 1968), p. 146; J. M. Fletcher, "Developments in the Faculty of Arts," in *History of the University of Oxford*, ed. Catto and Evans, p. 323.

[12] Kretzmann, Kenny, and Pinborg (eds.), *Cambridge History of Later Medieval Philosophy*, p. 666; Leff, *Paris and Oxford*, p. 156. This also appears to have been the case at the University of Freiburg im Breisgau at the end of the Middle Ages: J. M. Fletcher (ed.), *The Liber Taxatorum of Poor Students at the University of Freiburg im Breisgau* (Notre Dame, Ind., 1969), pp. 15–16, 20–3, 42.

[13] BN lat. 7695A and lat. 16583.

[14] Parkes, "Provision of Books," pp. 424–31. My thanks to Charles Burnett for providing me with a draft of his forthcoming article in *History of the Universities*, "Notes and Note-Taking in the Universities in the Twelfth and Thirteenth Centuries."

[15] For example, Cambridge, Sidney Sussex Coll. 98; BL Ar. 384; Roy. 5.C.iii; Bodleian Bodl. 589; Oxford, Jesus Coll. 98; BN lat. 6475, lat. 6478, lat. 10207, lat. 16123, and lat. 16124.

[16] C. Bremond, J. Le Goff, and J.-C. Schmitt, *L'"Exemplum,"* Typologie des sources du Moyen Age occidental, fasc. 40 (Turnhout, 1982), pp. 37–8.

[17] Scanlon, *Narrative, Authority and Power*, p. 57; J.-T. Welter, *L'exemplum dans la littérature religieuse et didactique du Moyen Age* (Paris, 1927; reprint, New York, 1973), p. 191.

regimine, where he relates the illustrative and cautionary stories of such figures as Hector of Troy, Dionysius of Syracuse, Julius Caesar, and Nero, to name but a few.[18] Related to the exemplum is the *similitudo*, or explanation by way of analogy, a device Giles often relies on to clarify or stress his arguments.[19] The medieval readers of *De regimine*, however, do not appear to have made these fine distinctions, and freely substituted the terms *exemplum, historia,* and *narratio* for both types of discourse.

ABRIDGMENTS

Several of the surviving manuscripts of *De regimine*, both in its Latin and vernacular forms, in fact contain abridgments.[20] The impetus behind their production doubtless resulted from the almost awe-inspiring breadth of field and thoroughness of *De regimine*. For if these qualities endowed Giles's mirror with the status of a veritable *summa* of moral philosophy, they also restricted access to its contents. It has already been shown how the careful reader could partially correct for this by inserting marginalia. Another means of effecting this was to cut out altogether what was considered to be extraneous material. The resulting abridgments, called *abbreviationes* or *compendia*, were designed to present their original's most important subject matter in largely the same narrative sequence, thus greatly speeding the act of gaining access to the text's *sententia*.[21] In doing so they could function in a sense like a glossed copy of the full text, but with an important difference. The full text of *De regimine* takes up roughly 125 leaves, or 250 pages, in a manuscript of average size where the text is written in double columns. A text of such length took considerable time to copy. This could be a liability either for the poor scholar wishing to do the work himself or for the better endowed cleric who commissioned someone else to do it, since in terms of manuscript book production time was money. An abridgment, then, would take less time to copy, though it should be

---

[18] *DRP* 1.1.10, 1.2.14 and 32.   [19] Bremond, Le Goff, and Schmitt, *L'"Exemplum,"* p. 158.
[20] For the vernacular abridgments, see above, pp. 43, 46–7. The Latin of the English Group are: BL Roy. 5.C.iii, Roy. 6.D.v, and Roy. 12.B.xxi; Bodleian Bodl. 234 and Laud Misc. 645. Two other manuscripts in this group (BL Ar. 384 and Oxford, Jesus Coll. 98) contain an alphabetically arranged abridgment, whose form is different enough to merit discussion in a separate section below, pp. 143–5. The several manuscripts in continental libraries containing Latin *De regimine* abridgments are listed in Del Punta and Luna, *Catalogo*, pp. xv–xvii; Bruni, *Le opere*, pp. 95–6; Zumkeller, *Manuskripte*, pp. 36–41. One should discount, however, the work by Paul Worczyn in Crakow Univ. Libr. 711, which was erroneously catalogued by Wislocki under the title *Lectura super Aegidii Romani De regimine principum*, as it is in fact entitled *Lectura super Aristotelis Secretum secretorum*: W. Wislocki, *Catalogus Codicum Manuscriptorum Bibliothecae Universitatis Jagellonicae Cracovensis* (Crakow, 1877–81).
[21] The benefits of abridgments were lauded by Giles's contemporary Pierre Dubois, who often preferred them over their *originalia* in the plan of instruction he proposed in his *De recuperatione terrae sanctae*: Thorndyke, *University Records*, pp. 138–9.

kept in mind that the initial preparation of an abridgment in some cases might require more time and effort than the less mentally rigorous act of copying the full text. There is no doubt, however, that a copy of the full text required more parchment or paper than an abridgment, thereby increasing the material cost of the manuscript.[22] Moreover a book's weight and bulk could very well enter into the potential owner's deliberations, particularly if he wanted to include his *De regimine* in a miscellany or to make it readily portable, which seems to have frequently been the case with abridgment copies.

The chief drawback of abridgments is that they leave things out. For the original owner, who might be well aware of what was being discarded, this might not have been such a problem. But these products of arbitrary selection could put subsequent owners at a disadvantage, since they might not always be aware of what they were missing. Moreover, the use of abridged texts could lead to overly reductive and simplistic arguments; again this might be a particular problem for second-hand owners. And yet the very arbitrariness which made these abbreviated texts a mixed blessing for their medieval readers is a boon for the modern-day scholar. For abridgments speak to us through what they both retain and discard, thereby revealing much about the needs, desires, and working methods of those who made and used them. This by extension will help us better to understand how at least some medieval readers approached and used *De regimine*.

An abridgment can in a sense be defined as occupying the vast grey area between the full text on the one extreme and the chapter list or contents summary, on the other. The briefest and least complicated of the Latin abridgments belonging to the English Group accompanies the full text in Bodleian Bodl. 234, a manuscript that belonged to, and may well have originally been intended for, the lay aristocrat William Lord Thorp. Occupying less than eight leaves, it has much more in common with a chapter list than with the full text, and indeed might better be called an analytical or expanded chapter list. Its form and the fact that it accompanies the full text strongly suggest that the model for this expanded chapter list's scribe/compiler (for the scribe of Bodl. 234 probably also compiled this expanded chapter list) was the consolidated chapter list, an apparatus that occasionally accompanies copies of *De regimine* (plate 10). For whatever reason, though, this scribe decided to go one step further by writing very brief summaries of each chapter's subject matter, rather than simply the chapter headings alone.

This process certainly required more effort on the scribe's part than the preparation of a straightforward consolidated chapter list. Compare, for example, the heading of *DRP* 1.1.1, "Quis sit modus procedendi in regimine principum," with the first entry in this expanded chapter list, "Quod modus procedendi in hoc libro

---

[22] J. Hamesse, "Les florilèges philosophiques, instruments de travail des intellectuels à la fin du Moyen Age et à la Renaissance," in *Filosofia e teologia nel Trecento: Studi in ricordo di Eugenio Randi*, ed. L. Bianchi (Louvain-la-Neuve, 1994), pp. 488–9.

10 Consolidated chapter list. Cambridge, Gonville and Caius College, MS 113/182, fol. 148r

sit figuralis et grossus, tum ex parte materie circa quam versatur huius ars, tum ex parte finis qui intenditur, dum ex parte populi qui eruditur; ac per hoc reddit lector benevolus." What, in effect, the scribe has given here is a brief description of the subject matter of *DRP* 1.1.1 by gathering together and paraphrasing the following bits of text from the chapter:

quod modum procedendi in hac sciencia oportet esse figuralem et grossum. Prima via sumitur ex parte materie, circa quam versatur huiusmodi ars; secunda ex parte finis qui intenditur in hac arte; tertia ex parte auditoris qui erudiendus est per talem artem . . . Tertia via sumitur ex parte auditoris qui erudiendus in hac arte. Nam licet intitulatus sit hic liber de eruditione principum, totus tamen populus erudiendus est per ipsum.

He then goes on to insert a paraphrase of a statement in *DRP* 1.1.3 which refers back to the purpose of the first chapter: "in primo capitulo reddidimus regiam maiestatem benivolam, ostendendo que dicenda sunt." This manipulation of the text with the aim of briefly conveying the key elements in it is the mark of an abridgment rather than a mere chapter list. Eventually, however, the scribe seems to have tired of the effort of preparing these extremely reductive chapter descriptions, since beginning with the entry for *DRP* 3.2.1 he abandoned the role of abbreviator and proceeded to copy the standard chapter headings instead.

At the other extreme from the expanded chapter list is an abridgment that survives in two copies, Bodleian Laud Misc. 645 and BL Roy. 6.B.v, both of which are of English origin, the former executed in the first quarter, and the latter in the first half of the fifteenth century. Because the compiler of this ambitious compendium has divided it into ten "tracts," which correspond to the ten parts of *De regimine*, I will refer to it here as the *Tractatus decem*. In a brief introduction that bears comparison with the colophon of the scribe Iacobinus, the compiler of the *Tractatus decem* explains that he has "brought together the authorities and propositions of *De regimine principum* in abbreviated form by leaving out the tiresome lengthy deductions that attend them" (*De regimine principum auctoritates et rationes compendiose collegi ad propositum pertinentes prolixas deducciones que fastidiunt relinquendo*).[23] A perusal of the fruits of his labors shows that he has largely managed to deliver on his claim since his abridgment treats almost all the original's fundamental subject matter and cites most of its principal authorities, while still managing to be only about one third as long. This condensation has been achieved by removing either entire chapters or parts thereof, and then compressing what remains into much more concise language.

The *Tractatus decem* is divided into 131 chapters, compared to the 209 of its source. Though this ostensibly leaves seventy-eight chapters unaccounted for, only the prologue and twenty *De regimine* chapters have actually been entirely dropped. These are *DRP* 1.1.1–3; 1.2.1 and 2; 1.3.2–6; 2.1.11–13, 19 and 20; 2.2.7; 3.1.4, 8, and 15;

---

23 Laud Misc. 645, fol. 84v.

3.2.25. The missing chapters from the first part of book I are those which introduce the entire work and discuss the mode of discourse most appropriate for moral philosophy, the order of subjects to be treated, and the utility in studying them. Those from the second part also serve an introductory function. Book 2, part 3, which is concerned with the passions, lacks those five chapters which treat respectively the order of the passions, love and hate, desire and abhorrence, hope and despair, and boldness and fear. The same number of chapters has been cut from book 2, part 1, which deals with the subject of women. The first of these missing chapters warns princes against marrying members of their immediate families or close kin; the next two both have to do with the exterior and interior goods of women; and the remainder are on the subject of how princes should rule their wives. The next part, on children, has been left largely intact, and even the one missing chapter, a discussion of the importance of teaching Latin to royal and noble boys, can still be found reiterated in the opening section of the *De regimine*'s next chapter, which has been included. The four other chapters that are missing from the *Tractatus decem* are all to some extent redundant, in that they treat subjects in greater detail that are brought up elsewhere.

Ninety-one of the *Tractatus decem*'s chapters correspond to individual chapters in *De regimine*. Of the remaining chapters in this abridgment, thirty-eight are composites of between two and four chapters from their source, and comprise ninety-eight *De regimine* chapters in total. The frequency and volume of composite chapters vary widely from one tract to another. In the first four tracts – those which correspond to *De regimine*'s first book – only three chapters are composites, whereas in the next three tracts, nineteen out of twenty-seven chapters are. This high rate continues in the eighth tract (five out of eight chapters), but then declines dramatically in tracts 9 and 10, with their respective ratios of eight composite chapters out of twenty-four and three out of nineteen respectively. The highest concentrations of these composite chapters occur in tracts 5, 6, and 8, which correspond to the parts in *De regimine* on women, children, and the opinions of ancient philosophers.

Almost invariably the composite chapters in the *Tractatus decem* are clusters of *De regimine* chapters united by a similar theme. In other words, the abbreviator took care to combine *De regimine* chapters in a way that corresponded to the major topical divisions in each part. This method is illustrated in table 7, where the chapter divisions in the sixth tract of the *Tractatus decem* are compared with the corresponding divisions in book 2, part 2 of its source.

It is apparent from this table that in his effort to compress his material while at the same time making it more accessible, the abbreviator has imposed a slightly different form on the text, one that makes explicit some of the implied thematic structures of his original. This attempt to impose a more rational system of chapter divisions has led the abbreviator at one point to reverse his usual practice of com-

Table 7. *Chapter divisions in* Tractatus decem *and* De regimine

Tractatus decem chapters	*DRP* 2.2 chapters	Topics
1	1–4	Parent–child relationship
2	5, 6, 8	Instruction in faith, habits, and liberal arts
3	9, 10	Choosing a tutor, how children should speak and use their sight and hearing
4	11–14	Instruction in good habits
5	15–18	The three phases of childhood
6	19–21	Behavior of daughters

bining chapters, and instead to devote two chapters of the *Tractatus decem* to a single chapter of his source (*DRP* 1.4.4), in which two topics are treated – the praiseworthy habits of old men and the habits of men of middle age. And while he almost universally follows the *ordo narrationis* of *De regimine*, he does on occasion rearrange the sequence of its material to suit the flow of his own narrative. For example, the fifth tract, first chapter, moves respectively through material from chapters 4, 3, 1, 2, and 4 again of the first part of *De regimine*'s second book. Yet as good a job as the abbreviator may have done, the margins of the copy in BL Roy. 6.B.v show that at least one of its readers felt the need to go back to the original in order to add material which the *Tractatus decem* is missing; and even here, the writer of these marginal additions has abbreviated and reorganized his borrowings from *De regimine*, perhaps in the interests of saving space.

This need of later readers to supplement their *De regimine* abridgments is also seen in BL Roy. 5.C.iii, a miscellany which contains not only an abridgment written during the first half of the fifteenth century, but also a consolidated chapter list of the unexpurgated text and a unique representative of a shortened recension of the *Abhominacio* type of alphabetical index. The hand responsible for the extensive marginal additions to this abridgment is contemporary with that of its mid fifteenth-century owner, Thomas Eborall, who may, then, have been responsible for them.[24] This same hand also compiled a list of the abridgment's chapters. It is not difficult to see why this reader would have wanted to supplement this heavily abbreviated version of *De regimine*, for the abbreviator had both entirely excised a very large number of chapters and removed large portions of text from the included chapters. And while the result of this effort was an extremely concise rendering of the text – the abridgment occupies a mere fifteen and a half leaves, written in double columns – its frequent and often substantial *lacunae* could well have frustrated anyone wanting better than a nodding acquaintance with the most heavily

---

[24] See above, pp. 98–9.

abbreviated sections of the text. Three general patterns of selection emerge from a perusal of this abridgment. First, each chapter entry tends to state the chapter's chief propositions but then discards Giles's elaborations of them, as well as the chapter's introductory and concluding matter. In order to see how he did this, compare the text of *DRP* 2.1.4 with the entry for the same chapter in the abridgment.

Rome 1556 edition

Est autem ex praecedenti capitulo aliqualiter declaratum, *qualis sit communitas domus*: cum ostensum sit quod homo est naturaliter animal domesticum, et quod communitas domus est quodammodo naturalis. Attamen quia per hoc non sufficienter habetur qualis sit huiusmodi communitas, ideo intendimus aliqua dicere de communitate domestica. Sciendum ergo, Philosophum I. Politicorum sic describere communitatem domus, videlicet, quod domus est communitas secundum naturam, constituta quidem in omnem diem. In hac autem descriptione aliquid declaratum est per praecedens capitulum, et aliquid restat ulterius declarandum. Nam quod domus sit communitas secundum naturam, superius grosse et figuraliter probabatur, et infra clarius ostendetur. Ubi distinguentur omnes partes domus, et probabitur quod quaelibet talis pars est aliquid naturale, restat ergo delarare in descriptione praedicta, quomodo domus sit communitas constituta in omnem diem. *Ad cuius euidentiam advertendum, quod humanorum operum, et eorum quae requiruntur ad sufficientiam vitae, ad quae ordinatur humana communitas, ut videtur distinguere Philosophus I. Politicorum, quaedam sunt diurnalia, ut illa, quibus indigemus omni die, cuiusmodi est commedere, bibere, et cuiusmodi* sunt alia sustentamenta, et servitia corporalia, quibus cotidie indigemus. Aliquia vero sunt non diurnalia, quibus non quotidie indigemus, ut emptio, et venditio. Nam et si aliqui existentes in aliqua domo, *ad sustentationem vitae quotidie indigent emptione, et venditione, videtur hoc esse ex defectu, et ex corruptione domus: non enim videntur se habere ut incolae nec ut cives, sed magis ut peregrini et ut viatores, si ad sustentationem vitae emptione vel venditione continue egeant. Communitas ergo domus facta fuit propter ea, quibus quotidie indigemus. Verum quia in una domo non reperiuntur omnia necessaria ad vitam, non sufficiebat communitas domestica, sed oportuit dare communitatem vici, ita quod cum vicus constet ex pluribus domibus, quod non reperitur in una domo, reperiatur in alia.* Propter quod Philosophus I. Poli. ait, quod sicut communitas domus constituta est in omnem

BL Roy. 5.C.iii, fol. 31v

Qualis sit communitas domus.

Communitas domus facta fuit propter ea quibus cotidie indigemus cuius sunt comedere et bibere.

Et si contingat aliquis indigere cotidiana empcione hoc est ex defectum eorum, quia non videntur se habere ut incole et cives sed magis ut peregrini et viatores.

Sed quia in una domo non reperiuntur omnia necessaria ad vitam, oportuit dare communitate vici ut quod non reperiatur in una domo reperiatur in alia.

diem, idest in opera diurnalia: sic in opera non diurnalia constituta est communitas vici. *Verum quam etiam in uno vico non reperiuntur omnia necessaria ad vitam, praeter communitatem vici oportuit dare communitatem civitatis. Communitas ergo civitatis esse videtur ad supplendam indigentiam in tota vita. Illa ergo videtur esse perfecta civitas (ut superius dicebatur) in qua reperiri possunt quae sunt necessaria universaliter ad totam vitam.* Rursus autem, quam contingit civitates habere guerras, *utile est uni civitati ad expugnandam civitatem aliam confoederare se alteri civitati.* Quare cum confoederatio civitatum utilis sit ad bellandum hostes, et ad removendum prohibentia corruptiva, praeter communitatem domus, vici, et civitatis, *inventa fuit communitas regni et principatus, quae est confoederatio plurium castrorum et civitatum existentium sub uno principe sive sub uno rege.* Erit ergo his ordo, quod domus est communitas secundum naturam constituta in omnem diem; vicus autem est communitas constituta in opera non diurnalia; civitas vero est communitas constituta ad sufficientiam in vita tota; sed regnum est communitas constituta non solum ad supplendum indigentias vitae, sed etiam ad removendum prohibentia corruptiva, ad quae removendum una civitas non potest plene sufficere, nisi ei sint adiunctae aliae plurimae civitates et castra. Patet ergo qualis sit communitas domus, quia est communitas naturalis constituta propter opera diurnalia et quotidiana. Quod autem oporteat domum ex pluribus constare personis, videre non est difficile. Nam cum domus (ut patet ex habitis) sit communitas quaedam et societas personarum, cum non sit, proprie communitas nec societas ad seipsum. Si in domo communitatem salvare volumus, oportet eam ex pluribus constare personis. Immo (ut infra patebit, et ut vult Philosophus I. Poli.) non solum domus est communitas quaedam, sed in domo oportet dare plures communitates, quod sine pluralitate personarum esse non potest. Patet ergo quod domus ex pluribus constat personis. Patet etiam qualis sit, et quomodo sit necessaria. Nam (ut est ex habitis manifestum) in vita humana non solum est expediens communitas domus, sed et vici, civitatis, et regni. Utrum autem propter alias causas, quam propter iam dictas, sit expediens communitas civitatis, et regni, in tertio libro plenius ostendetur. Ad praesens autem sufficiat in tantum tangere de regno et civitate, inquantum eorum notitia aliquo modo deservit ad cognoscendum domum, et ad sciendum qualiter sit regenda. Nam (ut superius tangebatur) in hoc secundo libro intenditur principaliter regimen domus, non autem regimen civitatis. His sic

Et quia non reperiuntur omnia necessaria in vico ideo oportuit dare communitatem civitatis ad supplendum indigenciam in tota vita; et sic civitas est perfecta in qua reperiri possunt que sunt necessaria ad totam vitam.

Et quia propter bella utile est unam communitatem alterius confederari;
ideo inventa fuit communitas regni sub uno rege.

Et patet iste processus primo politicorum.

123

pertractatis, cum communitas domus sit tam necessaria in
vita civili, spectat ad quemlibet civem scire debite regere
suam domum: tanto tamen magis hoc spectat ad reges et
principes, quanto ex incuria propriae domus magis potest
insurgere praeiudicium civitati et regno, quam ex incuria
aliorum.

Second, the abbreviator includes progressively fewer chapters as he goes along. In
the latter two books, moreover, the chapters that are included are often radically
pared down, sometimes to no more than a couple of lines (table 8). On the other
hand, some of the included chapters in these latter two books are largely intact.

Clearly, the abbreviator thought the material in the first book was the most
important, a principle, it will be recalled, which is consistent with that seen in *De
regimine* marginalia. But his decisions on what to preserve and what to leave out in
the latter two books were not made at random, and an examination of his choices in
the last book, where the cutting of chapters is most pronounced, provides ample
evidence of his interests. In book 3, part 1 he has included extracts from the first two
chapters, which state the book's chief proposition, which is that the city is the principal form of community and exists in order that people may not only live, but live
well. He then excises all the chapters that elaborate upon the initial proposition and
proceed to state the opinions of ancient philosophers regarding the proper disposi-
tion and rule of the city. Two chapters only remain, one of which (chapter 13)
admonishes kings and princes against allowing the same men to be repeatedly proposed for high offices of state, and the other (chapter 18) which states that the principal duty of the prince should be directed toward the suppression of covetousness,
rather than the equalizing of possessions. In the next part, whose subject is the rule
of the state in peacetime, all chapters have been removed that discuss forms of rule
other than a legitimate monarchy (chapters 1–7, 10–15), and that elaborate upon
matters of law (chapters 25, 27, 31), the constitution of the state (32, 33), and the
relationship between the prince and his people (34–6). What the abbreviator has
included are the chapters that define the office of the king (chapters 8, 9) and
discuss the chief means of legitimate governance, i.e. proper counsel (chapters
16–19), and the exercise of justice (chapters 20–24, 26, 28, 29). The final part, on
warfare, retains only those chapters which discuss fighting men and their weapons
(chapters 2–7), while discarding the chapters on tactics, strategy, and siegecraft
(chapters 8–22); and though the abbreviator has included the final chapter, he has
excised the entire first part on naval warfare, leaving only the final discussion on
why legitimate wars are fought.

Table 8 also lists the chapter extracts supplied by the reader, and thereby partially
reveals his efforts to supplement the abridgment. He also, however, frequently
amplified the chapters which the abbreviator had included, through the addition
of material from *De regimine*; he sometimes even corrected the text and provided

Table 8. *Contents of abridgment in BL Roy 5.C. iii*

Book and Part	Total chs. in full text	Total chs. missing	Percentage of chs. missing	Chs. excised	Chs. added	Cols. in MS	Pp. in DRP 1556 edn
1.1	13	1	7.7	no. 13	no. 13	5⅓	49
1.2	34	1	2.9	no. 4	no. 4	19	130
1.3	11	0	0			7	41
1.4	7	0	0			6	31
TOTAL	**65**	**2**	**3.1**			**37⅔**	**251**
2.1	24	4	16.7	nos. 3, 5, 11, 21	nos. 3, 5	4⅓	86
2.2	21	3	14.3	nos. 3, 6, 18	nos. 6, 18	4⅔	70
2.3	20	7	35	nos. 3, 4, 7, 13–15, 17	no. 3	3¼	62
TOTAL	**65**	**14**	**21.5**			**12¼**	**218**
3.1	20	16	80	nos. 3–12, 14–17, 19, 20		1	59
3.2	36	21	58.3	nos. 1–7, 10–15, 25, 27, 31–36		8½	125
3.3	23	16	69.7	nos. 1, 8–22		2	89
TOTAL	**79**	**53**	**67.1**			**11½**	**273**

cross-references to other chapters. For example, although the abbreviator included most of the chapters from the second part of book 2, whose subject is the care and education of children, he nevertheless radically shortened many of them. The last three chapters, which speak of the proper behavior of girls (essentially, that they should stay indoors, stay busy, and keep quiet), occupy seven and a half pages in the 1556 edition; in the abridgment, however, this subject has been reduced to a mere twenty-seven lines. Not satisfied with this scant treatment, the reader supplied additional material from *De regimine* (in italics) plus some notes of his own (italicized entries in margin).[25]

Capitulum 19

FILIE NOBILIUM A VAGACIONE SUNT COHIBENDE. Omne insollitum est quodammodo verecundum. *Maximum autem frenum feminarum ne prorumpant ad turpiam videtur esse verecundia.* Unde si puelle non fuerint assuete inter viros verecunde reddunt in aspectibus earum. Item ex hoc contrahunt quandam silvestritatem que optima est ad salvandam pudiciciam feminarum. Videmus enim quod animalia silvestria si assuescant conversacionibus hominum domesticantur et permittunt se tangi et palpari. Aliter si sint a conversacione remota, tactum hominum fugiunt. NON DEBENT VIVERE OCIOSE. Secundum Philosophum 10 Ethicorum absque omni delectactione vita nostra durare non possit (*potest*), unde oportet sumere aliqua opera licita et honesta circa que vacantes delectamur insistendo eisdem, et mens humana si non occupetur circa licita vagatur circa illicita, et mulieres pocius quam viri quia molliores sunt et magis deficiunt ab usu rationis. Et si queratur circa quod opus debent occupari distinguendum est secundum statum earum vel saltem si sint nobiles *et in alto gradu non esset dignum vel consuetum secundum morem patrie ut se circa utilia excitarent* occupentur circa studia litterarum. DE TACITURNITATE PUELLARUM. Filie eciam docende sunt ut sint taciturne. Nam, ut ait Philosophus <u>Primo Politicorum</u>, ornamentum mulierum est silencium propter hoc si modo debito sint taciturne magis appetuntur et amantur. Igitur nullum sermonem proferant nisi ipsum diligenter prius examinent et hec est racio potissima contra sermonem incautum. *Item quia sunt prone ad iurgia et lites et propter racionis defectum de facili loqui possunt pertinencia ad ea. Et postquam inceperint litigare nesciunt se abstinere sed augetur in eis concupiscencia licium eo quod ab usu racionis deficiunt et ut plurimum plus vivent passione quam racione.*

Capitulum 20
Et Rethorica
Nota de delectacione et occupatione investigamur 3ª 1.2. c 13 [i.e. *DRP* 2.1.13] *in fine.*

I have already mentioned that the date of the glossing hand raises the possibility of Thomas Eborall having been responsible for the marginal supplements in

25 BL Roy. 5.C.iii, fols. 33–33v.

this abridgment. Eborall's need to fulfill his pedagogical duties as master of Whittington College in London would certainly help to explain why the marginalia are particularly heavy in the portion of the text on education. Whosoever made these additions, however, their presence in the manuscript provides ample witness to the extent and kind of engagement which this late medieval reader had with Giles's manual on governance. His goal was to make the abridgment more suitable for his own purposes. This included making corrections, supplying extensive extracts from a copy of the full text of *De regimine*, and squeezing a list of chapters into the empty space between the explicit of the abridgment and the end of the quire. Moreover, on one occasion at least he used the alphabetical index found in another part of the manuscript (and in a hand other than that of the abridgment or the marginalia) in conjunction with his reading of the abridgment. At the bottom of folio 30, beneath the chapters in book 1, part 4 on the good and bad traits of youths and old men, he has added "Nota medii inter senes et iuvenes habent quicquid laudabilitatis est in iuvenibus et senibus." This refers to Giles's assertion in the latter part of *DRP* 1.4.4, but missing from the abridgment, that middle-aged men are naturally inclined to be the most virtuous. Immediately following this the reader has added a cross-reference to the section in *De regimine*'s third book where Giles recommends that the city or kingdom should have a large middle class: "Et illi qui sunt in medio statu sunt optimi in civitate, 3.2.33." This material, it should be recalled, is also missing from the abridgment. Yet these marginal additions were not taken directly from the full text of *De regimine* but rather from BL Roy. 5.C.iii's alphabetical index (fol. 17), where entries identical to those in the margin of folio 30 appear together and in the same sequential order. Finally, the *De regimine* abridgment and apparatus made up only a small part of a much larger whole, whose overall contents should not be ignored. For their inclusion, along with extracts from Aristotle's *Ethics* and *Politics*, in a miscellany largely stocked with devotional, penitential, and homiletic texts, and the fact that Eborall himself was a preacher of some note – he preached before the king at least once and wrote a work, now lost, entitled *Sermones in visitatione cleri Londiniensis* – could mean that Eborall closely associated texts of moral philosophy, including *De regimine*, with pastoral functions.

Judging from its contents and codicological situation, the abridgment in BL Roy. 12.B.xxi was meant to satisfy rather different expectations. Here the abridgment is paired with a copy of an abridged version of Vegetius' *De re militari*, a combination which suggests the former was meant to be read as a book of knighthood. The contents of the *De regimine* abridgment also support such a conclusion, for though the first two books and the first two parts of the third book have been heavily abbreviated, either by the excision of entire chapters or the radical paring down of the remaining chapters, the abbreviator has included the entire text of the last part, on warfare.[26] Interestingly, however, the abbreviator only made the decision to include the entire text on warfare after having already prepared abridged versions of that part's first six chapters. Then he shifted gears and decided to give the intended reader the part's full text from the beginning, or, as he put it: "Here begins the third part of the third book, at chapter thirty-seven, 'What is Warfare', in which it is shown how the city should be ruled in time of war. This part is not abbreviated but rather the text of Egidius word for word."[27]

Though military affairs were the primary matter of books of knighthood, texts of this genre also frequently concerned themselves with the management of the household and education of children. In keeping with these functions, this abridgment has cut only seven chapters from book 2, on the household and family, compared with its removal of thirteen chapters from book 1 and twenty-five from the first two parts of book 3. Though this manuscript provides no hint of its medieval ownership or provenance, its apparent role as a book of knighthood raises the possibility of its having been made for a lay aristocratic reader. As for its circumstances of production, its script is clearly English and dates from the first half of the fifteenth century, that is during the fifteenth-century phase of the Hundred Years War, when, I have argued, the English aristocracy, following the example of Henry V and his brothers, adopted *De regimine* as a military manual.

ALPHABETICAL INDEXES

Although marginalia and abbreviations certainly improved readers' access to *De regimine*'s contents, they each suffered from serious limitations. Marginal notes often lacked systematization, and were fundamentally arbitrary, being very much predicated on the peculiar concerns of the reader, or readers, who inscribed them. Abridgments were also arbitrary; and though usually more programmatic than marginalia, they tended to be customized to the needs of a particular reader, rather than being made for a general audience. Moreover, because they were invariably codicologically separate from copies of their source text, they denied access to more or less significant amounts of material to readers who were not in a position to lay their hands on the full text. These problems were largely avoided, however, if one

---

[26] The missing chapters are *DRP* 1.2.4, 6, 11, 18, 20, 21, 23, 24, 34; 1.3.2, 6, 9, 10; 2.1.23; 2.2.12, 17, 18; 2.3.2–4; 3.1.4, 6–10, 12, 14–17, 19, 20; and 3.2.4, 7, 10–15, 25, 27, 28, 31. Compare this with the abridgment in Florence, Bibl. Medicea Laurenziana, Plut. 78, 10, wherein the full text is given through 1.2.27.

[27] "Incipit tercia pars tercii libri in quo tractatur quomodo regenda sit civitas in tempore belli, Quid est milicia capitulo xxxvij°. Ista pars non est abbreviata sed est textus Egidii de verbo ad verbum": BL Roy. 12.B.xxi, fol. 52. The chapter numbering here is the result of sequential ordering of chapters throughout each book of the abridgment.

used the full text in conjunction with an alphabetical index.[28] The alphabetical index or, to use its Latin name, *tabula*, was a product of the new approach to texts that developed during the late twelfth and thirteenth centuries in response to the demands of the university curriculum and the pastoral responsibilities of the Church. They first began to be compiled during the 1230s and 1240s by the Dominicans of Saint-Jacques at Paris and Cistercian monks in some northern French houses who were looking to plunder *originalia* for moral exempla for sermons; by the early fourteenth century their use had become widespread, and scholars continued to refine their form.[29] They also continued to find new texts to index, one of them being *De regimine*.[30]

When viewed in aggregate, one of the most striking features of the English Group manuscripts is the large number and variety of alphabetical indexes they contain, there being four versions (one of which ramified into four recensions) surviving in twenty-three manuscripts (see table 5). Sixteen of these accompany the full Latin text of *De regimine*, another six appear in miscellanies of indexes and extracts, and one is bound into a manuscript also containing a copy of an abridgment. Perhaps even more impressive is the ratio of 1.7 to 1 between the forty copies of the full Latin text in the English Group and the total number of indexes. Such figures suggest that the compilation and use of alphabetical indexes were common features in the late medieval intellectual landscape. They support, moreover, the assertion of the Rouses that historians, chief among them Walter Ong, have drawn too sharp a distinction between the relative availability and utility of alphabetical indexes before and after the coming of print.[31] Nevertheless, the use of alphabetical indexes to *De regimine* seems to have been a particularly English habit, considering that the total number of surviving indexes in all Latin manuscripts of French and Italian origin is less than half that of those found in the English Group.[32] As I argued in the preceding chapter, the lion's share of compilation and copying of alphabetical indexes in England was done by English Augustinian friars and Black Monks, and the dissemination of these indexes happened largely at Oxford and

---

[28] On *De regimine* indexes, see also C. F. Briggs, "Late Medieval Texts and *Tabulae*: The Case of Giles of Rome, *De regimine principum*," *Manuscripta* 37 (1993), pp. 253–75.

[29] Rouse and Rouse, *Authentic Witnesses*, pp. 191–255; M. B. Parkes, "The Influence of the Concepts of *Ordinatio* and *Compilatio* on the Development of the Book," in *Medieval Learning and Literature: Essays Presented to Richard William Hunt*, ed. J. J. G. Alexander and M. T. Gibson (Oxford, 1976), pp. 131–2.

[30] None date before 1316. The earliest may be the "Concordantie in libro de Regimine principum per fratrem Jacobum de dacia" in Troyes, BM 989 (fols. 1–6v).

[31] Rouse and Rouse, *Authentic Witnesses*, pp. 254–5; W. J. Ong, *The Presence of the Word* (New Haven, 1967), pp. 85–6 and *Orality and Literacy: The Technologizing of the Word* (New York, 1982), p. 124; F. J. Witty, "The Beginnings of Indexing and Abstracting," in *The Indexer* 8 (1973), pp. 193–8.

[32] I do not know if alphabetical indexes were a regular feature in *De regimine* manuscripts produced in Germany. Rouse and Rouse, *Authentic Witnesses*, pp. 453–4, point to "the widespread appearance of subject indexes in fifteenth-century German manuscripts."

Cambridge. I also suggested that the more useful an index was, the more likely it was to proliferate. Now I would like to look more closely at the contents and structure of these indexes, for they, like marginalia and abridgments, provide important clues to the ways readers used *De regimine*.

The earliest surviving copy of an index is found in Oxford, Balliol Coll. 282. This index, which begins with the entry for *Amatores* and ends with either *Temperatus* or *Intemperatus*, may have been compiled by a scholar at Balliol College, since one of its other two surviving copies is also a Balliol manuscript.[33] In comparison with the other index versions, it is not a very impressive affair at all. For not only does it offer by far the fewest entries (some 100 subjects and 205 citations) of all the versions, but these entries have been alphabetized only according to their initial letter. Though at first glance it might appear that its compiler was simply less thorough and more haphazard than his counterparts, a consideration of the order of chapters cited in the entries reveals that his method was in fact perfectly in keeping with his goal, which was to construct an alphabetical index for use not with the text of *De regimine*, but rather with its chapter headings. The entries in each initial-letter group proceed serially according to the order in which their subjects appear in the rubrics. This can be demonstrated using the four entries under the letter E:

Alphabetical index	Chapter headings
EDIFICIA, qualia sunt pro tempore, libro 2°, parte 3ᵃ, capitulo 3° et 4°	(*DRP* 2.3.3) Qualia edificia debent habere reges et principes, et universaliter omnes cives quantum ad operis industriam et aeris temperamentum. (*DRP* 2.3.4) Qualia debent esse edificia, quantum ad ordinem universi.
In ELOQUIIS non habundare, libro 2°, parte 3ᵃ, capitulo 20°.	(*DRP* 2.3.20) Quod in mensis regum et principum, et universaliter nobilium tam recumbentes quam etiam ministrantes non decet in eloquiis habundare.
EDIFICIA lignea pro municione castrorum, libro 3°, parte 3ᵃ, capitulo 19°.	(*DRP* 3.3.19) Quomodo per edificia lignea impulsa ad muros civitatis et castri, impugnari possint munitiones obsesse.
EDIFICIA qualiter sunt castra et civitates, libro 3°, parte 3ᵃ, capitulo 20°.	(*DRP* 3.3.20) Qualiter edificanda sunt castra aut civitates, ne per pugnam ab obsidentibus facilius devincantur.

As one reads the entries in this index, one can imagine its anonymous compiler combing through the chapter headings in serial order, picking out what he considered to be their most important subjects, and then jotting them down in the order in which he found them in the appropriate letter sections of his copy-leaves. His source for the chapter headings could have been either the headings themselves as given at the beginnings of the chapters, the chapter lists that precede each of *De regimine*'s ten parts, or a consolidated chapter list of the whole work.

---

[33] Cambridge Univ. Libr. Ii.2.18 and Oxford, Balliol Coll. 146a.

By relying on these sources rather than on the text itself, the compiler produced a hybrid – part chapter list and part alphabetical subject index – in whose structure can be discerned differences in readers' approaches to the text. According to one approach, a reader might start at the beginning of a book, part, or chapter, and proceed to read in a serial fashion, following the *ordo narrationis* of the text. For such a reader the best reference tool would be the table of contents provided by a chapter list. A second approach might be one wherein a reader regards the text as a source of *sententiae* ripe for the plunder. This reader begins with a subject in mind, and he wants to cull his authorities rapidly, rather than lingering in the "vineyard of the text."[34] Because this approach involves an act of searching before that of reading, its proper tool is the alphabetical index. After the arrival of *De regimine* in England in the early fourteenth century, several decades passed during which time the text was disseminated and its contents read and absorbed by members of the scholarly community. The first approach would have been the most consonant with this process of absorption. By the third quarter of the fourteenth century, however, scholars had discerned the text's potential utility as a compendium of moral philosophy and source of moral precepts, *similitudines*, and exempla drawn from classical sources. This realization would have prompted the second sort of approach to the text and a concomitant desire to fashion tools with which they could exploit it more quickly and effectively.

The *Amatores* index's reliance on chapter headings made it a tool more useful for the first habit of reading than the second, and this would have frustrated anyone who was wanting to mine *De regimine* in the course of preparing a disputation, lecture, or sermon. On the one hand, they would have found that it refers to only a very narrow range of topics and misses several of the locations in which the subjects that it does mention can be found; on the other, its citations would not have been nearly exact enough for them, thus forcing them to hunt about in the chapters cited in order to find the appropriate passages. Such an index was, then, a tool of limited utility and, as often happens with such tools, it failed to "catch on" and was eventually superseded by more effective models. In the next two decades the *Abstinencia* index version would be compiled, probably by the Augustinians, while by 1390 scholars, probably of the Benedictine order, would have produced the *Avarus* type index and at least two of its *Abhominacio* recensions.

The *Abstinencia* index (plate II) survives in seven copies, the earliest of them being found in Cambridge Univ. Libr. Ii.4.22, a manuscript that appears to have been written in the 1380s.[35] This version with its 918 references to 382 subjects was a

---

[34] I. Illich, *In the Vineyard of the Text: A Commentary to Hugh's "Didascalicon"* (Chicago, 1993), pp. 57–8; R. H. Rouse and M. A. Rouse, *Preachers, Florilegia and Sermons: Studies on the "Manipulus florum" of Thomas of Ireland* (Toronto, 1979), pp. 40–2.

[35] The other manuscripts are: Bethesda, Nat. Libr. of Medicine 503; Cambridge, Peterhouse 208; London, Lambeth Palace Libr. Arc.L.40.2/L.26; Oxford, Lincoln Coll. Lat. 69; Bibl. Apost. Vat. Ottob. lat. 2071; and York Minster Library XVI.D.5.

11 Abstinentia *index. York, Minster Library, MS XVI.D.5, fol. 89v.*

substantial improvement over the *Amatores* type; moreover it alphabetizes its subjects throughout the word, and employs other referencing devices as well, as can be observed in the following sample:

COITU quando et in qua etate est utendum, 2.16 et 17. per totum. Quanta mala facit, 2.20.b. ubi *luxuria.*
COGITARE preterita quantum valet, 1.22.a.
COMMUNE bonum privato est preponendum, 1.50.bc. et 2.7.e. et 8.b. Communia omnia sunt secundum quosdam, 2.51. per totum et 3.7. per totum. Non omnia essent communia et quare, 3.8. per totum, et 10. et 11. per totum. ubi *proprium.*[36]

As can readily be seen here, the references each give a subject head-word, followed by one or more citations, each supplying a brief identifying phrase followed by its location. When there is more than one citation, these run in the order in which they appear in the text. Though the referencing system employed here is helpful in many ways, it does nevertheless employ the curious practice of giving only book and chapter numbers, ignoring the part divisions and numbering the chapters serially from the beginning through to the end of each book. I do not know why the compiler chose to number the chapters in this fashion. Perhaps he followed a copy of *De regimine* that used this system. If so, such a copy does not survive among the manuscripts of the English Group. There is no apparent advantage to using this system, since it would have forced the reader either to renumber the chapters of his copy or to take the additional step of making an arithmetic calculation in his head every time he looked up a citation. Either the compiler himself or a later copyist realized the confusion that this system might engender and so prefaced the index with the following cautionary guide:

Whosoever desires to turn to the table below on the books of the venerable Giles's On the Rule of Princes first should know that although the aforementioned volume ought to be divided into three principal books, and each book divided into several parts, and those parts into chapters, nevertheless this table does not observe this order but makes reference to books and chapters only. For example, the first number in the table stands for the book from which the usage is extracted and the second for the chapter of the book, so that the first chapter of the second part of the first book is the fourteenth chapter of the entire book from the beginning, and is thus cited in the table, and the first chapter of the third part of the first book is the forty-eighth chapter of the first book; and this is the way you ought to cite whatever book when searching this table.[37]

---

[36] The format used here is based on that in Lambeth Palace Arc.L.40.2/L.26, fols. 96–100, whose copy sets off the head-word for each subject from the rest of the entry by placing it first and underlining it in red.
[37] "Subscriptam tabulam super libros venerabilis Egidii de regimine principum volens advertere in primis sciat quod quamvis predictum volumen in tres libros sit divisum, et quilibet liber in plures partes dividatur, et partes in capitula, hunc tamen ordinem non observat presens tabula, sed tantum librorum et capitulorum facit quotaciones; verbi gratia, primus numerus in tabula stat pro libro a quo sensus extrahitur et secundum pro capitulo libri, ita quod primum capitulum secunde partis primi

Despite its cumbersome numbering system, however, the index has much to recommend it. For one thing, it directs its user swiftly to exact locations in the text by
means of a system whereby each chapter is divided into six roughly equal parts, designated A to F.[38] If, however, a subject is the matter of an entire chapter, the index
instructs the user to read the chapter "per totum." A system of cross-references
further aids the reader. With this, a reader looking for Giles's doctrine on sexual
intercourse who turned to the entry under *Coitus* would not only be told where to
look in the text for the time of year and at what age it should be engaged in, or what
evils might arise from it, he would also be directed to search the index for the
subject *Luxuria*. If he pursued this entry, he would find where to look in the text for
evidence of how contemptible it is, while also being given a further cross-reference
to *Incontinens*. Such a tool would certainly be a boon to someone looking to add fire
to a sermon on sexual vices.

A "contratabula" uniquely accompanies this index's earliest copy. It is a kind of
index's index, whose entries consist of the head-words for each subject in the index
listed seriatim in four vertical columns. Each head-word is followed by a number
corresponding to its position in the sequence of subjects in each initial-letter
group. These same numbers also appear in the index, in the margins beside the
beginning of each subject. This was a useful additional tool, since the index does
not distinguish the subject head-words, thereby making them hard to pick out
from the surrounding sea of black ink. Later copyists corrected for this by placing
the head-words at the beginning of each entry and further distinguishing them
either by writing them in rubrics or by underlining them, thus obviating the need
for a *contratabula*.

The *Avarus* type index shows signs of being an unfinished project.[39] To begin
with, its subject-designators are arranged alphabetically according only to their
initial letter. Moreover, the compiler has not even attempted to organize individual
subjects' entries either *en bloc* or in the sequential order in which they appear in the
text. Thus entries for the same subject end up being scattered throughout an initial-
letter group in a fashion that can best be characterized as random. A listing of
entries under the letter L will serve to illustrate this: *Liberalitas, Liberalis,
Liberalitas, Liberalis, Liberalitas, Lex, Lucrum, Lex, Ludus, Lex, Lancea, Loquela,*

libri est 14ᵐ capitulum tocius libri a principio, et sic quotatur in tabula, et primum captitulum 3ᵉ partis
primi libri est 48ᵐ capitulum primi libri a principio, et sic quemlibet librum quotare debes ad hanc
tabulam persequendam": Cambridge Univ. Libr. Ii.4.22, fol. 128.

[38] This system is a modification of the seven-part A–G system invented by the Dominicans of Saint-
Jacques, Paris in the first half of the thirteenth century. On this and competing systems of textual division in indexes and concordances, see Rouse and Rouse, *Preachers*, pp. 9–21, 33–4. B. Guenée, *Histoire
et culture historique dans l'Occident médiéval* (Paris, 1980), p. 234, provides another example of the A–F
system, in this case an index of Vincent of Beauvais's *Speculum historiale*.

[39] This index is found in Cambridge, Corpus Christi Coll. 283, fols. 149v–159v (missing one leaf);
Oxford Bodleian Libr. Bodl. 589, fol. 181v (first ten entries only); and San Marino, Huntington Libr.
EL 9.H.9, fols. 97v–103v.

Lucrum, Loquela, Latonienses, Lingua, Legiste, Litigio, Lex, Ludus, Locus, Lex, Latititivi, Lator legis, Lapidarium, Lupus, Ligna. This confused, rambling ordering of entries may have been the result of a poorly supervised communal effort or a desultory attempt by one compiler working over some considerable period of time, who occasionally searched in a serial fashion, noting down whatever subject happened to appear, and at other times took a topical approach, without regard for serial order. This would explain why the index contains evidence of serial searching in passages like this: "INCREDULI sunt senes, 1.4.3. ILLIBERALES, ibid. INVERECUNDI sunt, ibid. Per ILLIBERALITATEM magis peccant homines, 1.4.4."; whereas at other times the entries are purely topical: "FILIUS, filii nobilium debent instrui in artibus liberalibus, 2.2.8. De FILIORUM regimine, 2.2.6. FILIUS est testis perfectionis in patre, 2.2.4. Tria sunt consideranda in filiis, 2.2.9."[40]

This disorganization seriously impedes access to what is otherwise a very impressive index with over one thousand citations. Indeed the tremendous size of this index exacerbates the deleterious effect of its jumbled arrangement, since the eye can much more easily scan, and the mind can better comprehend, a small than a very large number of entries alphabetized by first letter only. A partial solution to this problem was achieved in the index's earliest surviving copy, in Huntington Libr. EL 9.H.9, where the scribe has written each entry's head-word immediately beside it in the margin. This simple strategy has created what amounts to a vertically arranged list of easily distinguishable lemmata. Yet despite this expedient, the index is still harder to use than a fully alphabetized one, and judging from the fact that it survives in only two other copies, one of which stops after only the first ten entries (plate 12), its limited utility seems also to have limited its appeal.[41]

The project whose first step was the *Avarus* index was completed in the long recension of the *Abhominacio* index, now surviving uniquely in BL Roy. 10.C.ix (plate 13). Its redactor must have had access to a copy of the *Avarus* index, either in the form of a fair copy or the compiler's sheaf of notes. Using this as his starting point, he alphabetized the entries throughout the word and put the citations for each subject in the order in which they appeared in the text.[42] Moreover, he also discarded and modified entries. A comparison of the two versions' entries for *Lex* and *Rex* shows some aspects of this selective process. The *Avarus* index provides thirty-two citations for *Lex*, whereas the *Abhominacio* long recension gives only seven. When, however, the number of chapters cited by each is compared, one finds much less discrepancy, since the *Abhominacio* long recension cites six of the nine

---

[40] This index actually cites the text according to book, chapter, and part. For the sake of regularity, and to avoid confusion, I have used the more common sequence of book, part, and chapter. The form of these entries has been adapted from that found in Cambridge, Corpus Christi Coll. 283, fols. 149v–159v.

[41] Cambridge, Corpus Christi Coll. 283 and Bodleian Bodl. 589 (first ten entries only).

[42] The redactor has idiosyncratically put words beginning "Pr" at the end of the **P** initial-letter group. Thus words beginning "Pr" come after those which begin "Pu."

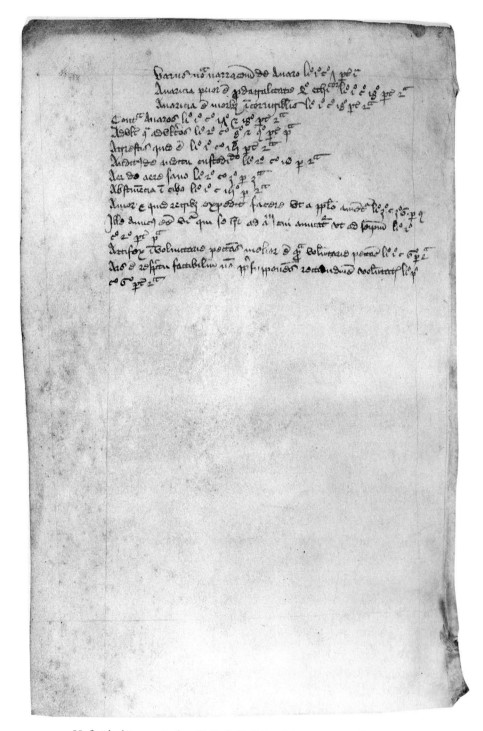

12 Unfinished Avarus *index. Oxford, Bodleian Library, MS Bodley 589, fol. 181v*

13 Abhominacio *index, long recension. London, British Library, MS Royal*
10.C.ix, fol. 22r

chapters cited in its predecessor. This suggests that the redactor selected those passages which he thought were the most important in these six chapters, and discarded the rest. In the case of the citations in his exemplar for *Rex*, the redactor was faced with the daunting task of reorganizing and copying some fifty-five entries, some with multiple citations, for this one subject. However, a perusal of these entries not only revealed that almost all the citations were from the second and third parts of book I, but also that most of the entries were in fact redundant, having been cited in entries for the virtues, vices, and passions. Thus he reduced this mass of entries to "de rege respice totum librum primum. partem 2^m. et 3^m. et in omnibus suis partibus et invenies multa de rege nobili et inprudente."

Soon the *Abhominacio* long recension would also be modified. This next, shorter generation of the index achieved considerable success, if its six, or possibly seven copies are anything to go by, and became what might be called its common recension.[43] The goal of this redactor seems to have been to produce a more compact, easier-to-copy version, yet one that retained what he thought would have been an acceptable degree of utility. In order to achieve this he discarded some 100 of his exemplar's 441 subject entries, as well as some of the citations for those subjects which he retained. The proliferation of this recension may have been due in part to its redactor having struck the right balance between brevity and copiousness. It may also, however, have been largely fortuitous, the result of its having found itself in an institutional milieu – namely the Benedictine colleges at Oxford – that promoted its availability and circulation. A still shorter recension survives in BL Roy. 5.C.iii (plate 14), which contains only 280 subject entries. It appears that the redactor of this short recension also used the long recension as his exemplar, since his recension occasionally includes entries or citations found in the long, but not in the common recension. A listing of the head-words for the letter E and their number of citations will help to show the relationship between these three recensions:

LONG	COMMON	SHORT
Ebrius		
Edificacio		
Edificium 3	Edificium 3	
Effici	Effici	Effici
Egenum		
Elacio	Elacio	
Elatus		
Eleccio 2	Eleccio	Eleccio
Emendacio		Emendacio
Emere	Emere	Emere

---

[43] Cambridge Univ. Libr. Ff.4.38; Canterbury Cath. Libr. B.II; Edinburgh Univ. Libr. 106; Bodleian Auct. F.3.2 and Bodl. 544; Oxford, All Souls Coll. 92. Verona, Bibl. Capitolare CCXXXIV, a fifteenth-century manuscript written in an Italian hand, but decorated by an English artist, appears also to have the same index. My thanks to Don Giuseppi Zivelonghi for this information.

LONG	COMMON	SHORT
Empcio	Empcione	
Epieikes	Epieykes	
Eroica		
Estivum		
Evangelium		
Ebula	Eubilia	Eubilia
Eutrapelia 2	Eutrapelia 2	Eutrapelia
Exercitacio 3	Exercitacio 3	Exercitacio
Exercitus	Exercitus	

A fragment of an index, beginning imperfectly at *Prudens* and ending *Zelotipus*, is found on the recto of one of the flyleaves at the end of Cambridge Univ. Libr. Ff.3.3 (plate 15). Although this manuscript and its text of *De regimine* almost certainly originated in France and date from the first half of the fourteenth century, the index is in a much later, mid fifteenth-century English hand. Surviving solely in this copy and unrelated to any other index that I know of, it is the only index that has established a separate category for words beginning with the letter **Y**. It also has a noteworthy layout. The page is divided into three columns, each measuring 60 mm in width; each of these columns is further divided into four columns ruled in ink, the widest being devoted to head-words and brief textual passages, and the three narrower ones citing book, part, and chapter. Here the compiler has achieved the clearest and most efficient mode of presentation of any of the *De regimine* indexes I have seen, and one that in many ways has the look of a modern-day table.

Like abridgments, alphabetical indexes are the result of a process of selection. They thus can reveal a great deal about their compilers' interests and methods of selection. The several redactors working in the *Avarus/Abhominacio* family of indexes kept material they thought was of particular value, while they discarded those items they thought they could do without or modified material they thought overly cumbersome. And, of course, the goals and method of a compiler could severely limit the number of subjects, as the *Amatores* index makes abundantly clear. Nevertheless, even the most thorough indexes differ significantly in their choices of subject matter. Appendix E, which compares the subject entries of the *Abstinencia* and *Abhominacio* long recension indexes, shows that although they share 239 subjects, the *Abstinencia* index includes 138 subjects not found in *Abhominacio*, which in turn contains entries for 173 subjects lacking in *Abstinencia*. Not surprisingly, both indexes have references to the virtues, vices, and passions, and to terms related to governance, like *civis, communitas, consilium, lex, ministrancium, nummisma, rex*, and *tirannus*. As for the entries that differ, some themes emerge like, for example, the *Abstinencia* compiler's interest in the liberal arts, or the penchant evinced in the *Abhominacio* (and *Avarus*) index for Greek words and the terminology of siegecraft. However, the indexes contrast most notably in their attention, or lack thereof, to exempla and *similitudines*. The

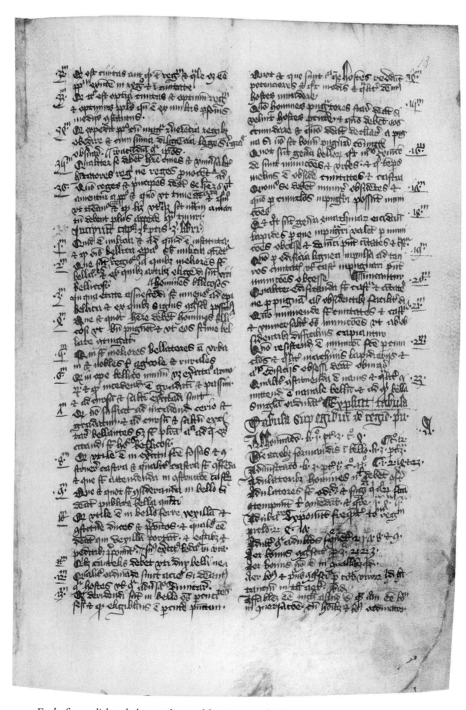

14 *End of consolidated chapter list and beginning of* Abhominacio *index, short recension.*
London, British Library, MS Royal 5.C.iii, fol. 13r

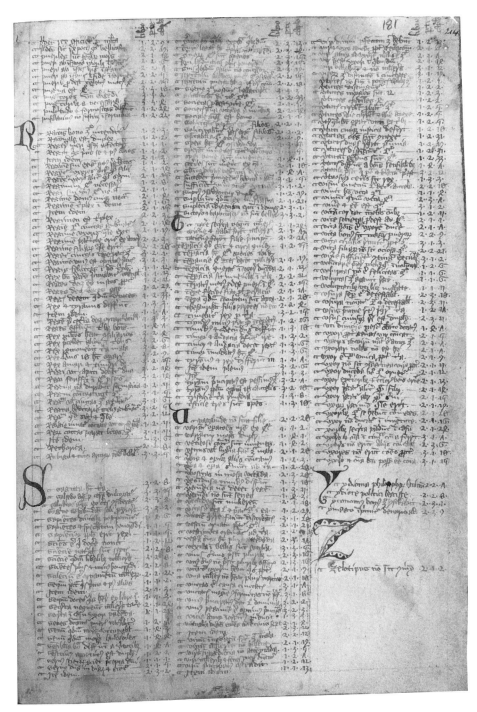

15 Alphabetical index, beginning imperfectly at prudens. *Cambridge, University Library, MS Ff.3.3, fol. 181r*

various recensions of the *Avarus*/*Abhominacio* family of indexes all take pains to point these out in such entries as "GULOSUS, de gulosis, 1.2.15, et nota ibidem optimam historiam de Philoseno," a reference to the glutton Phyloxenus, who asked the gods to make his neck as long as a crane's, so that he might take greater pleasure in the tactile sensation of food going down his throat. The *Avarus* index cites fifteen exempla and *similitudines*, while the long *Abhominacio* recension cites eighteen, some of which had previously been cited in *Avarus* but not specifically designated as such. The *Abstinencia* index, on the contrary, never once explicitly declares an exemplum or *similitudo*, though it occasionally cites the same passages of text.

Indexes so many and varied provide plenty of circumstantial evidence for English scholar-clerics having used them as a means to access the rich deposits of *sententiae, auctoritates,* and exempla buried in the quires of *De regimine* manuscripts. The margins of some manuscripts also bear testimony to their use. The borrowings from the short *Abhominacio* recension in the margins of Thomas Eborall's abridgment in BL Roy. 5.C.iii have already been discussed.[44] Elsewhere one finds that a reader used a plummet to re-number the chapters in Bodleian Hatton 15, so that they would correspond to the peculiar serial numbering system employed in the *Abstinencia* index; while in the margins of a copy of the same index in Bethesda, Nat. Libr. of Medicine 503, a fifteenth-century reader has added several entries not found in any other copy of the index.[45] Just as these indexes reveal the interests of their compilers, so too would their use have influenced and to some extent predetermined what their users would have looked for in the text. And since the contents of each version and recension were different, someone using one of them would have experienced that text in a slightly different way than if he had used another. The advent of printing would eventually change this by providing the same index to all readers of a given edition. Print would also further blur the medieval distinction between clerical and lay ways of reading, by making available to a much more diverse audience an apparatus that had for so long been confined largely to a clerical readership. In fourteenth- and fifteenth-century Europe, however, the use of alphabetical indexes in association with *De regimine* would remain the almost exclusive preserve of clerical readers; and even the one exception, Richard of York's *Abstinencia* index in Lambeth Palace Libr. Arc.L.40.2/L.26, proves the rule, since the duke was known to have had a high opinion of his latinity and *clergie*.[46]

---

[44] See above, p. 127.

[45] The entries, for *Amor, Civitas, Indigencia, Pecunie, Principatus, Usura,* and *Usus,* in the Bethesda manuscript are found on fols. 150, 150v, 152, 153v, 154, and 155v.

[46] See above, pp. 68–70.

COMPILATIONS

For someone who was very well acquainted with *De regimine*, it is conceivable that a glance at an index entry might be all that was needed to bring to mind the relevant portion of text.[47] I suspect, however, that more often than not the extreme brevity of the passages in these citations would have forced readers to turn to the text. Yet the same quest for searchable tools that led to the development of alphabetical indexes was also responsible for the creation of a tool called the *compilatio*, which combined the advantages of both the abridgment and index, thereby affording its users immediate access – both in time and space – to extensive extracts from *originalia*.[48] Most of these compilations were really alphabetized florilegia, and combined extracts from several different authors or works.[49] In the early fifteenth century, however, *De regimine* would be abridged and alphabetized into a compilation called the *Extractus per modum alphabeti*, which survives in BL Ar. 384 and Oxford, Jesus Coll. 12. The *Extractus* is a series of integral textual passages and occasional paraphrases that have been chosen according to what the compiler thought was their chief subject matter, and arranged alphabetically by initial letter only, beginning with an entry for *Amicabilia*, and ending with one for *Venia*. The subjects of these extracts appear as easily distinguishable lemmata in the margins, and the order of entries within each initial-letter group follows the serial *ordo narrationis* of the text. Typically the entries cite the book, part, and chapter of the source text and provide one or more cross-references, listing a subject, preceded by "vo." (i.e. *vocabulo*) and followed by a letter, or letters, from A to P. The letters A through P guide the reader to corresponding letters placed in the margins beside discrete passages of text. The compiler employed this device to alleviate the problem of finding the appropriate passage in its initial-letter group, since most of these contain very long strings of discontinuous extracts, which could in turn be quite lengthy. The following sample will help illustrate the content and form of these entries:

AMOR   Item sicut corpora naturalia per suas formas aut per gravitatem vel levitatem tendunt ad loca propria sic per amorem tendit quis in bonum si sit

[47] M. Carruthers, *The Book of Memory: A Study of Memory in Medieval Culture* (Cambridge, 1990), pp. 115–16.   [48] Parkes, "Influence," pp. 127–38.
[49] H. G. Pfander, "The Mediaeval Friars and Some Alphabetical Reference-Books for Sermons," *Medium Aevum* 3 (1934), pp. 19–29; M. A. Rouse and R. H. Rouse, "The Texts Called *Lumen Anime*," *Archivum Fratrum Praedicatorum* 41 (1971), pp. 5–113; J. Le Goff, "Le vocabulaire des *exempla* d'après l'*Alphabetum narrationum* (début XIVe siècle)," in *La lexicographie du latin médiéval et ses rapports avec les recherches actuelles sur la civilization du Moyen Age* (Paris, 1981), pp. 321–32; M. Grabmann, *Methoden und Hilfsmittel des Aristotelesstudiums im Mittelalter*, Sitzungsberichte der Bayerischen Akademie der Wissenschaften, Philosophisch-Historische Abteilung, Heft v (Munich, 1939), pp. 105–11.

PONDUS EST   sibi proporcionatum et conveniens. In gravibus igitur vel levibus sunt tria consideranda: primo forma gravis et levis per quam confirmatur sursum vel deorsum; 2° motus per quem tendunt in talem locum; 3° per

ODIUM   delectacionem quietamur in ipso. Amor ergo nos confortat, desiderium movet, et delectacio nos quietat. Sic malum, ut est oditum est aliquod displicens et difforme voluntati nostre, ut est abhominatum ab eo refugimus et si contingat ipsum adipisci dolemus et tristamur, <u>libro primo, parte 3ª, capitulo 4º</u>.

AUXILIUM ET

ADIUTORIUM   Nota qualiter natura providit animalibus per suo adiutorio et subsidio naturali arma, quibusdam de cornibus, quibusdam de dentibus, quibus-

ARMA   dam de agilitate, eciam de victu ut de fructibus et herbis de vestitu ad sui defensionem ut de lana et de pennis. Homini autem non sic sed quomodo sibi providit de 4, vo. HOMO. B.

An examination of this passage reveals the following features. First, the entries in the margins *Amor, Auxilium et Adiutorium*, and *Arma* are lemmata, whereas *Pondus est*, and *Odium* are notes to key words in the passage. Second, the length and character of extracts vary, the one for *Amor* being a verbatim transcription of a portion of *DRP* 1.3.4, while the passage for *Auxilium et Adiutorium* and *Arma* is a paraphrase of material found in *DRP* 2.1.1. Third, one of the extracts concludes with a reference to its location in *De regimine*, whereas the other provides a cross-reference to "HOMO. B." When one turns to this cross-referenced passage, there is indeed an extensive extract from *DRP* 2.1.1 that elaborates on the brief paraphrase for *Auxilium et Adiutorium* and *Arma*.

To further improve the utility of the *Extractus*, its compiler has included the marginal notation ".Ex^m." beside passages containing exempla and *similitudines* in entries for *Amor, Bellum, Cibus, Consilium* (twice), *Divicie, Experiencia, Iusticia, Iuventutis Condicio, Iudices, Iudicium, Iniuria, Mitis Mansuetus, Ornatus Mulierum, Obedire Maioribus, Prudens, Princeps, Regere, Tirannus, Virtus,* and *Verecundia Virgines*.[50] Thus here, as in the marginalia of several manuscripts and the *Abstinencia* index, we see the clerical audience of *De regimine*'s fascination with exempla. They probably marked these pithy stories in part because they would often have been familiar with them from having read or heard them before. For exempla and *similitudines*, like the seven deadly sins and four cardinal virtues, were the stock in trade of medieval sermons and florilegia, precisely because they aided the understanding and stayed fixed as commonplaces in the memory. There is also evidence, however, of medieval preachers having obtained their exempla either directly or indirectly from *De regimine*. The *Sertum florum moralium*, an alphabet-ically arranged collection of sermon exempla which was compiled at Paris in 1346 and circulated especially among the Cistercians, contained several exempla drawn

[50] In BL Ar. 384 (fol. 197v) a reader has added the note "narracio exemplaris" beside an entry for *Rex* taken from *DRP* 1.1.8, a cautionary tale against seeking honors.

from *De regimine*. In the fifteenth century an Italian Dominican friar named Gabriel Barletta (d. 1470) used Giles as a source of exempla in his sermons, as did the German preacher Meffreth (d. 1437).[51] I have not found similarly solid proof of borrowings from *De regimine* in the sermon literature of English preachers. This is hardly surprising, however, since almost any exemplum or *similitudo* found in Giles appears elsewhere in the plethora of florilegia and other preaching aids that appear in such abundance in the catalogues of medieval libraries. Nevertheless, the margins and indexes of the English Group manuscripts suggest that the English would have acted very much like the French, Italians, and Germans as far as *De regimine* and sermons were concerned.

Political motivations probably had more to do with the making of the *Extractus* than anything else, however. It was compiled at the Council of Constance in the winter of 1416–17, and since its contents include a sermon delivered there earlier that winter by Bishop Robert Hallum of Salisbury, the leader of the English delegation, it seems likely to have been produced for a member of that delegation, perhaps Hallum himself.[52] Though Hallum seems genuinely to have wanted to reform the Church, he and the other members of the English delegation were also charged by King Henry V to use the occasion of the Council to garner support for the English cause in the Hundred Years War. The earliest of the two surviving copies of the *Extractus*, Oxford, Jesus College 12, was written by a clerk from Cologne named Johannes Wydenroyde, who may also have been the compiler.[53] A few months prior to the completion of the *Extractus*, the archbishop of Cologne had agreed to assist the English in their war against France, and an alliance with the German emperor Sigismund followed shortly thereafter. Indeed, on January 27, 1417, just two days before the completion of the *Extractus*, the emperor had arrived in Constance and openly displayed his favor for the English.[54] Perhaps, then, the Anglo-German alliance supplied the impetus for the compilation of the *Extractus*, a tool that could be used by the English delegates to argue for their king's cause.

---

[51] Welter, *L'exemplum*, pp. 325–8, 417, 419–20.

[52] The colophon in Oxford, Jesus Coll. 12 (f. 202v) reads "Explicit extractus secundum alphabetum de libro Egidii de Regimine principum Constancie compilatus tempore concilii generalis. Et finitus sub anno domini millesimo quadringentesimo decimo sexto mensis Januarii die vicesima nona." According to E. F. Jacob, Hallum's sermon "which occurs in a number of manuscripts abroad, has apparently its sole English exemplar" in Oxford, Jesus Coll. 12: "Some English Documents of the Conciliar Movement," *Bulletin of the John Rylands Library* 15 (1931), p. 388. Hallum, who died at the Council in September 1417, made no mention of this manuscript in his will: *BRUO* 2, pp. 854–5.

[53] On the ascription to Wydenroyde, see C. M. D. Crowder, "Constance Acta in English Libraries," in *Das Konzil von Konstanz: Beiträge zu seiner Geschichte und Theologie*, ed. A. Franzen and W. Müller (Freiburg, 1964), pp. 516–17.   [54] Allmand, *Henry V*, pp. 233–56, esp. 243–5.

Conclusion

Þanne in þis wise þei þat wolle be princes scholde knowe moral mater: so þat þei knewe non oþer science, ȝut þei scholde bysiliche studie to lerne moral mater boistousliche in comyn langage and speche, for þerby a prince is ytauȝt at þe folle in what wise he scholde be prince and how he may brynge hymself and citeseyns to vertues and good maneres.[1]

With this sentence, which concludes his discussion of the education of princely and noble children in the liberal arts and theoretical and practical sciences, Giles both expresses the absolute necessity for the ruling classes of a knowledge of moral philosophy (if they are to rule legitimately and not as tyrants, that is), and implies the utility of his mirror, which, after all, is specifically designed as a means for them to acquire this knowledge. This same discussion, however, also largely sums up Giles's views on the proper functions of the different orders of society. To begin with, he sees the very division of the social orders as being intimately connected with the kinds of knowledge which the members of those orders possess. Thus clerics are distinct from the laity, thanks to their having been educated in the theoretical sciences of theology, metaphysics, and natural philosophy; and the ranks of distinction among the clergy conform to the hierarchy of these sciences, with theologians being the most worthy of honor, followed by the *metaphysici* and *naturales philosophi*. The practical, or moral, sciences of ethics, economics, and politics are, for their part, the proper province of princes and nobles, though to grasp these fully the members of the ruling classes should also be versed in the subjects of the *trivium* – grammar, dialectic, and rhetoric – as well as music "in so far as it serves good habits" (*inquantum deservit ad bonos mores*). Commoners, being ignorant for the most part of the liberal arts or the sciences, are deservedly unworthy to participate in governance, though they should be sufficiently informed in good habits by the example of their rulers.

Interestingly, Giles takes pains to explain that lawyers (*legistae*) are instruments of rulers but are themselves incapable of exercising rule, owing to their being *idiotae*

---

[1] Trevisa, *Governance*, p. 225 (*DRP* 2.2.8).

146

politici (or, as Trevisa put it, "lewede, maad, and nyse politici"). Giles reasons that just as law is an area of knowledge that falls under politics, so too are lawyers, who speak *narrative* and without reason regarding policy, subject to those who know politics and moral philosophy, since "those who know and give causes are more worthy of honor than those who speak but do not understand the cause of what they say."[2] Janet Coleman has recently asserted that this argument, which Giles appears to have taken from Albertus Magnus' commentary on the *Ethics*, fits in with the essentially rhetorical program of *De regimine*, which speaks in the fashion of an orator, that is, *grosse et figuraliter*, rather than in the "insufficient *modus narrativus*" of the civilian lawyers.[3] Giles does seem to have had a particularly strong interest in rhetoric, judging from his having written a commentary on the *Rhetoric* and the *De differentia ethicae, politicae, et rhetoricae*, and the fact that the quadripartite division of book 1 of *De regimine* conforms to the themes in books 1 and 2 of the *Rhetoric*.[4] Moreover, Giles derived most of his material for book 1, part 4, and for several chapters in book 3, part 2 of *De regimine* from book 2 of the *Rhetoric*.

Whether or not Giles's program was primarily rhetorical or based more broadly on the entire body of moral philosophy (to which rhetoric was attached, in so far as it served the ends of a well-ordered society), I concur with Coleman that *De regimine* both reflects the way moral philosophy was being studied by the arts faculty at Paris in the late thirteenth century and the artists' desire to bring their newly acquired knowledge of Aristotelian moral philosophy to bear on contemporary political issues. This desire to understand and use the Philosopher's moral philosophy would lead to its inclusion into the arts curriculum at Paris and the English universities by the middle of the fourteenth century, thus making the learning of moral philosophy a pursuit suitable and indeed expected of both clergy and the lay upper classes. Works of moral philosophy, then, became a chief textual site for that blurring of the long-maintained distinctions between the laity and clergy that was one of the most important cultural transformations of the later Middle Ages.[5]

[2] "Leges et iura, quae sunt de actibus hominum sub politica quae est de regimine civitatum . . . Sic legistae, quia ea de quibus est politica, dicunt narrative et sine ratione appellari possunt idiotae politici. Ex hoc autem patere potest quod magis honorandi sunt scientes politicam et morales sciencias, quam scientes leges et iura. Nam quanto scientes et dantes causam, honorabiliores sunt loquentibus et non reddentibus causam dicti, tanto tales honorabiliores sunt illis": *DRP* 2.2.8.

[3] J. Coleman, "Some Relations between the Study of Aristotle's *Rhetoric*, *Ethics* and *Politics* in Late 13th- and Early 14th-Century University Arts Courses and the Justification of Contemporary Civic Activities (Italy and France)," paper given in summer 1996 at a colloquium at the Max-Planck-Institut für Geschichte, Göttingen. This paper will be published in a forthcoming collection edited by J. Canning and G. Oexle. Dr. Coleman has kindly provided me with a copy of this paper prior to publication.   [4] Coleman, "Some Relations."

[5] Duby, *Three Orders*; G. de Lagarde, *La naissance de l'esprit laïque au déclin du Moyen Age*, vol. ii (Louvain and Paris, 1958); A. de Libera, *Penser au Moyen Age* (Paris, 1991); Murray, *Reason and Society*, pp. 213–404; J.-Ph. Genet, "Les auteurs politiques et leur maniement des sources en Angleterre à la fin du Moyen Age," in *Pratiques de la culture écrite en France au XVe siècle*, ed. M. Ornato and N. Pons (Louvain-la-Neuve, 1995), pp. 354–9.

From works like *De regimine* or Nicole Oresme's glossed translations of the *Ethics*, *Economics*, and *Politics* lay readers became familiar with the doctrine and methods of the schools, thus ending the long monopoly of clerical writers in the area of political discourse, while masters of arts and theology brought their knowledge of moral philosophy to bear on important political movements, like the attempted reforms of the French monarchy in 1356–58.[6]

The role of *De regimine* in this *translatio studii* is particularly apparent in the *Tractatus de regimine principum ad regem Henricum Sextum* written in all likelihood by one of the ecclesiastical ministers of Henry VI.[7] This work not only borrows extensively from *De regimine*, it also cites Aristotle's *Rhetoric, Ethics*, and *Politics* on thirty-four occasions. Of these citations, however, thirty came by way of *De regimine* and a further three from Aquinas's *Summa theologica*.[8] Here then, a university-educated cleric writes for his intended lay audience a mirror that itself cites Giles's mirror in order to transfer the doctrine of the Stagirite. Yet though the author of the *Tractatus de regimine principum* got most of his Aristotle by way of Giles, he did so tacitly, never acknowledging his immediate source. Contrarily, he does identify St. Thomas as his other intermediary. A similar "mélange d'honnêteté et d'hypocrisie," as Jean-Philippe Genet has characterized it, is seen in the author's use of another intermediary source, John of Wales's *Communoloquium*, which he only sometimes acknowledges. All of this suggests that he, like many of the other scholar-clerics I have discussed in this study, often had recourse to use *De regimine* and other compendious gatherings of *originalia*, instead of those *originalia* themselves, but that in doing so he sometimes hid his immediate sources in order to avoid giving his readers "le soupçon sinon d'un plagiat ou du moins celui d'une dépendence excessive" upon these sources.[9]

The discomfort among scholar-clerics regarding the use of *De regimine* resulted largely, I think, from their ambivalent attitude toward Giles's authorial status, at least in so far as *De regimine* was concerned. For if they frequently used it in lieu of, or in conjunction with, Aristotle's moral philosophical texts, it was the latter which were prescribed by the curriculum, and upon whose *auctor* a vast share of that cur-

---

[6] Perhaps the most striking example of a lay political writer is Christine de Pizan. See also J.-Ph. Genet, "Ecclesiastics and Political Theory in Late Medieval England: The End of a Monopoly," in *Church, Politics and Patronage in the Fifteenth Century*, ed. R. B. Dobson (New York, 1984), pp. 23–44; J. Krynen, "Aristotélisme et réforme de l'Etat en France, au XIVe siècle," in *Das Publikum politischer Theorie*, ed. Miethke, pp. 228–9.

[7] Genet, "Théorie politique," p. 271. The authorship of this work has most recently been treated by Genet, "Auteurs politiques," p. 346, who seems to agree with Ralph Griffith's assessment in *The Reign of Henry VI: The Exercise of Royal Authority, 1422–1461* (London, 1981), p. 265. Genet, "Théorie politique," p. 271, also seems to entertain the possibility of John Stafford, Henry VI's chancellor and archbishop of Canterbury, whose sermon preached in parliament in January 1441, "Rex et thronus eius sit innocens," has some close affinities with the *Tractatus de regimine principum*.

[8] Genet (ed.), *Four English Political Tracts*, p. 170.   [9] Genet, "Auteurs politiques," pp. 346–7.

riculum rested. Giles, on the other hand, was one of their own, a mere *modernus* who, moreover, unlike his more brilliant contemporary and teacher Aquinas, had failed to achieve the authorial status conferred by sainthood. This same ambivalence seems also to have been the chief cause of the text's eventual fall from favor at university, where scholars increasingly under the influence of humanist attitudes and approaches to learning, adhered ever more closely to Aristotle's *originalia* while relying less and less upon what they believed to be essentially derivative texts.[10] At least this was the case in England and probably France, for while the Latin *De regimine* was printed in four editions between 1473 and 1498 (one of which contained only book I, part 3, and was attributed to Albertus Magnus), and appeared in a further four editions in the sixteenth and seventeenth centuries, only the first and last of these, Günther Zainer's 1473 folio edition (which gives no place of publication but was undoubtedly printed in Augsburg) and the 1643 Leiden edition (mistakenly attributed to Aquinas), were printed outside Italy.[11]

Of course, just because England's early printers overlooked publishing *De regimine*, this should have been no bar to its having been imported, since the vast majority of early printed Latin texts in England were obtained from abroad.[12] Nevertheless, one searches in vain for copies of the early *De regimine* editions in the libraries of English scholars of the later fifteenth and sixteenth centuries, despite the fact that Venice, England's chief source of foreign-produced printed books, was also the center of production for editions of *De regimine*.[13] Conversely, these libraries were well stocked with editions of Aristotle's works of moral philosophy and the *Rhetoric*, as well as with several printed copies of Vegetius' *De re militari*, the other work from antiquity on which *De regimine* chiefly relied.[14] Yet the several printed editions do suggest that in Italy and Germany at least there continued to be

---

[10] On this phenomenon in England, see R. Weiss, *Humanism in England during the Fifteenth Century*, 3rd edn (Oxford, 1967).

[11] Bruni, *Le opere*, pp. 106–7, lists also a miscellany (Basel, 1516) attributed to Albertus Magnus, which contains excerpts from a few chapters of *DRP* I.3; he also mentions some other editions whose existence he thought doubtful. The 1643 edition is recorded in A. Potthast, *Bibliotheca Historica Medii Aevi* (Berlin, 1896), p. 17. On Zainer's activities, see S. Edmunds, "From Schoeffer to Vérard: Concerning the Scribes Who Became Printers," in *Printing the Written Word: The Social History of Books, circa 1450–1520*, ed. S. L. Hindman (Ithaca, 1991), pp. 21–40. Berges, *Fürstenspiegel*, p. 322, cautions that an edition printed at Paris in 1517, bearing the title *Miroir exemplaire selon la composition de Gilles de Rome, du régime et gouvernement des rois*, in fact contains Jean Golein's French translation of the anonymous *Liber de informatione principum*.

[12] L. Hellinga, "Importation of Books Printed on the Continent into England and Scotland before c. 1520," in *Printing the Written Word*, ed. Hindman, pp. 205–24; M. Lowry, "The Arrival and Use of Printed Books in Yorkist England," in *Le livre dans l'Europe de la Renaissance*, ed. P. Aquilon and H.-J. Martin (Paris, 1988), pp. 449–59.   [13] Hellinga, "Importation of Books," pp. 210–11, 221–4.

[14] This assessment is derived from the books listed in E. S. Leedham-Green, *Books in Cambridge Inventories: Book-Lists from Vice-Chancellor's Court Probate Inventories in the Tudor and Stuart Periods*, vol. II (Cambridge, 1986), esp. pp. 40–53, 695, 773; and the four currently published volumes in R. J. Fehrenbach and E. S. Leedham-Green (eds.), *Private Libraries in Renaissance England: A Collection and Catalogue of Tudor and Early Stuart Book-Lists* (Binghamton, N.Y., 1992–5).

a market for Giles's mirror well into the sixteenth century. This may have been owed in large part to the agency of the Augustinian friars, always a largely Italian order that managed to propagate itself most successfully in Germany, and whose charge to study the works of Giles may have been the principal cause of demand for printed copies of *De regimine*.[15]

The vernacular *De regimine* seems to have fared even worse. Vernacular translations were printed only in Spain, where two Castilian and two Catalan editions were published between 1480 and 1498.[16] The peculiar success of the mirror there at the end of the Middle Ages may also have resulted in part from Augustinian involvement, since it was "the country in which the Augustinian friars made most progress in the later Middle Ages."[17] A survey of the vernacular manuscripts tells a similar story. Only two of the thirty-four copies of French translations and none of the several Italian and German translations were produced after *c.* 1500.[18] In the case of the vernacular *De regimine*, its fate was sealed by a desire for both the old and the new. As lay readers like Charles V of France patronized vernacular translations of the classics or, like Humphrey, duke of Gloucester, developed a taste for the new Latin translations of Plato and Aristotle being made by the likes of Coluccio Salutati and Leonardo Bruni, so too were they receptive to a plethora of vernacular mirrors and advice literature of more contemporary vintage than *De regimine*, like Christine de Pizan's *Livre de corps de policie* or Thomas Hoccleve's *Regement of Princes*.[19] Moreover, in England especially, lay readers of the fifteenth and early sixteenth centuries evinced a strong affinity for the pseudo-Aristotelian *Secretum secretorum* (a work which among clerical readers seems to have fared little better than *De regimine* at this time), leading to its diffusion in several translations, adaptations, and an early printed edition (translated and published by Robert Copland in London, 1528).[20] This probably resulted from several factors, ranging from the relative brevity of the *Secretum* which made it easier and cheaper to translate, copy, or print, to the inclusion of advice on health and hygiene, to its claim to be a letter from Aristotle, the prince of the philosophers, to Alexander the Great, one of the greatest knights of all time.

Thus, *De regimine* was a text whose lifespan was largely confined within the "autumn" of the Middle Ages. Yet during the two centuries when it flourished it exercised a profound influence on the way medieval readers approached and con-

---

[15] Gwynn, *English Austin Friars*, esp. pp. 281–3.   [16] Bruni, *Le opere*, pp. 106–7.

[17] Gwynn, *English Austin Friars*, p. 282.

[18] BL Add. 22274 (*c.* 1500) and Bibl. de l'Arsenal 5062 (s. xvi[in]).

[19] C. R. Sherman, "Les thèmes humanistes dans le programme de traduction de Charles V: Compilation des textes et illustrations," in *Pratiques de la culture écrite*, ed. Ornato and Pons, pp. 527–37; Weiss, *Humanism*, pp. 46–9; Genet (ed.), *Four English Political Tracts*, pp. ix–xix; Green, *Poets and Princepleasers*, pp. 135–67.

[20] Green, *Poets and Princepleasers*, pp. 138–43; Manzalaoui (ed.), *Secretum Secretorum*, pp. 227–389; H. S. Bennett, *English Books and Readers, 1475 to 1557*, 2nd edn (Cambridge, 1969), p. 281.

ceived of moral philosophy, thanks in good measure to its being itself an entity conditioned by the attitudes and needs of its author, an aristocratic, university-educated friar who believed the business of governance was predicated on the moral, and thus spiritual, well-being of both the governor and the governed. His own curricular and pastoral concerns were reflected in the habits of his mirror's clerical readers, who modified the text to make it better serve their ends. As for lay readers like Thomas Lord Berkeley, it conferred attributes of good lordship through the authority imparted by its learning, and was a means to power through its lessons drawn from the conquering heroes and armies of antiquity. For Giles and all of his readers, politics was the most "perfect" of the sciences of human activity, since it encompassed everything to do with living, as Giles would say, *communicative et socialiter*, and in accordance with virtue.[21] For them, living politically meant something altogether more personal in one sense, and more universal, in another, than it means today. It began during the act of procreation, was informed by rigorous training and instruction in childhood, and was studiously practiced in adulthood in order to maintain peace, order, and concord; and at the time of passage into the next life, it aided the faithful Christian on his or her journey toward everlasting bliss.

[21] *DRP* 2.1.1; Lambertini, "'Costruzione dell'*Oecomonica*," p. 355; Coleman, "Some Relations."

Descriptive list of manuscripts of medieval English origin/provenance

This list attempts to strike a compromise between the brevity of a handlist (see C. F. Briggs, "Manuscripts of Giles of Rome's *De regimine principum* in England, 1300–1500: A Handlist," *Scriptorium* 47 [1993], pp. 60–73) and the exhaustive treatment of a descriptive catalogue. It concentrates primarily on those portions of each manuscript which are devoted to the text and apparatus of *De regimine principum*, and concerns itself with aspects of other items contained in the manuscripts only in so far as they are germane to the goals of this study. Moreover, it seeks to avoid duplication regarding material (e.g. details of illumination, ownership, incipits and explicits, and other textual characteristics) which is treated either in the body of this study or in the appendices which follow. Anonymous scribes are sometimes designated A, B, C, etc. as they appear in sequential order in a manuscript. The nomenclature of scripts employed here accords with those of Malcolm Parkes (*English Cursive Book Hands: 1200–1500*) and Michelle Brown (*A Guide to Western Historical Scripts from Antiquity to 1600*). The only evidence of ownership and provenance elaborated here is that contained in the manuscripts themselves, in the form of *ex libris* inscriptions, colophons, *cauciones*, and coats of arms; evidence of ownership derived from sources external to the manuscripts is also noted, however. References are made to published or unpublished library catalogues, standard reference works, and printed editions, as well as to monographs and articles in cases where these latter contain important information not found elsewhere. M. R. James's numerous catalogues are cited in abbreviated form. Manuscripts that I have not personally examined have been marked with an asterisk (*) if viewed on microfilm and with two asterisks (**) if I have viewed only photographs.

Baltimore, Walters Art Gallery, MS W. 144   *England, s. xiv[1]*

CONTENTS: Giles of Rome, *Li livres du gouvernement des rois et des princes* (fols. 2–120). STRUCTURE AND LAYOUT: parchment, fols. i + 119 + i; 1–8⁸, 9⁹, 10–14⁸, 15⁶; 300 × 205 mm, 2 cols. of 37 lines. Binding modern. 2° fo. -ment por saver. SCRIPT: Two contemporary hands. Fols. 2–106v, 115–119 in *textualis rotunda*; fols. 107–114v in *textualis rotunda* of inferior quality. ILLUMINATION: eleven miniatures at major textual divisions (fols. 2, 2v, 3v, 10, 28v, 35v, 41v, 51v, 63v, 73v, 92). One miniaturist was responsible for fols. 2, 3v, and 10; the other for the remainder. OWNERSHIP/PROVENANCE: inscription, 1463 (fol. 121), "Liber Monasterii Sancti Gualtheri [. . .] 16 novembris anno domini millesimo 463 et regis edwardi iiij^ti viij^vo pro x l. 10[?] s." REFERENCES: De Ricci, vol. 1 p. 846; Sandler, *Gothic Manuscripts*, pt. 1, pp. 25, 30–2, ills. 174, 176; pt. 2, p. 79.

Bethesda, National Library Of Medicine, MS 503*   *England, s. xiv^ex; index, s. xv^1*
CONTENTS: Giles of Rome, *De regimine principum* (fols. 1–149) with alphabetical index (fols. 150–155v). STRUCTURE AND LAYOUT: parchment, fols. 155; 1–11^12, 12–13^8, 14^{4+3}; 275 × 185 mm, 2 cols. of 50 lines. Binding modern. 2° fo. -dimus in tres. SCRIPT: two hands. Fols. 1–149 in *textualis semi-quadrata*, fols. 150–55v in Anglicana. ILLUMINATION: historiated initial and decorated border (fol. 1). Decorated initials at major textual divisions. OWNERSHIP/PROVENANCE: colophon, s. xv^1 (f. 155v), "Explicit tabula venerabilis egidii de regimine principum edita a fratre Galfrido Horsford ordinis fratrum heremitarum sancti augustini sacre theologie lectore." Possibly belonged to a convent of Augustinian friars. REFERENCES: D. M. Schullian and F. E. Sommer, *A Catalogue of Incunabula and Manuscripts in the Army Medical Library* (New York, 1948), pp. 230–1.

Cambridge, University Library, MS Dd.3.47   *England, s. xv^1*
CONTENTS: 1) Giles of Rome, *De regimine principum* (fols. 1–184v); 2) Francis de Maron, *De virtutibus moralibus*, 3) *Questiones de virtutibus moralibus*, 4) *De modo quo Apostoli habuerunt dominia in communi cum aliis*; 5) "Quaedam quaestio bene disputata, incipit 'utrum tendenti ad perfectionem necessaria sit abdicatio temporalium'"; 6) Duns Scotus, *De perfectione statuum*. STRUCTURE AND LAYOUT: parchment, fols. 256; 1–32^8; 270 × 185 mm, 2 cols. of 35 lines (fols. 1–56v) and 40 lines (fols. 57–184v). Binding modern. 2° fo. de amicabilitate. SCRIPT: several hands, all roughly contemporary. Fols. 1–184v in two hands: the first (fols. 1–56v), writes in Anglicana; the second (fols. 57–184v) seems to have been influenced by humanist script. Chapter headings in red. REFERENCES: *CCUL*, vol. 1, p. 102 (no. 134).

Cambridge, University Library, MS Ee.2.17   *France, s. xv^in*
CONTENTS: 1) fragment of Giles of Rome, *Le livre du gouvernement dez Roys et dez princes* (fols. 1–2): //murs ou as forteresces du chastel . . . et a ses loyauls Amys. E Cy fine le liure du gouuernement dez Roys et dez princes que frere gilles de rome de lordre st augustin a fait; 2) Vegetius, *Le livre de chevalerie*. STRUCTURE AND LAYOUT: parchment and paper; fols. 36; 1^3, 2^{10} (–6), 3–4^{12}; 280 × 210 mm; single block of 38–43 lines. Binding modern. 2° fo. (MS missing several gatherings). SCRIPT: single French secretary hand throughout. ILLUMINATION: miniature (fol. 3); decorated initials. OWNERSHIP/PROVENANCE: inscriptions, s. xv^1 and s. xv^2 (fol. 36v): 1) "Cest livre est a moy Homphrey duc de

Gloucestre du don Moss. Robert Roos chevalier mon cousin"; 2) Strangways. J. REFER-
ENCES: *CCUL*, vol. II, pp. 33–4 (no. 935).

Cambridge, University Library, MS Ff.3.3   *France, s. xiv^{in}; index England, s. xv*

CONTENTS: Giles of Rome, *De regimine principum* (fols. 1–180v), beginning imperfectly
(// -tare et rhetoricum demonstraciones expetere . . .), with alphabetical index fragment
(fol. 181): // Prudens rex efficietur per multa . . . Zelotipus non sit coniunx. STRUCTURE
AND LAYOUT: parchment, fols. 181; 1^8 (–1, 2, 7, 8), 2–7^8, 8^8 (–6), 9–16^8 (–4), 18–22^8, 23^6
(–1, 6); 295 × 205 mm; 2 cols. of 41 lines. Binding modern. 2° fo. (original fols. 1 and 2
excised). SCRIPT: Two hands. Fols. 1–180v in *textualis semi-quadrata*; fol. 181 in Anglicana.
ILLUMINATION: historiated initials (fols. 67 and 119v); decorated initials. OWNER-
SHIP/PROVENANCE: inscription, s. xv^2 (fol. 180v): "et iste idem liber constat Johanni
Catesby filio Hugonis Catesby." REFERENCES: *CCUL*, vol. II, pp. 410–11 (no. 1211).

Cambridge, University Library, MS Ff.4.38   *England, s. xv^{med}*

CONTENTS: 1–4) assorted indexes; 5) index of Giles of Rome, *De regimine principum* (fols.
134–42): Abhominacio . . . Zelotipia zelotipus; 6) index of Gregory's *Registrum*. STRUC-
TURE AND LAYOUT: parchment, fols. 162; 1^8, 2 (removed), 3^8, 4^{10}, 2–6^{16}, 7–8^{12}, 9–10^{16};
260 × 185 mm; single block of 39 lines (fols. 134–42). Binding early modern. 2° fo. in fine.
SCRIPT: index in several English hands of s. xv. Fols. 134–42 in Secretary. Last two items
executed and joined together at the same time, but in different hands. OWNER-
SHIP/PROVENANCE: colophon, s. xv^1 (fol. 142): "Explicit tabula domini Egidii de
regimine principum Edita a fratre Johanne Drayton." Inscription, s. xv^{ex}/xvi^{in} (fol. 1): "Ex
dono honorandi domini Thome episcopi Eboracensis domini Rotherham." REFER-
ENCES: *CCUL*, vol. II, p. 471 (no. 1281); *BRUO* I, p. 3.

Cambridge, University Library, MS Ii.2.8   *England, s. xv^{in}*

CONTENTS: 1) Walter Burley, commentary on the *Politics*; 2) Giles of Rome, *De regimine
principum* (fols. 61–126v), inc. "Rex regia . . .", with index (fols. 126v-129v): Amatores . . .
Intemperatum. STRUCTURE AND LAYOUT: parchment, fols. 129 + i; 1–10^{12}, 11^{10} (alter-
natively 11^8, 12^2); 335 × 230 mm; 2 cols. of 55–56 lines. Binding early modern. 2° fo. homo
naturaliter. SCRIPT: Anglicana/Secretary blend; one scribe. ILLUMINATION: decorated
initial and full border (fol. 61). OWNERSHIP/PROVENANCE: the "per manus magistri
Ricardi Bury" of the colophon (fol. 126v) does not refer to the bibliophile bishop of
Durham of the same name who died in 1345. REFERENCES: *CCUL*, vol. III, p. 378 (no.
1741).

Cambridge, University Library, MS Ii.4.22   *England, s. xiv^2*

CONTENTS: 1) Giles of Rome, *De regimine principum* (fols. 1–121v), inc. "De regia. . .",
with index (fols. 122–7): Abstinencia. . . . Zelotipus; and "contratabula" (fols. 127–8); 2)

Thomas Aquinas, *De regno ad regem Cipri.* STRUCTURE AND LAYOUT: parchment, fols. 178; 1–14^{12}, 15^{12} (–11, 12); 290 × 190 mm; 2 cols. of 45 lines. Binding early modern. 2° fo. debet industris. SCRIPT: Anglicana Formata; one scribe. OWNERSHIP/PROVENANCE: colophons: "Scripserat Egidium regum regimen referentem Swantoun, presidium poscendo cuncta regentem. Swanton. Jon." (fol. 121v); "Egidii tabula finit, dentur modo vina et sine qua fabula Swantoun pincerna propina. Swanton. Jon." (fol. 128); "Explicit liber de rege et regno. quod Swanton. Jon." (fol. 178v). REFERENCES: *CCUL*, vol. III, p. 457 (no. 1819).

Cambridge, University Library, MS Ii.4.37   *England, s. xiv^{1}*

CONTENTS: Giles of Rome, *De regimine principum* (fols. 3–145). STRUCTURE AND LAYOUT: parchment, fols. 146 + ii; 1–18^{8}; 255 × 190 mm; 2 cols. of 40 lines. Binding early modern. 2° fo. intellectus dicendorum. SCRIPT: *textualis semi-quadrata.* OWNERSHIP/PROVENANCE: Norwich Cathedral Priory. Inscriptions, s. xv: "Ego sum possessio fratris johannis moleti et verum est mediante pecunia et cetera viij" (fol. 146v); s. xv/xvi, "R. Catton" (fol. 3). REFERENCES: *CCUL*, vol. III, p. 471 (no. 1834); *MLGB*, p. 137; *BRUC*, p. 126.

Cambridge, University Library, MS Kk.2.11   *England, s. xv^{in}*

CONTENTS: 1) Thomas Aquinas, *Contra impugnantes religionem,* 2) *De perfectione spiritualis vite;* 3) Giles of Rome, *De regimine principum* (fols. 67–194v); 4) John of Wales, *Communiloquium.* STRUCTURE AND LAYOUT: parchment, fols. ii + 215 + iii; 1–7^{8}, 8^{8} (–7, 8), 9–26^{8}, 27^{8} (–8); 265 × 200 mm; 2 cols. of 50 lines. Binding modern. 2° fo. per hec. SCRIPT: MS four or five different hands. *DRP* in *textualis rotunda.* COMMENTS: Capitals flourished by same decorator, also same page layout (fols. 3–194v). Lists of contents, s. xv (fols. 1 and 217) list all four items. REFERENCES: *CCUL*, vol. III, p. 606 (no. 1974).

Cambridge, Corpus Christi College, MS 283   *England, s. xv^{in}*

CONTENTS: 1) Giles of Rome, *De regimine principum* (fols. 1–149), with index (fols. 149v–159v): Avarus . . . uncis ferreis; 2) copy of letter from John, duke of Norfolk, to Thomas Brouns, bishop of Norwich (1436–45). STRUCTURE AND LAYOUT: parchment, fols. v + 159 + ii; 1–13^{12}, 14^{6} (–5); 260 × 185 mm; 2 cols. of 40 lines. Binding early modern. 2° fo. nam licet. SCRIPT: Anglicana Formata. Same hand throughout. Verses, s. xv^{ex}, on recto of last flyleaf list of kings of England from Conquest to Henry VII. OWNERSHIP/PROVENANCE: letter of duke of Norfolk to Bishop Thomas (fol. 159v) and erased inscription of s. xv^{2} on verso of first flyleaf, "liber de dono fratris henr [*illegible*] cuius anime propicietur deus," suggest Norwich Cathedral Priory. ILLUMINATION: miniature and decorated initial with three-quarter foliate border (fol. 1). REFERENCES: James, *Cat. Corpus*, vol. II, pp. 48–9; *MLGB*, p. 137.

Cambridge, Gonville and Caius College, MS 113/182   *England, s. xv¹*

CONTENTS: Giles of Rome, *De regimine principum* (fols. 1–148), with chapter list (fols. 148–151v). STRUCTURE AND LAYOUT: parchment, fols. iii + 152; 263 × 185 mm; single block of 46 lines. Binding of s. xv. 2° fo. in primo. SCRIPT: Anglicana/Secretary blend. Same hand throughout. OWNERSHIP/PROVENANCE: inscription, s. xv¹ (fol. 152v), "Liber magistri Johannis Cranwys." Cranewys was sacrist of Bury St. Edmunds, 1426–27. REFERENCES: James, *Cat. Caius*, vol. I, pp. 118–19; *MLGB*, p. 17.

Cambridge, Gonville and Caius College, MS 508/387   *England, s. xiv^{in}*

CONTENTS: 1) Thomas Aquinas, commentary on the *Ethics*; 2) Giles of Rome, *De regimine principum* (fols. 153–255v). STRUCTURE AND LAYOUT: parchment, fols. 255; 1–12¹², 13⁸, 14–16¹², 17¹⁰, 18¹², 19⁴, 20¹² (+1 before 1), 21¹² (+3 leaves between 9 and 10), 22¹² (+1); 285 × 200 mm; 2 cols. of 53 lines (fols. 153–255v). Binding early modern. 2° fo. perfectio. SCRIPT: *textualis rotunda*. MS work of four scribes: A (item 1), B (fols. 153–88v), C (fols. 189–236v and 240–55v), and D (fols. 237–39v). Work of D added later, on three leaves glued into 21st gathering, to fill gap in text left by C. COMMENTS: single hand probably responsible for initial flourishes throughout MS (except fols. 237–39v). REFERENCES: James, *Cat. Caius*, vol. II, p. 578.

Cambridge, Jesus College, MS Q.B.9   *France, s. xiv²*

CONTENTS: Giles of Rome, *De regimine principum* (fols. 2–263v). STRUCTURE AND LAYOUT: parchment, fols. i + 262 + i; 1⁸ (1 removed and a leaf of s. xv substituted), 2–32⁸, 33⁸ (–1, 2, and 5; 8 blank); 245 × 170 mm; 2 cols. of 32 lines. Binding s. xvi. 2° fo. hac regitur. SCRIPT: *textualis quadrata*. Three scribes: A (fols. 2–2v), B (fol. 3, col. a, lines 1–10), C (fols. 3, col. a, line 11–263v). A and B have attempted to mimic the hand of C. ILLUMINATION: with the exception of fol. 2 (initial page), borders of fleurs-de-lis in gold and blue running along the left of both columns throughout. Three-quarter-page miniature and full border with Pert arms (quarterly azure and gules, four lions or rampant gardant; on a chief indented argent, three besants sable), s. xvi^{in} (fol. 2). OWNERSHIP/PROVENANCE: Erased inscription and autograph of King Charles V of France (fol. 263v). Arms executed s. xvi^{in} of English family surnamed Pert (fol. 2). REFERENCES: James, *Cat. Jesus*, p. 34; comments of Sydney Cockerell in the annotated copy of James's catalogue kept at Jesus College; Delisle, *Recherches*, pt. 2, pp. 87–8.

Cambridge, Pembroke College, MS 158   *England, s. xv¹*

CONTENTS: 1) Walter Burley, commentary on the *Politics*; 2) Giles of Rome, *De regimine principum* (fols. 46v–112v), inc. "E Regea . . ." STRUCTURE AND LAYOUT: parchment, fols. 112 + i; 1–14⁸; 360 × 250 mm; 2 cols. of 63–70 lines. Binding modern. 2° fo. et lignis. SCRIPT: MS work of two scribes, one of whom worked on both items. OWNERSHIP/PROVENANCE: inscriptions, s. xv¹, on recto and verso of end flyleaf: "Hic liber constat aule penbrochia in cantabrigia"; "Liber Aule valence marie Cantabrig' ex dono magistri Thome Lawenham quondam socii eiusdem aule cuius anima propicietur omnipotens deus." Lavenham was fellow of Pembroke Hall by 1408, precentor of Llandaff from 1421. REFERENCES: James, *Cat. Pembroke*, pp. 153–4; *BRUC*, p. 356.

Cambridge, Peterhouse, MS 208   *England, s. xv²*

CONTENTS: 1) *notabilia* from Albertus Magnus, Grosseteste, and Aquinas; 2) the *Ethics*, preceded by an index of contents; 3) "tabula Politicorum secundum sentenciam S. Thome"; 3) index of Giles of Rome, *De regimine principum* (fols. 201–5): Abstinentia . . . Zelotipus; 4) "Tractatus super Boethium de consolatione"; 5) *notabilia* from the *Ethics*; 6) index of Aristotle, *De animalibus*; 7) Thomas Aquinas, *De causis*; 8) *notabilia* from Aquinas, *Summa contra gentiles*; 9) *notabilia* from the *Ethics*; 10) *notabilia* from Giles of Rome, *De bona fortuna*, and from 11) *notabilia* from Giles of Rome's commentary on the *Rhetoric*; 12) *notabilia* from the *Politics* with an exposition of Peter of Auvergne. STRUCTURE AND LAYOUT: parchment and paper, fols. i + 255 + i; 1^{12}, 2^8, 3^{12}, 4–10^{14}, 11^2, 12–19^{14}, 20^{14} (–14); 290 × 200–10 mm; 2 cols. of 48 lines (fols. 201–5). Binding ca. 1500. 2° fo. accipere finem. SCRIPT: highly current Anglicana/Secretary blend. REFERENCES: James, *Cat. Peterhouse*, pp. 249–50.

Cambridge, Peterhouse, MS 233   *Italy, s. xiv¹*

CONTENTS: Giles of Rome, *De regimine principum* (fols. 1–290v). STRUCTURE AND LAYOUT: parchment, fols. i + 290 + ii; 1–24^{12}, 25^4 (3 and 4 glued in); 225 × 160 mm; 2 cols. of 28 lines. Binding modern. 2° fo. -mine principum. SCRIPT: *textualis rotunda*. MS heavily annotated in several hands of s. xiv and s. xv. OWNERSHIP/PROVENANCE: Peterhouse by 1418. REFERENCES: James, *Cat. Peterhouse*, pp. 14, 285.

Cambridge, St. John's College, MS A.12   *England, s. xv¹*

CONTENTS: Giles of Rome, *De regimine principum* (fols. 1–109v). STRUCTURE AND LAYOUT: parchment, fols. 109; 1–13^8, 14^8 (–6, 7, 8); 330 × 225 mm; 2 cols. of 52 lines. Binding early modern. 2° fo. quod ergo. SCRIPT: Anglicana/Secretary blend. MS today comprises two volumes, bound together in s. xvii; the other volume contains Higden's *Polychronicon*. REFERENCES: James, *Cat. St. John's*, p. 16.

Cambridge, Trinity College, MS B.15.20   *England, s. xiv²*

CONTENTS: 1–10) ten theological treatises and sermons of Robert Grosseteste; 11) fragment of Giles of Rome, *De regimine principum* (fols. 337–8v): Ex regia . . . magestatem implorare dei . . . STRUCTURE AND LAYOUT: parchment, fols. i + 338; 1–15^{12}, 16^{10}, 17^6, 18–19^{12}, 19^{12} (slip between 8 and 9), 21^{12+2} (+11, 12), 22–28^{12}, 29^{8+1} (–6, 7); 285 × 205 mm; 2 cols. of 53 lines. Binding early modern. 2° fo. podagram. SCRIPT: Anglicana Formata. ILLUMINATION: incipits from fol. 186v to the end have large decorated initials with springing foliate borders; this includes the initial (fol. 337). COMMENTS: MS is a composite of two separate MSS (referred to here as **I** and **II**), which were joined together no later than s. xvi, but no earlier than *c.* 1400. The first leaf of **II** has been carefully glued on to the last of **I**. **I** (fols. 1–186v) and **II** (fols. 186v-338) are roughly contemporary. **II** in that same hand throughout. On the verso of the front flyleaf is a contents list in two hands. The first part, which lists the first five items in the MS, dates to s. xiv^{ex}, the second part, listing the remaining items by Grosseteste, but not the fragment of *DRP*, is in an early modern hand. When **I** and **II** were joined, *DRP*'s inclusion was only incidental and the remainder of the text probably discarded at that time. REFERENCES: James, *Cat. Trinity*, vol. 1, pp. 483–5.

Canterbury, Cathedral Library, MS B.11   *England, s. xiv^{ex}/xv^{in}*

CONTENTS: 1 **and** 3) Giles of Rome, *De regimine principum* (fols.4–153v), with index (fols. 155–161v): Abhominacio . . . Zelotipia zelotipus; 2) letter of St. Bernard (fols. 154–54v). STRUCTURE AND LAYOUT: parchment, fols. iii + 158 + i; 1–19^8, 20^6; 270 × 195 mm; 2 cols. of 44 lines. Binding s. xv. 2° fo. nam sicut. SCRIPT: Anglicana/Secretary blend. MS is the work of three scribes, each responsible for a different item. OWNERSHIP/PROVENANCE: inscription, s. xv^{in} (fol. 3v), "Liber Egidii de regimine principum. Liber magistri Johannis Kynton monachi Ecclesie X. Cantuarie." And in upper left corner of pastedown, "J Kynton." John Kyngton (d. 1416) was queen's chancellor, and became a monk of Christchurch in 1408. Colophon of index, s. xv^1 (fol. 161v), "Explicit tabula super Egidium de regimine principum per J.S." may refer to John Sarysbury, warden of Canterbury College, Oxford (1428) and later prior of Christchurch. REFERENCES: *MLGB*, p. 34; *MMBL*, vol. 11, pp. 272–3; note, dated February 15, 1951, of A. B. Emden in the copy of C. E. Woodruff's *A Catalogue of the Manuscript Books in the Library of Christ-Church, Canterbury* (Canterbury, 1911) kept at the Cathedral Library.

Chicago, University of Chicago Library, MS 533–v**   *France, s. xiv^{in}*

CONTENTS: Giles of Rome, *Le livre du gouvernement des rois et des princes* (fols. 3–129). STRUCTURE AND LAYOUT: parchment, fols. 133; collation unavailable; 280 × 190 mm; 2 cols. of 39 lines. Binding modern. 2° fo. la meniere. SCRIPT: *textualis rotunda.* ILLUMINA-TION: historiated initial with three-quarter border and drolleries (fol. 3); decorated initials and partial borders at beginning of each part. OWNERSHIP/PROVENANCE: Garshall arms (probably) with the motto "Nul autre espoir," s. xv^{med}, on one of the front flyleaves. Arms of earlier owner (folio not available), s. xiv: per fesse sable and argent, a lion rampant counter-charged, with the motto "Avisiowel." COMMENTS: on an end flyleaf "a drawing in color of an oak tree (unfinished) on which are hung six pairs of heraldic shields, and each shield has above it a helmet with the name of a distinguished family – Cleves, Blois, Des Barres, Florines, Strangort, Chauvegni, Pomponne, Montfort, Boulogne, Lessigniun, Mello, and Longuespee. At the top of the leaf are the royal arms of England and the word (divided) 'engle terre'." REFERENCES: De Ricci, vol. 1, p. 589; description of manuscript from the unpublished catalogue of manuscripts in the Department of Special Collections, University of Chicago Library.

Durham, Cathedral Library, MS B.III.24   *England, s. xiv^{ex}*

CONTENTS: 1) Giles of Rome, *De regimine principum* (fols. 1–105v); 2) William of Monte Lauduno (?), *De imperatore, rege et milite*; 3) Roger of Waltham, *Compendium morale*. STRUCTURE AND LAYOUT: parchment, fols. ii + 207 + ii; 1–13^8, 14^8 (–8), 15^{8+1}, 16–22^{12}, 23^6 (–5); 335 × 235 mm; 2 cols. of 49 lines (fols. 1–105). Binding early modern. 2° fo. se det. SCRIPT: MS work of three scribes, each responsible for a different item. Fols. 1–105v in Anglicana Formata. ILLUMINATION: large decorated initial with springing foliate border (fol. 1). OWNERSHIP/PROVENANCE: inscription, *c.* 1400 (fol. 1), "De communi lib. monachorum dunelm." COMMENTS: List of contents, *c.* 1500, on verso of second front flyleaf by Thomas Swalwell, monk of Durham, is identical to MS's present contents. REFERENCES: T. Rud, *Codicum Manuscriptorum Ecclesiae Cathedralis Dunelmensis Catalogus Classicus* (Durham, 1825), p. 167; *MLGB*, p. 68; comments of Alan J. Piper.

Durham, Cathedral Library, MS B.IV.31   *Italy, s. xiv^{1}*

CONTENTS: Giles of Rome, *De regimine principum* (fols. 2–173v). STRUCTURE AND LAYOUT: parchment, fols. i + 172; 1–21^8, 22^4; 295 × 190 mm; single block of 33 lines. Binding early modern. 2° fo. qui erudiendus. SCRIPT: Italian cursive book hand. OWNERSHIP/PROVENANCE: inscription, s. xv (fol. 2), "Liber sancti Cuthberti assignatus communi armarialo [*sic*] de dunelm." COMMENTS: Contents on verso of first flyleaf, *c.* 1500, in hand of Thomas Swalwell, monk of Durham. REFERENCES: Rud, *Codicum Manuscriptorum*, p. 236; *MLGB*, p. 69.

Durham, University Library, MS Cosin V.I.9   *England, s. xiv^{ex}*

CONTENTS: 1) Giles of Rome, *Governement dez Roys et dez princes*, bk. I only (fols. 2–203); 2) verses in English, inc. "Allemy3ty and alle mercyable qwene." STRUCTURE AND LAYOUT: paper, fols. 203; 1–20^{10}, 21^2; 290 × 190 mm; single block of 18 lines. Binding early modern. 2° fo. qui ad force. SCRIPT: item 1 in very large Anglicana. Hand of item 2 slightly later and much smaller with some Secretary graphs. ILLUMINATION: historiated initial and full foliate border (fol. 2); inhabited initials (fols. 41 and 138). OWNERSHIP/PROVENANCE: The dialect of item 2 suggests an East Anglian influence on the scribe or his exemplar. COMMENTS: This is the only all-paper MS treated in this study, and one of the earliest examples of a paper manuscript book written in England; Italian watermark of a triple mount surmounted by a cross (cf. Briquet nos. 11678–11728). REFERENCES: typescript of the catalogue of the University Library's manuscripts now being prepared by A. I. Doyle; C. M. Briquet, *Les filigranes: Dictionnaire historique des marques du papier*, 2nd edn (Leipzig, 1923; reprint, New York, 1977).

Edinburgh, University Library, MS 106   *England, s. xiv^{ex}*

CONTENTS: 1–9) assorted indexes; 10) index of Giles of Rome, *De regimine principum* (fols. 139v-46): Abhominacio . . . Zelotipia zelotipus; 11 and 12) assorted indexes. STRUCTURE AND LAYOUT: parchment, fols. 142 (though modern foliation counts first six missing leaves, for a total of fols. 148); 1^6 (–1 through 6), 2–12^{12}, 13^8, 14^2; 300 × 195 mm; 2 cols. of 51 lines. Binding modern. 2° fo. fuisse uexatam. SCRIPT: Anglicana. Items 1–10 in same hand. Last two items in a slightly later and more current hand. OWNERSHIP/PROVENANCE: Durham Cathedral Priory. COMMENTS: Ker believed MS was "of the type classified as of Oxford by Destrez in *La pecia*, 1935." REFERENCES: C. R. Borland, *A Descriptive Catalogue of the Western Medieval Manuscripts in the Edinburgh University Library* (Edinburgh, 1916), pp. 166–7; *MLGB Supplement*, p. 29.

Glasgow, University Library Hamilton, MS 141   *France (probably the south), s. xv^1*

CONTENTS: Giles of Rome, *De regimine principum* (fols. 1–172v), with list of chapters (fols. 173–6). STRUCTURE AND LAYOUT: parchment and paper, fols. i + 176; 1–10^{16}, 11^{16} (–3, 4, and 16), 12^3; 280 × 200 mm; 2 cols. of 43 lines. Binding of s. xv stamped with fleurs-de-lis and the Lamb of God. 2° fo. cum ergo. SCRIPT: MS in the same current hand throughout. Chapter headings in rubrics; lists of chapters precede each part. OWNERSHIP/PROVENANCE: inscription recording MS's use as a pledge in an Oxford loan-chest: "Caro suo cognato cristofero forster committantur hii 2° libri sub assecuracione Magistri Been. Hic liber cum alio tabularum est michi pignus pro vj s. viij d." A Christopher Forster was at Oxford in 1481–82 when Thomas Benne was keeper of the Guildford chest. Another inscription, *c.* 1500 (fol. 176), "Clayton meus verus possessor est." REFERENCES: *MMBL*, vol. ii, p. 931; *BRUO* 2, p. 707.

Hereford, Cathedral Library, MS P.V.7   *England, s. xiv^{ex}*

CONTENTS: Giles of Rome, *De regimine principum* (fols. 1–130v). STRUCTURE AND LAYOUT: parchment, fols. i + 131; 1^{14}, 2–10^{12}, 11^{12} (–10, 11); 330 × 240 mm; 2 cols. of 48 lines. Binding of s. xv. 2° fo. -lie nec. SCRIPT: *textualis semi-quadrata*. MS in same hand throughout. Extensive marginal notes and corrections in several hands, though mostly in a single hand of s. xv, also responsible for a summary of *De regimine*'s contents on the front flyleaf verso, and a copy of letter from John Booth, bishop of Exeter (1465–78). OWNERSHIP/PROVENANCE: inscription, s. xv^{ex} (fol. 2), "Ex dono magistri Oweyni lloyd legum doctoris," and in the same hand under horn on outside of back cover, "Egidium de regimine principum ex dono magistri Oweyni lloyd quondam canonis huius Ecclesie." Owen Lloyd, prebendary of Exeter Cathedral (1469–78) and archdeacon of Totnes (1476) and Barnstaple (1476–8). MS bequeathed by Lloyd to Hereford Cathedral Chapter. REFERENCES: Mynors and Thomson, *Catalogue*, p. 98; A. T. Bannister, *A Descriptive Catalogue of the Manuscripts in the Hereford Cathedral Library* (Hereford, 1927), p. 153; *MLGB*, p. 98.

London, British Library, MS Arundel 384   *England, s. xv^1*

CONTENTS: 1) Nicholas de Interamne, *Collationes epistolarum dominicalium*; 2) Five sermons on the Old and New Testaments; 3) Robert Holcote, *Moralitates sive Historiae in usum predicatorum*; 4) *Lumen anime*; 5) alphabetical abridgment of Giles of Rome, *De regimine principum* (fols. 136–222v): Extractus quidam per modum alphabeti super Egidio de Regimine principum. Amicabilia que sunt. . . . debite taxande sunt, vo. CONSILIA. K.; 6) Ovid, *Ars amatoria*, bk. III, with marginal notes; 7–33) several *carmina* on love, the seasons, and nature; 34) *sententiae* on Cicero's *De officiis*; 35) "tractatulus de usu astrolabii"; 36) index of Boethius, *De consolatione philosophiae*. STRUCTURE AND LAYOUT: parchment, fols. 247; 1–10⁸, 11⁸ (–8) (fols. 136–222v); 225 × 160 mm; single block of 31 lines (fols. 136–222v). Binding modern. 2° fo. circa primum (MS); continuat (*DRP*). SCRIPT: Secretary with several Anglicana graphs (fols. 136–222v) COMMENTS: MS a composite volume of several works in several hands of s. xiv¹ and s. xv². *DRP* appears to have been bound in with the other works at a fairly late date, as evidenced by the worn appearance of fols. 136 and 222v; also, signatures in *DRP* begin with "**a**." REFERENCES: *Catalogue of the Manuscripts in the British Museum, the Arundel Manuscripts* (London, 1834), pp. 112–14.

London, British Library, MS Royal 4.D.iv   *England, s. xv¹*

CONTENTS: 1) Bertrand de la Tour, *postillae* on Gospel lections for the entire year; 2) John of Wales, *Tractatus de septem viciis*; 3) John of Wales, *Tractatus de penitentia*; 4) Giles of Rome, *De regimine principum* (fols. 262–348v), ending imperfectly, "et societate hominum est dare plures personas et plures homines et . . ." STRUCTURE AND LAYOUT: parchment, fols. 348 (two numbered leaves missing); 1–9¹², 10¹² (–2 fols.), 11–29¹²; 367 × 260 mm; 2 cols. of 61 lines. Binding modern. 2° fo. exponi possunt. SCRIPT: *textualis semi-quadrata*. Scribe stops in *DRP* 3.3.23. OWNERSHIP/PROVENANCE: inscription, s. xv (fol. 1), "Iste liber est de conventu fratrum minorum Londinii." REFERENCES: G. F. Warner and J. P. Gilson, *Catalogue of the Old Royal and King's Collection in the British Museum* (London, 1921), vol. 1, p. 89; *MLGB*, p. 123.

London, British Library, MS Royal 5.C.iii   *England, s. xv^med*

CONTENTS: 1) anonymous treatise "De modo docendi"; 2) chapter list of Giles of Rome, *De regimine principum* followed by index (fols. 11–17): Abhominacio . . . Zelotopus [*sic*] zelotipia; 3) index of Urso, *Liber aphorismorum*; 4) abridgment with chapter list of Giles of Rome, *De regimine principum* (fols. 22–37v), inc. "Oportet ut latitudo. . ."; 5) propositions from principal works of Aristotle, including the *Ethics* and *Politics*; 6) Prosper of Aquitaine, *Liber sentenciarum*; 7) propositions extracted from theological works of Augustine; 8) Hugh of Strasbourg (?), *Compendium theologie*; 9–11) abridgments and extracts of three works of Grosseteste; 12) abridgment of Boethius, *De consolatione philosophiae*; 13) extracts from a work entitled *Speculum peccatorum*, wrongly attributed to Augustine; 14) Bonaventure, *Meditationes*; 15) extracts from Henry Suso, *Horologium eternae sapientis*; 16) Simon of Ghent, *Meditationes*; 17) letter of Roger Freton, dean of Chichester, concerning the implementation of a deanery, dated August 4, 1374; 18) license from Pope Boniface IX to King Richard II to alienate the possessions of alien priories for the purpose of founding a college of clerics; 19) "Meditatio" of Bonaventure; 20) "Tractatus de elemosina"; 21) Richard Rolle, *Incendium amoris*; 22) *Forma predicandi*; 23) Short homiletic paragraphs; 24) Bernard, sermons on the Song of Songs; 25) four epistles of Jerome. STRUCTURE AND

LAYOUT: parchment, fols. 381; 1^{10}, 2^{8+3}, $3–14^8$, 15^{10}, $16–35^8$, 36^{8+1}, 37^8, $38–43^{12}$, 44^{10} (–3 fols.); $330–35 \times 230$ mm; 2 cols. of 59 lines (fols. 22–37v). Binding modern. 2° fo. sed quia. SCRIPT: Bastard Secretary (item 2); Anglicana/Secretary blend (item 4). MS a composite volume of several originally separate items in many different hands. *DRP* index and chapter list in a different hand from that of the abridgment and its chapter list. OWNER-SHIP/PROVENANCE: according to an early catalogue, an inscription at the end, now lost, read: "Liber T. Eyburhale, emptus a Iohanne Pye pro 27s. 6d. Do Henrico Mosie, quondam scolari meo, si contingat eum presbyterari; aliter erit Liber Domini Iohannis Sory, sic quod non vendatur, sed transeat inter cognatos meos, si fuerint aliqui inventi; sin autem, ab uno presbytero ad alium." Thomas Eyburhale, or Eborall, Oxford D.Th. by 1443, master of Whittington College, London. COMMENTS: Although the date when the items were assembled is unknown, the price quoted in the lost inscription is high enough to suggest that it was already a substantial volume when purchased by Eborall. REFERENCES: Warner and Gilson, *Catalogue*, vol. 1, pp. 105–6; *BRUO* 1, pp. 622–3.

London, British Library, MS Royal 6.B.v   *England, s. xv¹*

CONTENTS: 1) Gregory, *Omelie*; 2) Isidore, *De summo bono*; 3) abridgment of Giles of Rome, *De regimine principum* (fols. 127–71): De regimine principum autoritates et raciones . . . pacem civium supernorum et gloriam perpetuam bonorum. Explicit liber Egidii de regimine principum abbreviatus; 4) Bernard (though more probably Hugh of St. Victor), *Speculum conscientie*; 5) treatise on the priestly office including quotations from the *Decretum*. STRUCTURE AND LAYOUT: parchment, fols. i + 185; $1–10^{12}$, 11^{10} (–9), $12–14^{12}$, 15^{12} (–11), 16^{12} (–10), 17^6; 300×215 mm; 2 cols. of 46–57 lines. Binding modern. 2° fo. debemus. SCRIPT: Anglicana/Secretary blend (items 2 and 3). MS is several hands, though items 2 and 3 in same hand. OWNERSHIP/PROVENANCE: inscription, s. xv (fol. 185), "Iste liber constat Iohanni Broughton domino de Todyngton qui sit benedictus. Amen." John Broughton, esquire, of Toddington, Beds. (fl. s. xv^med). COMMENTS: List of contents, s. xiv² (flyleaf verso), "contentus omelie beati gregorii cum ysidero [sic] de summo bono et egidio de Regimine principum cum aliis presentibus – viginti solidi." REFERENCES: Warner and Gilson, *Catalogue*, vol. 1, p. 135; *CCR* 1441–47, pp. 223, 267, 478; *CPR* 1441–46, p. 467.

London, British Library, MS Royal 10.C.ix   *England, s. xv¹*

CONTENTS: 1–2) indexes of Augustine, *City of God* and *Retractationes*; 3) chapter list of Peter of Limoges, *Oculus moralis*; 4) Giles of Rome, *De regimine principum* (fols. 32–144v), with index (fols. 22–9) and chapter list (fols. 29v–31v): Abhominacio . . . Zelus duplex; 5) abridgment of the *Politics*; 6) treatise on the *Enigmata Aristotelis*. STRUCTURE AND LAYOUT: parchment, fols. 175; $1–2^8$, 3^8 (–6, 7, 8), 4^{10+8}, $5–21^8$; 340×260 mm; 2 cols. of 51 lines. Binding modern. 2° fo. tempore 12 (MS); sive monastica (*DRP*). SCRIPT: Anglicana Formata with several Secretary graphs (*DRP* text), and Anglicana (*DRP* index and chapter list). MS the work of two scribes, A (fols. 1–21v, 32–174) B (fols. 22–31v). ILLUMINATION: decorated initial and border (fol. 22); large decorated initial with full foliate border (fol.

32). The same artist may have been responsible for both. COMMENTS: *DRP* is complete but the chapter list leaves out twenty-one chapters of book 3, part 2 and seven chapters of book 3, part 3. This and the collation of gathering 4 suggest it may not have been intended for the *DRP* in this MS. REFERENCES: Warner and Gilson, *Catalogue*, vol. 1, p. 328.

London, British Library, MS Royal 12.B.xxi   *England, s. xv¹*

CONTENTS: 1) abridgment of Giles of Rome, *De regimine principum* (fols. 1–79), beginning imperfectly in 1.1.9: //felicitas tantum inest bonis et beatis. . .; 2) Vegetius, *De re militari*. STRUCTURE AND LAYOUT: parchment, fols. 120; 1⁸ (−1, 2, 3), 2–10⁸, 11⁸ (−5 through 8), 12–15⁸, 16⁸⁺¹; 215 × 160 mm; 2 cols. of 33 lines. Binding modern. 2° fo. (MS missing first several leaves). SCRIPT: Anglicana. MS in the same hand throughout. REFERENCES: Warner and Gilson, *Catalogue*, vol. 11, p. 18.

London, British Library, MS Royal 15.E.vi   *France, Rouen, 1445*

CONTENTS: 1) dedicatory verses to Margaret of Anjou; 2) Genealogical tree of Henry VI; 3) pseudo-Callisthenes, *Le liure de la conqueste du roy Alixandre*; 4) "Le liuure [*sic*] du roy Charlemaine"; 5) Rainault de Montaubain, *Quatre fils Aimon*; 6) prose romance of Pontus and Sidoine, entitled "Le noble liure du Roy pontus"; 7–8) two prose romances of Guy of Warwick and the Heraud d'Ardennes; 9) *Lystoire du chevalier au Signe*; 10) Honoré Bovet, *L'Arbre des batailles*; 11) Giles of Rome, abridged French *De regimine principum*, entitled "Le liure de politique" (fols. 327–61); 12) *Chroniques Normandes*; 13) Alain Chartier, *Le brèviaire des nobles*; 14) Christine de Pisan, *Le livre des fais d'armes et de chévalerie*; 15) statutes of the Order of the Garter in French. STRUCTURE AND LAYOUT: parchment, fols. 440; 1–55⁸; 470 × 330 mm; 2 cols. of 69 lines. Binding modern. SCRIPT: French Bastard Secretary. ILLUMINATION: MS lavishly illustrated with several decorated borders and more than a hundred miniatures of very high quality. *DRP* has introductory miniature (fol. 327). OWNERSHIP/PROVENANCE: dedicatory verses (fol. 2v), "Princesse tres excellente/Ce liure cy vous presente/De schrosbery le conte." Wedding gift of John Talbot, earl of Shrewsbury, to Margaret of Anjou. REFERENCES: Warner and Gilson, *Catalogue*, vol. 11, pp. 177–9.

London, Lambeth Palace Library, MS 150   *England, s. xiv^{med}*

CONTENTS: 1) Giles of Rome, *De regimine principum* (fols. 1–178v), with schematic contents summary (fols. 179–79v); 2) Giles of Rome, *De peccato originali*; 3) Nicholas Trevet, *De officio missae*. STRUCTURE AND LAYOUT: parchment, fols. i + 216 + i; 1¹², 2¹² (−1), 3–6¹², 7–8¹⁰, 9¹², 10⁸, 11–14¹², 15¹⁰, 16¹², 17⁸, 18–19¹², 20⁴; 285 × 205 mm; 2 cols. of 40 lines. Binding modern. 2° fo. summo opere. SCRIPT: Anglicana. MS by two roughly contemporary scribes, the first responsible for items 1 and 2. OWNERSHIP/PROVENANCE: inscription, front flyleaf verso, "Istum librum legavit Magister Johannes Lech' ecclesie Lanth. iuxta Glouc. cuius anima per misericordiam Dei requiescat in pace. Amen. Qui eum alienaverit a dicta domo anathema sit fiat fiat. Amen." John Lecche (d. 1361), chancellor of

Oxford (1338), official at the court of Canterbury, and king's clerk (1347–53). MS bequeathed to Lanthony. COMMENTS: On front flyleaf recto is a *provocatio* of Michael Northburgh, advocate of the court of the archbishop of Canterbury, dated February 16, 1338. REFERENCES: James, *Cat. Lambeth*, pp. 239–40; *MLGB*, p. 110; *BRUO* 2, pp. 1118–19.

London, Lambeth Palace Library, MS 184   *England, 1460–61*

CONTENTS: 1) Giles of Rome, *De regimine principum* (fols. 1–179v); 2) letter of Bernard; 3) Peter Thomas, *Formalitates*, inc. "Ad evidentiam . . ." STRUCTURE AND LAYOUT: parchment, fols. iii + 240 + iv; 1–30⁸, 31⁴ (all blank); 288 × 195 mm; single block of 37 lines. Binding modern. 2° fo. et grosse. SCRIPT: Secretary. MS by one scribe. Date of execution given in the colophons of *DRP* and the last item. ILLUMINATION: decorated initial, full border, and arms of Edward the Confessor impaled with the arms of the see of St. Peter (fol. 1). OWNERSHIP/PROVENANCE: the coat of arms (fol. 1) identifies the MS with Westminster Abbey, and most likely with one of its abbots, cf. the arms of George Fascet (prior, 1491–98, and abbot, 1498–1500), displayed on the Cotehele Annunciation panel. A later inscription (fol. 1), "J. Foxus"; probably the John Foxe installed as a prebendary at Westminster in 1606. REFERENCES: James, *Cat. Lambeth*, pp. 288–9.

London, Lambeth Palace Library, MS Arc.L.40.2/L.26   *England, s. xv¹*

CONTENTS: Giles of Rome, *De regimine principum* (fols. 1–96), inc. "Egregia ac sanctissima. . .", with index (fols. 96–100): Abstinencia . . . Zelus. STRUCTURE AND LAYOUT: parchment, fols. 100 + i; 1–8⁸, 9⁸ (–4), 10–11⁸, 12¹⁰, 13⁴; 405 × 275 mm; 2 cols. of 52 lines. Binding early modern. 2° fo. quis plene. SCRIPT: Secretary. ILLUMINATION: large decorated initial inhabited by arms of Richard II, a full foliate border, and four other coats of arms (fol. 1). Decorated initials inhabited by coats of arms (fols. 6v, 22, 27v, 32, 42, 51v, 60v, 68, 84, and 84v). OWNERSHIP/PROVENANCE: inscription, s. xv² (fol. 1), "Egidius de Regimine. Liber illustrissimus Principis Ducis gloucestr'." The last three words of inscription erased but visible under ultra-violet light. Illumination program suggests Richard, duke of York, as the original owner; inscription belongs to King Richard III. COMMENTS: MS formerly at Sion College, London. REFERENCES: *MMBL*, vol. 1, pp. 282–3.

New York, Pierpont Morgan Library, MS M. 122   *France, s. xivⁱⁿ*

CONTENTS: Giles of Rome, *Le livre du gouvernment des rois et des princes* (fols. 1–106). STRUCTURE AND LAYOUT: parchment, fols. 106; 345 × 230 mm; 2 cols. of 40–1 lines. Binding modern. 2° fo. comment il. SCRIPT: *textualis semi-quadrata*. ILLUMINATION: historiated initial with springing foliate border inhabited by several grotesques (fol. 1). Decorated initials throughout. OWNERSHIP/PROVENANCE: inscription, s. xv (fol. 106): "Cest liure parteent au gylliam Sonnyng, alderman de Calleis et a son fyz." William Sonnyng, alderman of Calais, s. xv². REFERENCES: De Ricci, vol. 11, p. 1405; unpublished catalogue of MSS in the Pierpont Morgan Library; Molenaer (ed.), *Li livres du Gouvernement*; *CCR* 1435–1441, pp. 285–6.

Oxford, All Souls College, MS 92   *England, s. xv^{med}*

CONTENTS: Giles of Rome, *De regimine principum* (fols. 1–159), with index (fols. 159v-66): Abhominacio ... Zelotipia. STRUCTURE AND LAYOUT: parchment, fols. 166; 1–16¹⁰, 17⁶; 280 × 190 mm; 2 cols. of 45–51 lines. Binding modern. 2° fo. Cum omnis. SCRIPT: Anglicana. OWNERSHIP/PROVENANCE: inscription (fol. 1v), "Liber collegii animarum omnium fidelium defunctorum, ex dono M. Thome Lay. Oretis pro bono statu eiusdem." Lay, fellow of All Souls (*c.* 1437–*c.* 1450). Index colophon (fol. 166), "Explicit liber de regimine principum secundum Egidium edita a fratre Thoma Abyndon." COMMENTS: single gloss "contra reges qui sunt pueri" (fol. 24) beside text "secundo intemperancia est vicium maxime puerile" in *DRP* 1.2.16. REFERENCES: H. O. Coxe, *Catalogus Codicum MSS, Qui in Collegiis Aulisque Oxoniensibus Hodie Adservantur* (Oxford, 1852), vol. II, p. 28; *BRUO* 2, p. 1114.

Oxford, Balliol College, MS 146a   *England, s. xv^{in}*

CONTENTS: 1) Vegetius, *De re militari*; 2) *Secretum secretorum*; 3) extracts from Pliny, *Historia naturalis*; 4) John of Paris, *De potestate regia et papali*; 5) Giles of Rome, *De regimine principum* (fols. 120–235v), with index (fols. 236–7): Amatores ... Intemperatus; 6) extracts from Aristotle, *Politics*; 7) copy of letter, dated 1446 from Wolfard Koer, physician, to Thomas Gascoigne. STRUCTURE AND LAYOUT: parchment, fols. i + 280; 1¹², 2¹² (–7 through 12), 3¹² (–12), 4–8¹², 9¹⁶ (–16), 10¹²⁺², 11–19¹², 20¹² (–11, 12), 21–23², 24¹² (–9 through 12); 300 × 215 mm; 2 cols. of 50–61 lines. Binding early modern. 2° fo. dolis atque. SCRIPT: Anglicana (items 1 and 5). MS in several roughly contemporary hands (except the last item, which is later). Same scribe responsible for items 1 and 5. COMMENTS: list of contents, s. xv (flyleaf verso), "Flavius Vegesius de re militari / Aliud opus / Egidius de Regimine principum / Bonum opus super libros Politicorum." REFERENCES: Mynors, *Catalogue*, pp. 123–5.

Oxford, Balliol College, MS 282   *England, s. xiv^{med}*

CONTENTS: 1) Giles of Rome, *De regimine principum* (fols. 2–123v), followed by index (fols. 123v-25): Amatores ... Temperancia; 2) Walter Burley, commentary on the *Politics*. STRUCTURE AND LAYOUT: parchment, fols. i + 203; 1–5¹², 6¹² (–4), 7–16¹², 17¹² (–12); 305 × 205 mm; 2 cols. of 52–6 lines. Binding early modern. 2° fo. tercio diversificantur. SCRIPT: Anglicana. COMMENTS: list of contents, s. xiv (flyleaf verso), "In isto volumine continentur libri infra scripti / Egidius de Regimine principum / Item Burley super Octos libros politicorum / Item Afforismi Ursonis / Item tractatus nobilis de effectibus qualitatum primarum." REFERENCES: Mynors, *Catalogue*, p. 298.

Oxford, Bodleian Library, MS Auct. F.3.2   *England, s. xiv^{med}*

CONTENTS: 1) Giles of Rome, *De regimine principum* (fols. 2–117) beginning imperfectly (//capitulum ii quis sit...), with *index* (fols. 117–24v): Abhominacio ... Zelotipia zelotipus; 2) Vegetius, *De re militari*. STRUCTURE AND LAYOUT: parchment, fols. i + 145; 1¹² (–1),

$2-7^{12}$, slip insert, 8^{12}, 9^{14+1} (−5), 10^{10+3}, 11^{6+1}, 12^8, 13^8 (−8); 290 × 185 mm; 2 cols. of 41–2 lines (fols. 2–117). Binding modern. 2° fo. Cum omnis. SCRIPT: Anglicana. MS by three scribes, one responsible for *DRP*, another (s. xv) for the index, and a third (s. xiv¹) for the Vegetius. OWNERSHIP/PROVENANCE: Canterbury College, Oxford, by 1501. Index colphon (fol. 124v), "Explicit tabula Egidii de regimine principum edita a Fratre Thoma Abendon." REFERENCES: *SC*, pt. 2, pp. 818–19; *BRUO*, vol. 1, p. 3; James, *Ancient Libraries*, p. 169.

Oxford, Bodleian Library, MS Auct. F.3.3   *England, s. xiv^med*

CONTENTS: 1) Giles of Rome, *De regimine principum* (fols. 1–105v); 2) Vegetius, *De re militari*; 3) *Liber de gestis Alexandri Magni*; 4) Thomas Aquinas, commentary on the *Ethics*. STRUCTURE AND LAYOUT: parchment, fols. i+268; $1-7^{12}$, 8^9 (originally ten leaves, then five excised, four of which were replaced), $9-22^{12}$, 23^8 (−1 leaf); 305 × 190 mm; 2 cols. of 56 lines. Binding of s. xv. 2° fo. -beat imitari. SCRIPT: *textualis semi-quadrata* (*DRP*). MS by three contemporary scribes: A (item 1), B (item 2), and C (items 3 and 4). ILLUMINATION: decorated initials and borders for all items by same artist. OWNERSHIP/PROVENANCE: Reading Abbey (?). Abbey accounts appear on flyleaf and binding. COMMENTS: brief summary, s. xiv (flyleaf verso), of *DRP*'s contents and a list of the twelve moral virtues. REFERENCES: *SC*, pt. 1, pp. 239–40; *MLGB*, p. 156.

Oxford, Bodleian Library, MS Bodley 181   *England, s. xv*

CONTENTS: 1) Giles of Rome, *De regimine principum* (fols. 1–97); 2) *Secretum secretorum*, with a note on human longevity at the end, inc. "Noe vero cum vixisset"; 3) *Regimen corporale*, inc. "Cum mane surrexeritis. . ."; 4) pseudo-Aristotle, *De pomo*, inc. "Cum homo creaturarum dignissima. . . ." STRUCTURE AND LAYOUT: parchment, fols. 123; 1^4, $2-4^8$, $4-6^6$, $7-8^8$, 9^8, 10 missing, $11-13^8$, 14^{8+1}, $15-17^8$, 19^2; 300 × 205 mm; 2 cols. of 52–4 lines. Binding early modern. 2° fo. scire suam. ILLUMINATION: pen and ink illustrations, s. xvi^med (fol. 97v), with an anti-monastic theme. SCRIPT: Secretary. MS by one scribe. REFERENCES: *SC*, pt. 1, pp. 201–2; O. Pächt and J. J. G. Alexander, *Illuminated Manuscripts in the Bodleian Library, Oxford*, vol. III (Oxford, 1973), p. 102, pl. cviii.

Oxford, Bodleian Library, MS Bodley 234   *England, s. xiv^ex*

CONTENTS: Giles of Rome, *De regimine principum* (fols. 1–240v), with chapter summary (fols. 241–8). STRUCTURE AND LAYOUT: parchment, fols. iv+248+iii; $1-31^8$; 260 × 170 mm; 2 cols. of 46 lines. Contemporary red binding decorated with red fleurs-de-lys. 2° fo. -gis illuminent. SCRIPT: *textualis semi-quadrata*. MS is in the same competent hand throughout. ILLUMINATION: historiated initial and decorated border (fol. 1) containing Thorp arms (gules, a fess argent between six fleurs-de-lys argent). OWNERSHIP/PROVENANCE: arms (fol. 1) of William Lord Thorp (d. 1391). REFERENCES: *SC*, pt. 1, pp. 254–5; Pächt and Alexander, *Illuminated Manuscripts*, vol. III, p. 70, pl. lxxiv.

Oxford, Bodleian Library, MS Bodley 544 England, *s. xv^med*

CONTENTS: Giles of Rome, *De regimine principum* (fols. 1–122v), with index (fols. 223–31v): Abhominacio . . . Zelotipus zelotipia. STRUCTURE AND LAYOUT: parchment, fols. iii + 231 + v; 1–29^8; 190 × 135 mm; single block of 38 lines. Binding contemporary, original clasps intact. 2° fo. subtilem sed. SCRIPT: Secretary. MS by one scribe. OWNERSHIP/PROVENANCE: St. George's, Windsor before 1612. Inscription (second flyleaf verso), "Iste liber constat magistro [. . .] cuius pretium xxx s." REFERENCES: *SC*, pt. 1, pp. 440–1; *MLGB*, p. 204.

Oxford, Bodleian Library, MS Bodley 589 England, *s. xv^1*

CONTENTS: Giles of Rome, *De regimine principum* (fols. 1–181), with unfinished index (fol. 181v): Avarus. . . . Ars est respectu factibilium non presupponens rectitudinem voluntatis, li. 1, c. 6, p. 2. STRUCTURE AND LAYOUT: parchment, fols. iv + 181 + ii; 1–22^8, 23^8 (–6, 7, 8); 235 × 135 mm; single block of 37–43 lines. Binding contemporary. 2° fo. sit hic. SCRIPT: Anglicana/Secretary blend. MS by one scribe. OWNERSHIP/PROVENANCE: scribal colophon (fol. 181), "Explicit liber de regimine principum fratris Egidii ordinis eremitarum sancti Augustini episcopi et doctoris gloriosi quod Burgh." Inscription, *s. xv^ex* (first flyleaf recto), "Memorandum quod Robertus thystilton debet rectori de Rothwell xvii d." Copy of will, dated April 30, 1528 (fol. 182), "I William Kyghtone of Brigeforde at ye brige end . . ." REFERENCES: *SC*, pt. 1, p. 329.

Oxford, Bodleian Library, MS Digby 233 England, *s. xv^in*

CONTENTS: 1) Middle English translation by John Trevisa of Giles of Rome, *De regimine principum* (fols. 1–182v): To his special lord icome of kinges blood and of most holy kyn, Sire Phelyp þe eldest sone and herre. . . . þe whiche pees God graunteþ and byhoteþ to his owne trewe seruantes þat is iblessed for euermore. Amen; 2) Middle English translation of Vegetius, *De re militari*. STRUCTURE AND LAYOUT: parchment, fols. ii + 227 + iii; 1–14^8, 15^8 (–5), 16–28^8, 29^6; 460 × 325 mm; binding early modern. 2° fo. as the comentour. SCRIPT: Anglicana Formata. Two contemporary text scribes. Scribe A responsible for original campaign of entire MS and for most corrections in text space. Scribe B, writing in a more angular hand, responsible for some corrections in text space. Several corrections (most now erased) and additions in several hands of s. xv–xvi appear in the margins. ILLUMINATION: miniature and full border (fol. 1), miniature (fol. 62), and probably a third miniature, now lost (on excised leaf between fols. 116 and 117). Large decorated initials with springing partial borders at the beginnings of parts and decorated initials beginning each chapter. Both miniatures appear to be the work of the same artist. OWNERSHIP/PROVENANCE: probably commissioned by Thomas fourth Lord Berkeley. Inscription, *c.* 1500 (fol. 228), "loyallte me ley / Mary Hastyngs Hungreford / bottreaux mollens and Mulles / god help me." Mary Lady Hastings and Hungerford, daughter-in-law of William Lord Hastings, chamberlain of Edward IV. The swan badge (fol. 199v) suggests intended ownership of Thomas Berkeley's daughter, Elizabeth, and her husband, Richard Beauchamp, earl of Warwick. REFERENCES: Trevisa, *Governance*; Pächt and Alexander, *Illuminated Manuscripts*, vol. III, p. 72, ill. lxxx.

Oxford, Bodleian Library, MS Hatton 15   *England, s. xiv²*

CONTENTS: 1) Giles of Rome, *De regimine principum* (fols. 5–83v); 2) Thomas Aquinas, commentary on the *Ethics*; 3) Giles of Rome, sentences on Aristotle's *De anima*. STRUCTURE AND LAYOUT: parchment, fols. iii + 220 + i; $1–7^{12}, 8^{12}$ (–8 through 12), $9–13^{12}, 14^4$, $15–19^{12}, 20^5$; 350 × 230 mm; 2 cols. of 60 lines. Binding modern. 2° fo. nam quia. SCRIPT: *textualis semi-quadrata*; MS by one scribe. OWNERSHIP/PROVENANCE: *cauciones* (fol. 3v) of three deposits in Oxford loan-chests: 1461 "in cista de Thecheley," 1463 "in cista Warwici," and 1465 "in cista de Warwyk." Erased inscription (fol. 5), "Conventus Wygornie." COMMENTS: List of contents, *c.* 1400 (fol. 4), lists all three items. REFERENCES: *SC*, pt. 2, pp. 851–2.

Oxford, Bodleian Library, MS Laud Misc. 645   *England, s. xv^{in}*

CONTENTS: 1) Guido da Colonna, *De casu Trojae historia*; 2) Malachy of Armagh, *De venenis*; 3) *Secretum secretorum*; 4) Giles of Rome, abridgment of *De regimine principum* (fols. 84v–117v): De regimine principum auctoritates et raciones compendiose collegi . . . ad quam nos perducat qui sine fine vivit et regnat. Amen. Explicit Liber egidii de Regimine principum et continet Tractatus decem; 5) "Epistolae legatinae ad res in Anglia et alibi," inc. "sponsa Christi patrum clamoribus. . ."; 6) "De septem ineptis," inc. "Septem hec inepta vidi. . ."; 7) A few verses on the six vices of drinking, inc. "Post potum primum mens declinabit ad ymum"; 8) "Epistola ad canonicum quendam gratulatoria," inc. "Pauca bone. . ."; 9) "Epistola ad regem congratulatoria"; 10) "L. Episcopi Cenomanensis, ad M. venerabilem Anglorum reginam"; 11) index on the Bible, inc. "Abstinentia . . ." STRUCTURE AND LAYOUT: parchment, fols. i + 170 + i; $1^6, 2–6^{12}, 7^{12}$ (–1, 2, 11, and 12), $8–13^{12}, 14^{12}$ (–10), 15^8 (–6 leaves); 360 × 250 mm; 2 cols. of 61 lines. Binding *c.* 1500. 2° fo. a magno. SCRIPT: Secretary; MS by one scribe. ILLUMINATION: incipit pages have decorated initials and borders. OWNERSHIP/PROVENANCE: inscription, 1528 (fol. 1), "Iste liber est domini Everardi Dygby militis comitatus Rutlandie. Orate pro eo et pro suis parentibus anno salutis nostre millesimo quingentesimo vicesimo octavo." COMMENTS: List of MS contents (fol. 1) and chapter lists of *DRP* and *Secretum secretorum* (fols. 3–5), and chapter numbers in *DRP* in the same hand as that of the inscription. REFERENCES: H. O. Coxe, *Catalogi Codicum Manuscriptorum Bibliothecae Bodleianae, Pars Secunda, Codices Latinos et Miscellaneos Laudianos Complectens* (Oxford, 1858–85; reprint, Oxford, 1973), cols. 468–70.

Oxford, Bodleian Library, MS Laud Misc. 652   *England, s. xiv^{ex}/xv^{in}*

CONTENTS: 1) Giles of Rome, *De regimine principum* (fols. 1–104v); 2) John Chrysostom, letter to a bishop, inc. "Novam tibi dominus dignitatem contulit. . ."; 3) brief sermons by Grosseteste, inc. "Spiritus sanctus per os salamonis beate virginis ait. . ."; 4) morals drawn from several authorities, inc. "Secundum Aristotelem sapor videtur fieri. . . ." STRUCTURE AND LAYOUT: parchment, fols. i + 222 + i; $1–8^{12}, 9^{10}, 10–14^8, 15–17^{10}, 18^8, 19^{10}, 20^{12}$, $21^{10}, 22^6$; 355 × 240 mm; 2 cols. of 52 lines. Binding, *c.* 1500. 2° fo. quoniam ut. SCRIPT: Anglicana/*textualis* blend. MS a composite volume in at least five hands, all roughly contemporary. One scribe responsible for item 1's text and marginal notes. OWNER-

SHIP/PROVENANCE: Hugh Tapton, Cambridge B.Th. by 1451, prebendary of Stoke in Rutland, died 1481. Also, inscription, 1536 (fol. 223), "Memorandum that A.E. of Stoke in the comitis of Roteland . . . the xiii day of aprill in the xxvii yere of the reygn of kyng harry the viij." COMMENTS: Exhaustive set of schematic distinctions on health and the virtues and vices (fols. 216–21v) REFERENCES: Coxe, *Catalogi*, col. 475; *BRUC*, p. 576.

Oxford, Bodleian Library, MS Laud Misc. 702   *France, s. xiv^{in}*

CONTENTS: Giles of Rome, *De regimine principum* (fols. 2–206v). STRUCTURE AND LAYOUT: parchment, fols. v + 206 + iii; 1–16^{12}, 17^{14}; 200 × 145 mm; 2 cols. of 36 lines. Binding s. xiv^{ex}. 2° fo. finis qui. SCRIPT: *textualis semi-quadrata*; one scribe. ILLUMINATION: historiated initial and inhabited three-quarter border with drolleries (fol. 2). Decorated initial and half border (fol. 2v). OWNERSHIP/PROVENANCE: inscription (fol. iv), "Hunc librum contulit dominus Henricus Percy, inclitus comes Northumbrie, fratri Willelmo de Norham confessori eiusdem domini et sacre theologie doctori, xiij die Aprilis, 1419." Henry V Lord Percy (d. 1455), to William de Norham, O.P., Oxford D.Th. (fl. s. xiv^{ex} -s. xv^1). COMMENTS: inscription, extensive marginalia, and brief desciption of contents (fol. iv) in same hand of s. xv^1. REFERENCES: Coxe, *Catalogi*, cols. 502–3; Pächt and Alexander, *Illuminated Manuscripts*, vol. III, p. 51, ill. lxi.

Oxford, Jesus College, MS 12   *Council of Constance, 1416*

CONTENTS: 1) Jacques de Cessoles, *De ludo scacchorum*; 2) alphabetical abridgment of Giles of Rome, *De regimine principum* (fols. 84–202v): Extractus secundum alphabetum de libro Egidii de Regimine principum . . . Quod pondera et mensure vendencium debite taxande sunt, vo. Concilia. K.; 3) Sermon preached by Robert Hallum on the second Sunday of Advent, 1415: inc. "Erunt signa." STRUCTURE AND LAYOUT: parchment and paper, fols. 228 (foliation in MS skips a leaf between fols. 57 and 58); 1–8^{12}, 9^{12} (–6), 10^{12} (–7), 11^{14} (–8), 12^{14} (–8), 13^{14} (–7), 14^{12} (–7), 15^{14} (–7, 14), 16^{14} (–7), 17^{14} (–8), 18^{12}, 19^{12} (–12); 210 × 155 mm; single block of 24–7 lines. Binding s. xv. 2° fo. ludus scachorum *or* inter omnia. SCRIPT: German *hybrida cursiva*, by Johannes Wydenroyde. OWNERSHIP/PROVENANCE: inscription, s. xvi^1 (fol. 2), "Codex magistri Davidis Rice in legibus baccallarii, sacellani domini regis henrici octavi, ac rectoris de llandettye." David Rice, Oxford B.C.L. Original owner a member of the English delegation at the Council (?). REFERENCES: Coxe, *Catalogus*, vol. II, p. 84; A. G. Watson, *Catalogue of Dated and Datable Manuscripts, ca. 435–1600, in Oxford Libraries*, vol. I (Oxford, 1984), p. 132; *BRUO 1501–40*, p. 10.

Oxford, Lincoln College, MS Lat. 69   *England, s. xv^1*

CONTENTS: 1–4) assorted indexes; 5) index of Giles of Rome, *De regimine principum* (fols. 132v-37v): Abstinencia . . . Zelotipus; 6–22) assorted indexes. STRUCTURE AND LAYOUT: paper, fols. 272 + ii (parchment), anvil, cloche, unicorn, and monts watermarks; 1^4, 2–4^{24}, 5^{12}, 6^{30}, 7^{28}, 8^{26}, 9–10^{34}, 11^{32}; 295 × 210 mm; single block of 48 lines (item 5). Binding s. xv.

2° fo. utrum legem. SCRIPT: Anglicana/Secretary blend; one, possibly two, scribes. REFERENCES: Coxe, *Catalogus*, vol. 1, pp. 38–9; comments of N. G. Wilson of Lincoln College and Martin Kauffmann of the Department of Western Manuscripts, Bodleian Library.

San Marino, Huntington Library, MS EL 9.H.9   *England, s. xiv²*

CONTENTS: 1) Giles of Rome, *De regimine principum* (fols. 1–97v), beginning imperfectly (//opera faciamus. Quarto etiam ipsi mores opera diversificare videntur. . .), with index (fols. 97v–103v): Avarus . . . Uncis Ferreis; 2) Nicholas Trevet, *Super quinque libros Boeicii de consolacione philosophie*; 3) anonymous treatise on metrics, inc. "Ad designandas metrorum diversitates . . ." STRUCTURE AND LAYOUT: parchment, fols. 198 + i; 1^{12} (–1, 7), 2–3^{12}, 4^{12} (–3), 5–8^{12}, 9^{12} (–11, fifth and sixth bifolia reversed), 10–16^{12}, 17^{12} (–11, 12); 345 × 245 mm; 2 cols. of 56 lines. Binding modern. 2° fo. opera faciamus. SCRIPT: *textualis*; one scribe. OWNERSHIP/PROVENANCE: House of Bonshommes at, Ashridge, at the time of the Dissolution. Inscription, s. xvii^1 (fol. 1), "liber Fra. Combe ex cenobio Ash ex dono Avunculi ibidem Abbatis Domini Thomas Waterhouse." Francis Combes, grandnephew of Thomas Waterhouse, last rector of Ashridge, who surrendered the house in 1539, after which it was leased by his nephew Richard Combes, Francis's father. REFERENCES: C. W. Dutschke, *Guide to the Medieval and Renaissance Manuscripts in the Huntington Library* (San Marino, 1989), pp. 15–17; *MLGB*, p. 5.

Vatican, Biblioteca Apostolica Vaticana, MS Ottob. lat. 1102 **   *England, s. xiv^{ex}*

CONTENTS: Giles of Rome, *De regimine principum* (fols. 1–164). STRUCTURE AND LAYOUT: Parchment, fols. 164; 1–10^8, 11^6, 12^8, 13^{10}, 14^8, $15^{(8-1)+2}$, 16–20^8, 21^{4-1}; 300–4 × 205–10 mm; 2 cols. of 43 lines. Binding modern. 2° fo. si de talibus. SCRIPT: *textualis semi-quadrata*; one scribe. ILLUMINATION: decorated initial and full border (fol. 1), and decorated initials for each part. OWNERSHIP/PROVENANCE: perhaps Cambridge; Marcello Cervini (Pope Marcellus II) by *c.* 1545. REFERENCES: Del Punta and Luna, *Catalogo*, pp. 10–13; Ker, "Cardinal Cervini's Manuscripts," p. 60.

Vatican, Biblioteca Apostolica Vaticana, MS Ottob. Lat. 1166 **   *England, s. xiv*

CONTENTS: Giles of Rome, *De regimine principum* (fols. 1–208v). STRUCTURE AND LAYOUT: Parchment, fols. 208; 1–3^{12}, 4^{16}, 5–16^{12}, 17^{12+1}; 198 × 134 mm; single block of 37 lines. Binding modern. 2° fo. si sit manifestatio. SCRIPT: *textualis rotunda*; one scribe. OWNERSHIP/PROVENANCE: perhaps Cambridge; Marcello Cervini (Pope Marcellus II) by *c.* 1545. REFERENCES: Del Punta and Luna, *Catalogo*, pp. 13–16; Ker, "Cardinal Cervini's Manuscripts," p. 60.

Vatican, Bibliotheca Apostolica Vaticana, MS Ottob. Lat. 2071 **   *England, s. xiv/xv*

CONTENTS: 1) index of Augustine, *Ennaratio Psalmorum*; 2) index of Gregory the Great,

Homilias; 3) index of Giles of Rome, *De regimine principum* (fols. 66–9v): Abstinencia . . .
Zelotipus; 4) index of Augustine, *De civitate Dei*. STRUCTURE AND LAYOUT: parchment,
fols. 85; 1–3¹², 4¹²⁺¹, 5–7¹²; 358 × 270 mm; 2 cols. of 58 lines (*DRP*). SCRIPT: highly
current Anglicana/*textualis* blend (*DRP*). MS composed of two parts, of which the second
(fols. 49–84) was executed by four English scribes, one of which was responsible for the first
three items (with the exception of one and a half columns on fol. 64). OWNER-
SHIP/PROVENANCE: pressmark "G.Q." of Cambridge Austin friars; Marcello Cervini
(Pope Marcellus II) by *c.* 1545. REFERENCES: Del Punta and Luna, *Catalogo*, pp. 305–6;
Ker, "Cardinal Cervini's Manuscripts," p. 69.

Verona, Biblioteca Capitolare, MS CCXXXIV**   *Italy; English decoration, s. xv*
CONTENTS: Giles of Rome, *De regimine principum* (fols. 7–200), with chapter list (fols.
1–6v) and index (fols. 201–17): Abhominatio . . . Zelotophia. STRUCTURE AND LAYOUT:
parchment, fols. i + 217 + i; 1⁶, 2–20¹⁰, 21⁸⁻⁴, 22¹⁰, 23⁸⁻¹; 280 × 197 mm; single block of 34
lines. Binding medieval. 2° fo. Quot sunt. SCRIPT: *textualis* with some traits of Italian bas-
tarda; scribe Petrus Lomer of Colorno. ILLUMINATION: decorated initials by English
artist at beginnings of parts. COMMENTS: the index appears to be of the *Abhominatio* type
found in several manuscripts of English origin. REFERENCES: Del Punta and Luna,
Catalogo, pp. 301–4; comments of Don Giuseppe Zivelonghi, vicedirettore of the
Biblioteca Capitolare.

York, Minster Library, MS XVI.D.5**   *England, s. xivᵉˣ/xvⁱⁿ*
CONTENTS: Giles of Rome, *De regimine principum* (fols. 1–89v), beginning imperfectly
(//decet eas esse pudicas et honestas. . .), with index (fols. 89v–95v): Abstinencia . . .
Zelotipus. STRUCTURE AND LAYOUT: parchment, fols. 96; 1–12⁸; 290 × 190 mm; 2 cols.
of 45 lines. Binding modern. 2° fo. (first several leaves missing). OWNERSHIP/
PROVENANCE: Oxford or Cambridge, s. xv¹. Erased *cauciones* (fol. 95v), "Caucio [. . .]
Anno domini MᵒCCCCxxiiij in vigilia exaltationis sancte crucis et habet supplementum
[. . .] pr xxxij s. iiij d / Caucio M. [. . .]." SCRIPT: *textualis*; one scribe. REFERENCES:
MMBL, vol. IV, p. 696.

Latin De regimine *manuscripts of French origin*

Arras, Bibl. mun. 586 (s. xiv[1])
Auxerre, Bibl. mun. 234 (s. xiv[2])
Avignon, Bibl. mun. 763 (s. xiv[2])
   764 (s. xv)
   765 (s. xv)
Bergamo, Bibl. Civica. I.32 (MA 499) (s. xiv)
Besançon, Bibl. mun. 433 (s. xiv[1])
Bologna, Bibl. del Collegio di Spagna 62 (s. xiv[in])
Cambrai, Bibl. mun. 958 (1424)
Cambridge, Univ. Libr. Fols.3.3 (s. xiv[in]) [English Group MS]
   Jesus Coll. Q.B.9 (*c.* 1372) [English Group MS]
Douai, Bibl. mun. 425 (s. xiv)
Florence, Bibl. Medicea Laurenziana S. Marco 452 (s. xiv[med])
Glasgow, Univ. Libr. Hamilton 141 (s. xv 1) [English Group MS]
Grenoble, Bibl. mun. 869 (xiv/xv)
Lille, Bibl. mun. 321 (s. xiv)
London, BL Harley 4802 (s. xiv)
Marseille, Bibl. mun. 735 (1448)
Massa Lombarda, Bibl. Communale 24 (s. xiv[1])
Metz, Bibl. mun. 273 (s. xiv)
Milan, Bibl. Ambrosiana C 84 sup. (s. xv)
   R 45 sup. (s. xiv)
Montpellier, Bibl. Interuniversitaire (Section de Médecine) H 210 (s. xiv[1])
   Bibl. mun, 9 (s. xiv)
Oxford, Bodleian Libr., Laud Misc. 702 (s. xiii/xiv) [English Group MS]
Paris, Bibl. de l'Arsenal 743 (s. xiv[2])
   744 (s. xiv[ex])
   Bibl. Mazarine 838 (s. xiii[ex])
     3494 (s. xiv[1])
   BN lat. 2191 (s. xv)
    lat. 2925 (s. xiv)
    lat. 6466 (s. xv[1])
    lat. 6475 (s. xiv[1])
    lat. 6476 (s. xiv[2])

lat. 6478 (s. xiv)
lat. 6479 (s. xv¹)
lat. 6480 (s. xv¹)
lat. 6481 (s. xv¹)
lat. 6482 (s. xv)
lat. 6695 (s. xiv^{in})
lat. 6696 (s. xiv^{in-1})
lat. 6697 (s. xv^{ex})
lat. 10208 (s. xv¹)
lat. 12431 (s. xv^{ex})
lat. 15101 (s. xiii/xiv)
lat. 15449 (s. xiii/xiv)
lat. 16123 (s. xiv^{in-1})
lat. 16124 (s. xiii^{ex})
lat. 18428 (s. xiv^{in})
lat. 18429 (s. xiv^{1-med})
n.a.l. 1912 (s. xiv¹)
Bibl. de la Sorbonne 1035 (s. xiv)
Reims, Bibl. mun. 882 (s. xiv)
883 (s. xiv²)
884 (s. xiv)
Rouen, Bibl. mun. 935 (s. xiv)
Saint-Omer, Bibl. mun. 517 (s. xiv)
Toulouse, Bibl. mun. 740 (s. xiv¹)
Tours, Bibl. mun. 764 (s. xv¹)
765 (s. xv) [destroyed in Second World War]
766 (s. xv) [destroyed in Second World War]
Troyes, Bibl. mun. 989 (1301)
1602 (s. xiv)
2137 (s. xiv)
Turin, Archivio di Stato J.a.VII.29 (s. xiv^{in})
Vatican, Bibl. Apost. Vat. Chig. B.VI.92 (s. xiv)
Pal. lat. 727 (s. xiv¹)
Ross. 523 (s. xiv^{in-1})

Origin unknown, but certainly French or Italian: Bern, Burgerbibliothek Bongars 182
(s. xiii^{ex})

APPENDIX C

Manuscripts containing French translations of De regimine

Baltimore, Walters Art Gallery W. 144 (England, s. xiv¹, probably 1320s)
Barcelona, Bibl. de D. Carlos de Aragon 43 (?, s. xiv)
Besançon, Bibl. mun. 434 (Paris, 1372)
Cambridge, Univ. Libr. Ee.2.17 (France, s. xv^in)
Chicago, Univ. of Chicago Libr. 533–v (France, s. xiv^in)
Dôle, Bibl. mun. 157 (Paris, 1282)
Durham, Univ. Libr. Cosin V.I.9 (England, s. xiv^ex)
London, BL Add. 22274 (France, s. xv/xvi)
     Egerton 811 (France, s. xv¹)
     Harley 4385 (Paris, s. xv¹)
     Roy. 15.E.vi (Rouen, 1445)
   Lambeth Palace Libr. 266 (France, s. xiv^in)
Lyons, Bibl. mun. 951/857 (France, s. xiv/xv)
Madrid, Bibl. Nacional 50 (?, s. xiv)
Modena, Bibl. Estense 43 (?, s. xv)
Mons, Stadtbibl. 103/123 (?, s. xv)
New York, Pierpont Morgan Libr. M. 122 (France, s. xiv^in)
     M. 123 (France, 1412)
Paris, Bibl. de l'Arsenal 2690 (France, s. xiv¹, probably 1330s)
     5062 (France, s. xvi^in)
   BN fr. 213 (Paris, s. xv², 3rd quarter, after 1469)
     fr. 573 (Paris, s. xv^in)
     fr. 581 (Paris, s. xv^in)
     fr. 1201 (northern France, s. xiii/xiv)
     fr. 1202 (Paris, s. xv^in)
     fr. 1203 (Italy, s. xiii^ex)
     fr. 19920 (France, probably Paris, s. xiv^in)
     fr. 24233 (Italy, s. xiii^ex)
   Bibl. Ste-Geneviève 1015 (France, s. xv)
   Institut de France 314 (France, s. xv)
Rennes, Bibl. mun. 153 (France, s. xv)
Troyes, Bibl. mun. 898 (France, s. xiv)
Turin, Bibl. Naz. 1562 (?, s. xv)
Vatican, Bibl. Apost. Vat. Ross. 457 (France, s. xiv¹)

APPENDIX D

Cambridge, Jesus College, MS Q.B.9

A manuscript conserved since 1633 in the library of Jesus College, Cambridge has a number of curious features that reveal, at least in part, an equally curious history.[1] The manuscript was produced in Paris between 1373 and September 1380 for King Charles V of France, who added it to his newly founded royal library in the Louvre.[2] Its first leaf (fol. 2) is, however, a replacement, very probably made in Paris in or just before 1423, but not illuminated until the beginning of the sixteenth century, probably also in Paris. The iconography of this half-page miniature (plate 16) is unlike that found in any other *De regimine* manuscript, and is entirely unrelated to the subject matter of the text. The scene is divided into two registers, the lower of which depicts the Virgin Mary kneeling in prayer before a book, and surrounded by a group of seventeen men (also kneeling in prayer), while the upper register, now partially erased, represents the first two Persons of the Trinity enthroned beside one another and sending down the dove of the Holy Spirit. This miniature seems to have been painted for a member of the Essex gentry family of Pert, whose coat of arms appears in the border of the opening page. Perhaps this was William Pert, gentleman of "Alrechelay," who was twice mentioned in the Close Rolls during the last quarter of the fifteenth century.[3]

The earliest surviving record of Jesus Coll. Q.B.9 appears in the catalogue of the Louvre compiled in 1411 by the keeper of the royal library, Antoine des Essarts, which describes it as

---

[1] According to a lengthy entry by Sydney Cockerell in the annotated James *Catalogue* in Jesus College Library, the book belonged to the Elizabethan poet, Edward Dyer, who may have acquired it by way of Fulke Greville or Sir Philip Sidney. Dyer gave the book to John Barker of Trinity College, Cambridge, after which it came into the possession of Francis Hughes, who presented it to Jesus College on December 17, 1633. Cockerell was the first person to identify Jesus Coll. Q.B.9 as having been a part of Charles V's library. Léopold Delisle published Cockerell's discovery in "Un manuscrit de Charles V et un double feuillet d'images de la bible retrouvés en Angleterre," *Bibliothèque de l'Ecole des Chartes* 71 (1910), p. 468.

[2] It is not recorded in the first catalogue of the library compiled by Gilles Malet in 1373, but must have entered the collection by the time of Charles V's death in September 1380.

[3] Cockerell first identified the coat of arms as belonging to the Perts. On William Pert, see above, p. 70.

16 Pentecost scene with other iconographic elements; Pert arms in lower border.
Cambridge, Jesus College, MS Q.B.9, fol. 2r

a very lovely book . . . well written in Latin in *lettres de forme* in two columns, and illuminated all along these columns with *fleurs-de-lis* of gold and blue. The second leaf begins
"nesta quam michi reputo," and the last "um quibus ex impetu." And it is signed CHARLES
at the end. It is covered in rosy silk patterned with white swans, and has a silvergilt clasp
decorated with *fleurs-de-lis*, and a silvergilt bookmark.[4]

The same description is repeated in the catalogue compiled two years later by
Garnier de Saint-Yon. Between 1413 and when the library was again catalogued, in
1423 at the request of John, duke of Bedford, who had been made regent of France
on the death of Charles VI, Jesus Coll. Q.B.9 appears to have been stolen – or at
least borrowed with no intention of its being returned – and then recovered. In the
1423 catalogue, prepared under the direction of Garnier de Saint-Yon, the compiler
repeats verbatim the description from the 1411 and 1413 catalogues, and then adds:

said book originally was just as described, and since has been recovered; but the first leaf has
been lost and the opening words of the second leaf have been scraped away with a penknife,
and the opening words now found there are made to look as though they have been there
from the beginning; and there is neither the original clasp, nor bookmark, nor binding;
and since then the first leaf has been refashioned, and the book has been re-bound in
stamped red leather. The second folio begins "hic regitur [*sic*]." ——— viii l.[5]

All of these changes are apparent upon inspection of Jesus Q.B.9. The slightly
different ruling pattern, script, and ink of the recto and verso of the opening leaf
(fol. 2) bear witness to its being a replacement, while the first ten lines of text on the
next leaf have been written over an erasure in a hand that attempts to mimic that of
the manuscript's scribe (plate 17). Indeed the likeness achieved is so close that it is
not the script itself that reveals this act of scribal legerdemain. Rather one must turn
to the physical evidence – the erasure itself, the ink's slightly more gray color, and
the fact that the ruling of these ten lines of text does not match up exactly with that
of the right-hand column. Moreover, the scribe had to cram almost two more lines
of text into this space, thus forcing him to abbreviate more heavily and to write a
slightly longer line of approximately 45 mm as opposed to the 40 mm column
width found in the remainder of the manuscript. One suspects, then, that the
volume was stolen, and that the binding, the first leaf which may well have borne a
miniature of a king looking much like Charles V, and the first several lines of the

---

[4] "Un très bel livre . . . très bien escript en latin, de lettre de forme et à deux coulombes, enluminé
tout au long des dites coulombes de fleures de lis d'or et d'asur. Comm.: *nesta quam michi reputo*. Fin.:
um quibus ex impetu. Et est signé CHARLES en la fin. Couvert d'une chemise de soie vermeille à cygnes
blancs, à ung fermoir d'argent doré hachié aux armes de France, et une pipe d'argent doré": Delisle,
Recherches, pt. 2, pp. 87–8.

[5] "Ledit livre avoit esté emblé comme l'en dit, et depuis a esté recouvré, mais le premier fueillet a esté
osté et le commancement dudit iie fo. a esté rasé au canivet, et le commencement relié est comme tout
neuf, et n'y a ne fermouers ne pipe ne couverture, et a depuis ledit premier fueillet refait, et est recou-
vert de cuir rouge emprint. Comm^t ou iie fo. 'hic regitur'———— viii l.": Douët d'Arcq (ed.),
Inventaire, p. 176.

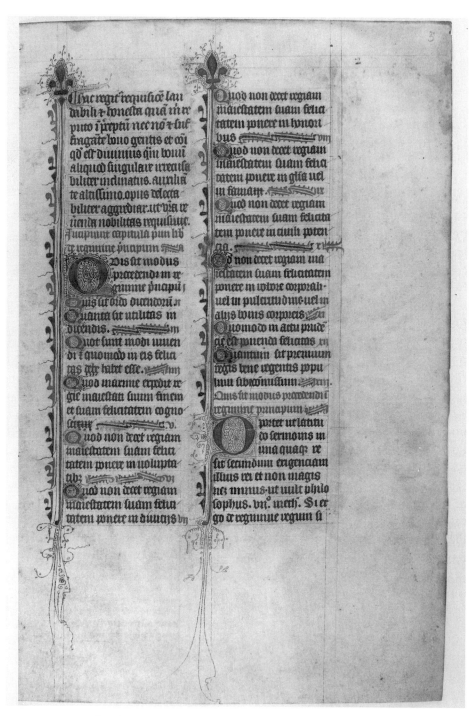

17 Erased and overwritten explicit of prologue. Cambridge, Jesus College, MS Q.B.9, fol. 3r

next leaf were removed in order to hide the evidence. And though the 1423 inventory does not support this, it could be that it was also at this time that Charles V's autograph was erased.[6]

Jesus Coll. Q.B.9 was certainly not the only manuscript taken from the royal library during the reign of Charles VI. According to Delisle, it became common practice during this time "de ne point réintégrer dans le dépôt les livres qu'on voulait lire ou consulter," and the relatives of the king participated in what amounted to "un vrai pillage" of books. In the last two or three months of 1413 alone, some fifty-five manuscripts disappeared from the library.[7] The circumstances of the Jesus College manuscript's restoration are as mysterious as those surrounding its disappearance. However this may have been effected, the book was again in the Louvre by 1423; and from the wording of the catalogue entry, it was only after its return that the new first leaf and red binding were added. Although Jesus Q.B.9 was almost certainly among the hoard of books purchased by Bedford two years later, like most of Bedford's books, it apparently was dispersed by or shortly after his death in 1435.[8] How it later came into Pert's possession can only be a matter of conjecture, though it seems likely he acquired it in France, and there had its opening page illuminated.

Assuming that Pert was responsible for commissioning the curious miniature that now graces its first page, what might have been his motivation? Perhaps as a member of that middling class that made up the bulk of England's new reading public at the end of the Middle Ages, Pert's idea of what constituted the appropriate subject matter for a book's illustration was informed by the books which he and others of his social milieu would most frequently have come across, that is books of hours. Yet one looks in vain for any one scene in books of hours or other liturgical books designed for personal use, like breviaries, for an exact parallel, for though the miniature in Jesus Coll. Q.B.9 depicts for the most part a Pentecost scene, the artist has also added iconographic elements that put one in mind of scenes associated with the feasts of All Saints, Trinity, and the Coronation of the Virgin.[9] Perhaps, then, Pert regarded his book as a kind of devotional object, despite the fact that its text was almost entirely devoid of scriptural content.

---

[6] Delisle, *Recherches*, pt. 1, p. 3, mentions ten other manuscripts that bore the king's autograph. The autograph can be found in only two of the five manuscripts, besides Jesus Coll. Q.B.9, which survive.

[7] Delisle, *Recherches*, pt. 1, pp. 131–7.

[8] Barber, "Books and Patronage," p. 313. No inventory exists of the books which Bedford purchased from the Louvre. They are mentioned only in passing in one of the three surviving inventories of the duke's personal effects: J. Stratford, *The Bedford Inventories: The Worldly Goods of John, Duke of Bedford, Regent of France (1389–1435)* (London, 1993), p. 226.

[9] My thanks to Kathleen Scott for pointing out these parallels.

Comparison of subject designators
in the Abstinencia and the Abhominacio
long recension indexes

Common subject designators	Subject designators only in *Abstinencia* index	Subject designators only in *Abhominacio* long recension
A	A	A
abstinencia	adquiritur	abhominacio
acies	altior	administracio
actiones	ars metrica	additum
adulatores	augmentatur	adulter
aer		affabilitas
affectiones		agrestis
agentibus		alleator
altitudo		alere
amare		alimenta
amicus		ancillaris
amicabilitas		animal
amicicia		animositas
amor		arbitrium
anima		archus
appetitus		aristocracia
aque		articulus
aries		artifex
arma		assuescere
ars		avis
avaricia		
avarus		
audacia		
auditum		
B	B	B
barbarus	bene	barbitonsores
belli	bestie	bifa
bellator	borialis	bomolocus
beneficium		

The *Abstinencia* and *Abhominacio* long recension indexes

Common subject designators	Subject designators only in *Abstinencia* index	Subject designators only in *Abhominacio* long recension
B	B	B
bestialis		
bonitas		
bonum		
C	C	C
calidi	caput	calx
castrum	cardinales	caro
cautele	castitas	cassa
cibum	cecus	cataracta
cives	circumdare	caymus
civilis	coitu	cerebrum
civitas	cogitare	creditivus
clemencia	cognoscitur	crines
commune	congregacio	commutacio
communitas	contemplativi	connubium
cummunicacio	contrariatur	conservacio
concupiscencia	cor	constructio
concupiscibilia	credendi	conversari
coniugium	cupiditas	conversando
consilium	custodia	contemptus
consuetudo		contumeliosus
continens		corpus
cunniculus		corriguntur
curia		coronari
curialitas		cura
cursus		
D	D	D
defensio	dare	decanus
delectacio	dantis	delinquens
denarius	debilitas	democracia
deus	decipitur	demos
diliget	defectus	desperacio
delectio	desiderium	Dyonisius
divicie	dialectica	dispocicio
divitum	dignitas	docilis
doctor	dirigentibus	dominium
docendus	diversitas	
doctrine	dona	
dolor	dormienti	
dominari	ductores	
dominus	dux	
domus		

Common subject designators	Subject designators only in *Abstinencia* index	Subject designators only in *Abhominacio* long recension
E	E	E
ebrietas	equalitas	effici
edificacioni	equus	egenum
eligere	erubescencia	elacio
estas	esse	elatus
evangelica	etatum	emendacio
exercicium	expense	emere
	experimentum	empcio
	experiencia	epieikes
	exploratores	eroica
	extrema	ebula
		eutrapelia
		excercitacio
F	F	F
fama	fatigacio	facere
fames	flumen	familiaritas
felicitas	fons	familiarem
felix	forisfacere	ferrum
femina	furtum	filum
fides		forma
fidelitas		furor
filia		futura
filiorum		
finis		
fornicacio		
fortis		
fortitudo		
fortunam		
fossa		
frigus		
fugere		
funda		
G	G	G
generacio	geometria	galea
gratia	gloria	gentes
gubernans	gramatica	gentiles
gubernaculum		gesta
gula		gradus
		gustus

Common subject designators	Subject designators only in *Abstinencia* index	Subject designators only in *Abhominacio* long recension
H	H	H
homo	habere	Helena
homore	hereditarie	histrio
hostes	hereditas	
humilitas	habitacio	
	hyemps	
I	I	I
incontinens	imperfectum	iactatores
intemperancia	industris	ignis
invidia	inferiora	illiberales
ira	imparitas	illiberalitas
irascibilis	insidie	inconsuetum
iudicium	intellectus	incredulus
iudex		inimicicia
iusticia		iniuria
iustus		iniusticia
ius		insensibilis
iuvenum		insensibilitas
		intencio
		inverecundus
		iocundus
		iocus
		irracionale
		iuventus
L	L	L
laus	labor	lancea
laudibile	lac	lapidarium
legiste	largitas	latitivus
lex	Latinum	Latomenses
liberalitas	lectio	lator legis
lingua	lepra	lignum
loquaces	lesio	litigium
loqui	libertas	lupus
lucrandi	lis	
ludus	litteras	
	locus	
	luxuria	
M	M	M
machinarum	magna	manus
magister	maior	mappa
magnanimitas	maculorum	mendacium

Common subject designators	Subject designators only in *Abstinencia* index	Subject designators only in *Abhominacio* long recension
M	M	M
magnificencia	matres	mens
malus	membra	mensurare
mansuetudo	memoria	milum
medium	methaphisicam	miserativus
mense		mititas
mercatores		monopolia
mercenarius		multitudo
milicia		musculos
ministrancium		
misericordiam		
mollis		
morale		
mores		
mors		
motus		
mulierum		
municiones		
muri		
musica		
mutacio		
N	N	N
natare	narracio	nemesis
natura	nascuntur	nupciale
naturalia		nutrimentum
navale		
navis		
nobilium		
noticia		
nummisma		
O	O	O
obediencia	obliviscenda	observatum
obedire	ocium	ociosum
obsidio	officum	oligarchia
oculi	officiales	opinio
odium	oportunitas	oppugnacio
operaciones		
ordo		
organa		
ornatus		

The *Abstinencia* and *Abhominacio* long recension indexes

Common subject designators	Subject designators only in *Abstinencia* index	Subject designators only in *Abhominacio* long recension
P	P	P
paciencia	parcere	parvificencia/parvificus
passiones	parentibus	passus
pater	paterfamilias	paucitas
pauper	particularia	pensio
pax	pericula	persona
peccatum	philosophia	persuadens
pecuniam	pigricia	placere
percussionum	pisces	placidus
perfectum	pluralitas	positivum
permittere	pluvialis	posterius
perseverancia	pondus	potus
plorare	porta	puella
policia	portarium	presumptuosus
populi	portanda	pretorium
possessio	pontus	procedere
potencie	percipere	proventus
princeps	preceptum	
prodigalitas	premiare	
prohibere	premium	
prudencia	proprias	
puer	providencia	
pugne	pulchritudo	
punire		
pudor		
R	R	R
racio	regiones	rector
racionale	racio regendi	recordari
regere	regula	
regimen	rethorica	
regni	rurales	
rex		
rigor		
S	S	S
sagitta	salvacio	sal
saltare	sanitas	sapienciam
sanguinis	saturari	sapo
sapiens	seipsum	Sardanapallus
scientibus	sensualitas	sedicio
sciencia	sensus	septennium
secreta	separari	severitas
senum	similis	sinesis

Appendix E

Common subject designators	Subject designators only in *Abstinencia* index	Subject designators only in *Abhominacio* long recension
S (*cont.*)	S (*cont.*)	S (*cont.*)
sermonis	solitudo	situs
servus	solitaria	sobrietas
signa	speculari	sobrius
silencium	spes	societas/sociis
stare	sterilitas	superbia
studio	superati	suspiciosus
subici	superiora	statu
sufficiencia	sustinere	studiosus
T	T	T
tacere		tabula
temperancia		tactus
tempus		telum
theologia		trabes
timor		tranquillitas
timidus		trabucium
tirannus		transgressio
tristicia		
turris		
V	V	V
vendencium	valle	vas
ventus	vini	velum
verba	universalis	vertibilis
verecundia	volutum	victus
veritatem		vinea
vestimentorum		virga
vexillum		voluntas
vexillifer		uncus
via		unicus
vicus		
victoria		
vir		
virtus		
visioni		
vita		
una		
unitas		
voluptas		
usura		
uti		
uxor		

The *Abstinencia* and *Abhominacio* long recension indexes

Common subject designators	Subject designators only in *Abstinencia* index	Subject designators only in *Abhominacio* long recension
X/Z		
xelotipus/zelotipus		
zelus		
TOTAL=239	TOTAL=138	TOTAL=173

Bibliography

PRIMARY SOURCES

Anstey, H., ed. *Munimenta Academica, or Documents Illustrative of the Academical Life and Studies at Oxford.* Vol. II. Rolls Series. London, 1868.

Aquinas, Thomas. *In octo libros Politicorum Aristotelis expositio.* Edited by R. M. Spiazzi. Turin and Rome, 1966.

    On Kingship to the King of Cyprus. Translated and edited by G. B. Phelan and I. T. Eschmann. Toronto, 1949; reprint, 1982.

Auweele, D. Van den. "Un abrégé flamand du 'De regimine principum' de Gilles de Rome." In *"Sapientiae Doctrina": Mélanges de théologie et de littérature médiévales offerts à Dom Hildebrand Bascour O.S.B.*, ed. R. Hissette, G. Michiels, and D. Van den Auweele, pp. 327–58. Louvain, 1980.

Beauvoir, H. de, ed. *La librairie de Jean de Berry au Chateau de Mehun-sur-Yevre, 1416.* Paris, 1860.

Bell, D. N. *The Libraries of the Cistercians, Gilbertines and Premonstratensians.* Corpus of British Medieval Library Catalogues 3. London, 1992.

Bouvet, Honoré de. *The Tree of Battles of Honoré de Bonet.* Edited by G. W. Coopland. Liverpool, 1949.

Botfield, B., ed. *Catalogi veteres librorum ecclesiae cathedralis Dunelm.* Surtees Society, vol. VII (1838).

Bradshaw, H. "Two Lists of Books in the University Library." Chapter in *Collected Papers.* Cambridge, 1889.

Bury, Richard de. *The Philobiblon.* Translated by Archer Taylor. Berkeley, 1948.

Calendar of the Close Rolls Preserved in the Public Record Office. London.

Calendar of the Patent Rolls Preserved in the Public Record Office. London.

Capgrave, John. *The Chronicle of England.* Edited by F.-C. Hingeston. Rolls Series. London, 1858.

Cheney, C. R. "A Register of MSS Borrowed from a College Library, 1440–1517." *Transactions of the Cambridge Bibliographical Society* 9 (1987), pp. 103–29.

Christine de Pizan. *The Book of the Body Politic.* Translated by K. L. Forhan. Cambridge, 1994.

Corazzini, F., ed. *Del Reggimento de' principi di Egidio Romano, volgarizzamento trascritto nel MCCLXXXVIII.* Florence, 1858.

Denifle, H. and A. Chatelain. *Chartularium Universitatis Parisiensis*. Vol. 11 Paris, 1891; reprint, Brussels, 1964.

Dillon, H. A. and W. H. St. John Hope. "Inventory of the Goods and Chattels Belonging to Thomas, Duke of Gloucester." *Archaeological Review* 54 (1897), pp. 275–308.

Douët d'Arcq, L., ed. *Inventaire de la bibliothèque du roi Charles VI fait au Louvre en 1423 par ordre du Régent duc de Bedford.* Paris, 1867.

  ed. *Nouveau recueil de comptes de l'argenterie.* Paris, 1874.

Dugdale, W. *Monasticon Anglicanum.* Vol. 11. Edited by J. Caley, H. Ellis, and B. Bandinel. London, 1846.

Fehrenbach, R. J. and E. S. Leedham-Green, eds. *Private Libraries in Renaissance England: A Collection and Catalogue of Tudor and Early Stuart Book-Lists.* 4 vols. Binghampton, N.Y., 1992–95.

Fletcher, J. M., ed. *The Liber Taxatorum of Poor Students at the University of Freiburg im Breisgau.* Notre Dame, Ind., 1969.

Fortescue, Sir John. *The Governance of England.* Edited by C. Plummer. Oxford, 1885.

Fraijs de Veubeke, A.-C. "Un catalogue des manuscrits de la collégiale Saint-Paul, Liège au milieu du XVᶜ siècle." *Revue d'histoire des textes* 4 (1974), pp. 359–424.

Genet, J.-Ph., ed. *Four English Political Tracts of the Later Middle Ages.* Camden Fourth Series 18 (1977).

Giles of Rome. *D. Aegidii Romani, Archiepiscopi Biturcensis, Ordinis Fratrum Eremitarum Sancti Augustini, De regimine principum Libri III.* Rome, 1556.

Hingeston-Randolph, F. C., ed. *The Register of Walter de Stapeldon, Bishop of Exeter (A.D. 1307–1326).* London, 1892.

Hoccleve, Thomas. *Hoccleve's Works, The Regement of Princes.* Edited by F. J. Furnivall. EETS, extra ser., 72 (1897).

Horstmann, C., ed. *Osbert Bockenhams Legenden.* Heilbronn, 1883.

Humphreys, K. W. *The Friars' Libraries.* Corpus of British Medieval Library Catalogues 1. London, 1990.

James, M. R. *The Ancient Libraries of Canterbury and Dover.* Cambridge, 1903.

  "The Catalogue of the Library of the Augustinian Friars at York." In *Fasciculus Ioanni Willis Clark Dicatus*, pp. 2–96. Cambridge, 1909.

James, M. R. ed. *The Treatise of Walter de Milemete De Nobilitatibus, Sapientiis, et Prudentiis Regum.* Oxford: Roxburghe Club, 1913.

Ker, N. R. *Records of All Souls College Library, 1437–1600.* Oxford Bibliographical Society Publications, new ser., 16 (1971).

Leedham-Green, E. S. *Books in Cambridge Inventories: Book-Lists from Vice-Chancellor's Court Probate Inventories in the Tudor and Stuart Periods.* 2 vols. Cambridge, 1986.

Lester, G. A., ed. *The Earliest English Translation of Vegetius' "De re militari."* Heidelberg, 1988.

Mante, A., ed. "Aegidius Romanus: De regimine principum." [Middle Low German translation of Johann von Brakel.] Ph.D. dissertation, Lund, 1929.

Manzalaoui, M. A., ed. *Secretum Secretorum: Nine English Versions.* Vol. 1. EETS, orig. ser. 276 (1977).

McMahon, J. V., ed. "Das Puech von der Ordnung der Fuersten: A Critical Text-Edition of Book I of the MHG Version of the De regimine principum of Aegidius Romanus." Ph.D. dissertation, University of Texas at Austin, 1967.

Menzel, M., ed. *Die "Katharina divina" des Johann von Vippach: Ein Fürstenspiegel des 14. Jahrhunderts.* Cologne and Vienna, 1989.

Molenaer, S. P., ed. *Li Livres du Gouvernement des Rois: A XIIIth Century French Version of Egidio Colonna's Treatise De regimine principum.* New York and London, 1899.

Müller, H., ed. "Aegidii Romani de regimine Principum libri III, abbreviati per M. Leoninum de Padua." *Zeitschrift für die gesamte Staatswissenschaft* 36 (1880), pp. 96–114, 568–78, 673–749.

Nicolas, N. H., ed. *Privy Purse Expenses of Elizabeth of York: Wardrobe Accounts of Edward the Fourth.* London, 1830.

———, ed. *Testamenta Vetusta.* Vol. 1. London, 1826.

Palgrave, F., ed. *The Antient Kalendars and Inventories of the Treasury of His Majesty's Exchequer.* Vol. 1. London, 1836.

Pantin, W. A., ed. *Documents Illustrating the Activities of the General and Provincial Chapters of the English Black Monks, 1215–1540.* Vol. II of 3. Camden Third Series 47 (1933).

Perez, J. B., ed. *Glosa Castellana al "Regimiento de Príncipes" de Egidio Romano.* 3 vols. Madrid, 1947.

Ross, W. O., ed. *Middle English Sermons Edited from British Museum MS. Royal 18.B.XXIII.* EETS, orig. ser. 209 (1960).

Rud, T. *Codicum Manuscriptorum Ecclesiae Cathedralis Dunelmensis Catalogus Classicus.* Durham, 1825.

Scattergood, V. J. "Two Medieval Book Lists." *The Library,* 5th ser., 23 (1968), pp. 236–9.

Seymour, M. C. *et al.,* eds. *On the Properties of Things: John Trevisa's Translation of Bartholomeus Anglicus, De Proprietatibus Rerum.* Vol. III. Oxford, 1988.

Sharpe, R., J. P. Carley, R. M. Thomson, and A. G. Watson. *English Benedictine Libraries: The Shorter Catalogues.* Corpus of British Medieval Library Catalogues 4. London, 1996.

Störmer, U., ed. "Der ostmitteldeutsche Traktat *Welch Furste Sich vnde syne Erbin wil in synem Furstethum festin* nach Aegidius Romanus, *De regimine principum.*" In *Zwei ostmitteldeutsche Bearbeitungen lateinischer Prosadenkmäler.* Berlin, 1990.

Stratford, J. *The Bedford Inventories: The Worldly Goods of John, Duke of Bedford, Regent of France (1389–1435).* London, 1993.

Taylor, F. and J. S. Roskell, eds. and trans. *Gesta Henrici Quinti: The Deeds of Henry the Fifth.* Oxford, 1975.

Thorndyke, L., ed. and trans. *University Records and Life in the Middle Ages.* New York, 1972.

Tille, A., ed. "Aegidius Romanus: De regimine principum" [Fragment of lower Rhenish German translation]. *Zeitschrift für die gesamte Staatswissenschaft* 57 (1901), pp. 484–96.

Trevisa, John. *The Governance of Kings and Princes: John Trevisa's Middle English Translation of the "De regimine principum" of Aegidius Romanus.* Edited by D. C. Fowler, C. F. Briggs, and P. G. Remley. New York, 1997.

Walcott, M. E. C. "Medieval Libraries." *Transactions of the Royal Society of Literature,* 2nd ser., 9 (1870), pp. 68–86.

Weiss, R. "The Earliest Catalogues of the Library of Lincoln College." *Bodleian Quarterly Record* 8 (1937), pp. 343–59.

Bibliography

CATALOGUES OF MANUSCRIPTS

Bannister, A. T. *A Descriptive Catalogue of the Manuscripts in the Hereford Cathedral Library.* Hereford, 1927.

Borland, C. R. *A Descriptive Catalogue of the Western Medieval Manuscripts in the Edinburgh University Library.* Edinburgh, 1916.

Catalogue général des manuscrits des bibliothèques publiques de France: Départements. 43 vols. Paris, 1885–1904.

Catalogue of Manuscripts in the British Museum, the Arundel Manuscripts. London, 1834.

Catalogue of Manuscripts Preserved in the Library of the University of Cambridge. Vols. I-III. 1856–58.

Coxe, H. O. *Catalogi Codicum Manuscriptorum Bibliothecae Bodleianae, Pars Secunda, Codices Latinos et Miscellaneos Laudianos Complectens.* Oxford, 1858–85; reprint with corrections, additions, and a historical introduction by R. W. Hunt, Oxford, 1973.

   Catalogus Codicum MSS, Qui in Collegiis Aulisque Oxoniensibus Hodie Adservantur. 2 vols. Oxford, 1852.

Del Punta, F. and C. Luna. *Aegidii Romani Opera Omnia: I.1/II, Catalogo dei manoscritti (1001–1075) "De regimine principum": Città del Vaticano – Italia.* Florence, 1993.

De Ricci, S. and W. J. Wilson. *Census of Medieval and Renaissance Manuscripts in the United States and Canada.* 3 vols. New York, 1935–40.

James, M. R. *A Descriptive Catalogue of the Manuscripts in the Library of Corpus Christi College, Cambridge.* Cambridge, 1912.

   A Descriptive Catalogue of the Manuscripts in the Library of Gonville and Caius College, Cambridge. 2 vols. Cambridge, 1907–8.

   A Descriptive Catalogue of the Manuscripts in the Library of Jesus College, Cambridge. Cambridge, 1895.

   A Descriptive Catalogue of the Manuscripts in the Library of Lambeth Palace: The Medieval Manuscripts. Cambridge, 1930–32.

   A Descriptive Catalogue of the Manuscripts in the Library of Pembroke College, Cambridge. Cambridge, 1905.

   A Descriptive Catalogue of the Manuscripts in the Library of Peterhouse. Cambridge, 1899.

   A Descriptive Catalogue of the Manuscripts in the Library of St. John's College, Cambridge. Cambridge, 1913.

   A Descriptive Catalogue of the Manuscripts in the Library of Trinity College, Cambridge. Vol. I. Cambridge, 1900.

   A Descriptive Catalogue of the Manuscripts other than Oriental in the Library of King's College, Cambridge. Cambridge, 1895.

Ker, N. R. and A. J. Piper. *Medieval Manuscripts in British Libraries.* 4 vols. Oxford, 1969–92.

Mynors, R. A. B. *Catalogue of the Manuscripts of Balliol College, Oxford.* Oxford, 1963.

Mynors, R. A. B. and R. M. Thomson. *Catalogue of the Manuscripts of Hereford Cathedral Library.* Cambridge, 1993.

Schullian, D. M. and F. E. Sommer. *A Catalogue of Incunabula and Manuscripts in the Army Medical Library.* New York, 1948.

Summary Catalogue of Western Manuscripts in the Bodleian Library at Oxford. Vol. II. Oxford, 1922.

Bibliography

Warner, G. F. and J. P. Gilson. *Catalogue of the Old Royal and King's Collection in the British Museum.* 4 vols. London, 1921.

Watson, A. G. *Catalogue of Dated and Datable Manuscripts, ca. 435–1600, in Oxford Libraries.* Vol. I. Oxford, 1984.

Wislocki, W. *Catalogus Codicum Manuscriptorum Bibliothecae Universitatis Jagellonicae Cracovensis.* Crakow, 1877–81.

Woodruff, C. E. *A Catalogue of the Manuscript Books in the Library of Christ-Church, Canterbury.* Canterbury, 1911.

SECONDARY SOURCES

Alexander, J. J. G. *Medieval Illuminators and Their Methods of Work.* New Haven, 1992.
  "Painting and Manuscript Illumination for Royal Patrons in the Later Middle Ages." In *English Court Culture in the Later Middle Ages,* ed. V. J. Scattergood and J. W. Sherborne, pp. 141–62. London, 1983.

Allmand, C. T. *Henry V.* Berkeley, 1992.

Avril, F. and M.-Th. Gousset. *Manuscrits enluminés d'origine italienne.* Vol. II. Paris, 1984.

Backhouse, J. "Founders of the Royal Library: Edward IV and Henry VII as Collectors of Illuminated Manuscripts." In *England in the Fifteenth Century,* ed. D. Williams, pp. 23–41. Woodbridge, Suffolk, 1986.

Barber, M. J. "The Books and Patronage of Learning of a Fifteenth-Century Prince." *The Book Collector* 12 (1963), pp. 308–15.

Bell, D. M. *L'Idéal éthique de la royauté en France au Moyen Age.* Geneva and Paris, 1962.

Bennett, H. S. *English Books and Their Readers, 1475 to 1557.* 2nd edn. Cambridge, 1969.

Berges, W. *Die Fürstenspiegel des hohen und späten Mittelalters.* Leipzig, 1938.

Bornstein, D. "Military Manuals in Fifteenth-Century England." *Mediaeval Studies* 37 (1975), pp. 469–77.
  Mirrors of Courtesy. New York, 1975.

Bozzolo, C. and E. Ornato. *Pour une histoire du livre manuscrit au Moyen Age.* Paris, 1983.

Bremond, C., J. Le Goff, and J.-C. Schmitt. *L'"Exemplum".* Typologie des sources du Moyen Age occidental, Fasc. 40. Turnhout, 1982.

Briggs, C. F. "Late Medieval Texts and *Tabulae*: The Case of Giles of Rome, *De regimine principum.*" *Manuscripta* 37 (1993), pp. 253–75.
  "Manuscripts of Giles of Rome's *De regimine principum* in England, 1300–1500: A Handlist." *Scriptorium* 47 (1993), pp. 60–73.
  "MS Digby 233: and the Patronage of John Trevisa's, *De regimine principum.*" *English Manuscript Studies, 1100–1700* (1998). Forthcoming.

Briquet, C. M. *Les filigranes: Dictionnaire historique des marques du papier.* 2nd edn. Leipzig, 1923; reprint, New York, 1977.

Brown, E. A. R. "Persona et Gesta: The Image and Deeds of the Thirteenth-Century Capetians: The Case of Philip the Fair." *Viator* 19 (1988), pp. 219–46.

Brown, M. P. *A Guide to Western Historical Scripts from Antiquity to 1600.* Toronto, 1990.

Bruni, G. "Il *De regimine principum* di Egidio Romano." *Aevum* 6 (1932), pp. 339–70.
  Le opere di Egidio Romano. Florence, 1936.

Burnett, C. "[Give Him the White Cow:] Notes and Note-Taking in the Universities in the Twelfth and Thirteenth Centuries." *History of the Universities.* Forthcoming.

Burns, J. H., ed. *The Cambridge History of Medieval Political Thought: c. 350–c. 1450.* Cambridge, 1988.

Carley, J. P. "John Leland and the Contents of English Pre-Dissolution Libraries: Lincolnshire." *Transactions of the Cambridge Bibliographical Society* 9 (1989), pp. 330–57.

Carruthers, M. *The Book of Memory: A Study of Memory in Medieval Culture.* Cambridge, 1990.

Catto, J. I. and R. Evans, eds. *The History of the University of Oxford.* Vol. II. Oxford, 1992.

Cavanaugh, S. H. "Royal Books: King John to Richard II." *The Library,* 5th ser., 10 (1988), pp. 304–16.

    "A Study of Books Privately Owned in England, 1300–1450." Ph.D. dissertation, University of Pennsylvania, 1980.

Christianson, C. P. *A Directory of London Stationers and Book Artisans, 1300–1500.* New York, 1990.

Cokayne, G. E. *The Complete Peerage.* Revised and edited by Vicary Gibbs. 12 vols. London, 1910–59.

Coleman, Janet. "Some Relations between the Study of Aristotle's *Rhetoric, Ethics* and *Politics* in Late 13th- and Early 14th-Century Arts Courses and the Justification of Contemporary Civic Activities (Italy and France)." Forthcoming.

Coleman, Joyce. *Public Reading and the Reading Public in Late Medieval England and France.* Cambridge, 1996.

Contamine, P. *War in the Middle Ages.* Translated by M. Jones. Oxford, 1984.

Courdaveaux, V. *Aegidii Romani de Regimine Principum Doctrina.* Paris, 1857.

Courtenay, W. J. *Schools and Scholars in Fourteenth-Century England.* Princeton, 1987.

Crowder, C. M. D. "Constance Acta in English Libraries." In *Das Konzil von Konstanz: Beiträge zu seiner Geschichte und Theologie,* ed. A. Franzen and W. Müller, pp. 477–517. Freiburg, 1964.

Delisle, L. *Recherches sur la librairie de Charles V.* Paris, 1907.

    "Un manuscrit de Charles V et un double feuillet d'images de la bible retrouvés en Angleterre." *Bibliothèque de l'Ecole des Chartes* 71 (1910), pp. 468–9.

Dembowski, P. F. "Learned Latin Treatises in French: Inspiration, Plagiarism, and Translation." *Viator* 17 (1986), pp. 255–69.

Denholm-Young, N. "Richard de Bury." *Transactions of the Royal Historical Society,* 4th ser., 20 (1937), pp. 135–63.

Destrez, J. *La pecia dans les manuscrits universitaires du XIIIᵉ et XIVᵉ siècle.* Paris, 1935.

Dictionary of National Biography. Oxford: Oxford University Press, 1917–.

Dizionario biografico degli italiani. Vols. VI and XLII. Rome, 1964.

Dobson, R. B. *Durham Priory, 1400–1450.* Cambridge, 1973.

Doyle, A. I. "English Books In and Out of Court from Edward III to Henry VII." In *English Court Culture in the Later Middle Ages,* ed. V. J. Scattergood and J. W. Sherborne, pp. 163–81. London, 1983.

Duby, G. *The Three Orders: Feudal Society Imagined.* Translated by A. Goldhammer. Chicago, 1980.

Dutschke, C. W. *Guide to the Medieval and Renaissance Manuscripts in the Huntington Library.* San Marino, 1989.

Eastman, J. R. "Relating Martin Luther to Giles of Rome: How to Proceed!" *Medieval Perspectives* 8 (1993), pp. 41–52.

Edmunds, S. "From Schoeffer to Vérard: Concerning the Scribes Who Became Printers." In *Printing the Written Word: The Social History of Books, circa 1450–1520*, ed. S. L. Hindman, pp. 21–40. Ithaca, 1991.

Edwards, A. S. G. "John Trevisa." In *Middle English Prose: A Critical Guide to Major Authors and Genres*, ed. A. S. G. Edwards, pp. 133–46. New Brunswick, N.J., 1984.

Edwards, K. "Bishops and Learning in the Reign of Edward II." *Church Quarterly Review* 138 (1944), pp. 57–86.

Emden, A. B. *A Biographical Register of the University of Cambridge to 1500*. Cambridge, 1963.
  A Biographical Register of the University of Oxford, A.D. 1501–1540. Oxford, 1974.
  A Biographical Register of the University of Oxford to 1500. 3 vols. Oxford, 1957–59.
  A Biographical Register of the University of Oxford, Appendix. Oxford.

Febvre, L. and H.-J. Martin. *The Coming of the Book: The Impact of Printing, 1450–1800*. Translated by D. Gerard. London and New York, 1990.

Ferguson, A. B. *The Indian Summer of English Chivalry*. Durham, N.C., 1960.

Fletcher, J. M. "Developments in the Faculty of Arts." In *The History of the University of Oxford*, vol. 11, ed. J. I. Catto and R. Evans, pp. 315–45. Oxford, 1992.

Flüeler, C. *Rezeption und Interpretation der aristotelischen "Politica" im späten Mittelalter*. 2 vols. Amsterdam and Philadelphia, 1992.

Fowler, D. C. "John Trevisa and the English Bible." *Modern Philology* 58 (1960), pp. 81–98.
  The Life and Times of John Trevisa, Medieval Scholar. Seattle, 1995.

Fristedt, S. L. *The Wycliffe Bible: Part III*. Stockholm, 1973.

Garand, M.-C. "Les copistes de Jean Budé (1430–1502)." *Bulletin de l'Institut de Recherche et d'Histoire des Textes* 15 (1967–68), pp. 293–332.

Genet, J.-Ph. "Les auteurs politiques et leur maniement des sources en Angleterre à la fin du Moyen Age." In *Pratiques de la culture écrite en France au XVe siècle*, ed. M. Ornato and N. Pons, pp. 345–59. Louvain-la-Neuve, 1995.
  "Ecclesiastics and Political Theory in Late Medieval England: The End of a Monopoly." In *Church, Politics and Patronage in the Fifteenth Century*, ed. R. B. Dobson, pp. 23–44. New York, 1984.
  "La théorie politique en Angleterre au XIVe siècle: sa diffusion, son public." In *Das Publikum politischer Theorie im 14. Jahrhundert*, ed. J. Miethke, pp. 269–91. Munich, 1992.

Gilbert, A. H. "Notes on the Influence of the *Secretum Secretorum*." *Speculum* 3 (1928), pp. 84–98.

Glenisson, J., ed. *Le livre au Moyen Age*. Paris, 1988.

Grabmann, M. *Methoden und Hilfsmittel des Aristotelesstudiums im Mittelalter*. Sitzungsberichte der Bayerischen Akademie der Wissenschaft, Philosophisch-Historische Abteilung, Heft v. Munich, 1939.

Green, D. H. *Medieval Listening and Reading: The Primary Reception of German Literature, 800–1300*. Cambridge, 1994.

Green, R. F. "King Richard II's Books Revisited." *The Library*, 5th ser., 31 (1976), pp. 235–9.
  Poets and Princepleasers: Literature and the English Court in the Late Middle Ages. Toronto, 1980.

Griffiths, J. and D. Pearsall, eds. *Book Production and Publishing in Britain, 1375–1475*. Cambridge, 1989.

Griffiths, R. *The Reign of Henry VI: The Exercise of Royal Authority, 1422–1461.* London, 1981.

Guenée, B. *Histoire et culture historique dans l'Occident médiéval.* Paris, 1980.

Gwynn, A. *The English Austin Friars in the Time of Wyclif.* London, 1940.

Hamesse, J. "Les florilèges philosophiques, instruments de travail des intellectuels à la fin du Moyen Age et à la Renaissance." In *Filosofia e teologia nel Trecento: Studi in ricordo di Eugenio Randi,* ed. L. Bianchi, pp. 479–508. Louvain-la-Neuve, 1994.

Hanna, R. III. "Sir Thomas Berkeley and His Patronage." *Speculum* 64 (1989), pp. 878–916.

Harris, K. "Patrons, Buyers and Owners: The Evidence for Ownership and the Role of Book Owners in Book Production and the Book Trade." In *Book Production and Publishing in Britain, 1375–1475,* ed. J. Griffiths and D. Pearsall, pp. 163–99. Cambridge, 1989.

Harriss, G. L. *Henry V: The Practice of Kingship.* Oxford, 1985.

Harvey, B. "The Monks of Westminster and the University of Oxford." In *The Reign of Richard II: Essays in Honour of May McKisack,* ed. F. R. H. Du Boulay and C. M. Barron, pp. 108–30. London, 1971.

Hellinga, L. "Importation of Books Printed on the Continent into England and Scotland before *c.* 1520." In *Printing the Written Word: The Social History of Books, circa 1450–1520,* ed. S. L. Hindman, pp. 205–24. Ithaca, 1991.

Hindman, S. L., ed. *Printing the Written Word: The Social History of Books, circa 1450–1520.* Ithaca, 1991.

Hudson, A. *The Premature Reformation: Wycliffite Texts and Lollard History.* Oxford, 1988.

Hunt, T. *Teaching and Learning Latin in Thirteenth-Century England.* 3 vols. Cambridge, 1991.

Illich, I. *In the Vineyard of the Text: A Commentary to Hugh's "Didascalicon."* Chicago, 1993.

Ivy, G. S. "The Bibliography of the Manuscript-Book." In *The English Library before 1700,* ed. F. Wormald and C. E. Wright, pp. 32–65. London, 1958.

Jacob, E. F. "Some English Documents of the Conciliar Movement." *Bulletin of the John Rylands Library* 15 (1931), pp. 358–94.

James, M. R. "The Manuscripts of St. George's Chapel, Windsor." *The Library,* 4th ser., 13 (1932), pp. 55–76.

Jones, R. H. *The Royal Policy of Richard II: Absolutism in the Later Middle Ages.* Oxford, 1968.

Keen, M. H. *Chivalry.* New Haven, 1984.

Ker, N. R. "Cardinal Cervini's Manuscripts from the Cambridge Friars." In *Xenia Medii Aevi Historiam Illustrantia Oblata Thomae Kaeppeli, O.P.,* ed. R. Creytens and P. Künzle, pp. 51–71. Rome, 1978.

Medieval Libraries of Great Britain. 2nd edn. London, 1964.

"Medieval Manuscripts from Norwich Cathedral Priory." *Transactions of the Cambridge Bibliographical Society* 1 (1949), pp. 1–28.

"The Migration of Manuscripts from the English Medieval Libraries." *The Library,* 4th ser., 23 (1942–3), pp. 1–11.

"Oxford College Libraries before 1500." In *The Universities in the Late Middle Ages,* ed. J. Ijsewijn and J. Paquet, pp. 293–311. Mediaevalia Lovaniensia, ser. 1, studia 6 (1973).

"Oxford College Libraries in the Sixteenth Century." *Bodleian Library Record* 6 (1957–61).

"Sir John Prise." *The Library,* 5th ser., 10 (1955), pp. 1–24.

Knowles, D. *The Religious Orders in England.* Vol. 1. Cambridge, 1948.

Kretzmann, N., A. Kenny, and J. Pinborg, eds. *The Cambridge History of Later Medieval Philosophy.* Cambridge, 1982.

Krynen, J. "Aristotélisme et réforme de l'État en France, au XIVe siècle." In *Das Publikum politischer Theorie im 14. Jahrhundert*, ed. J. Miethke, pp. 225–36. Munich, 1992.

Lagarde, G. de. *La naissance de l'esprit laïque au déclin du Moyen Age*. Vol. II. Louvain and Paris, 1958.

Lajard, F. "Gilles de Rome." In *Histoire littéraire de la France*, vol. XXX, pp. 421–566. Paris, 1888.

Lambertini, R. "A proposito della 'costruzione' dell'*Oeconomica* in Egidio Romano." *Medioevo* 14 (1988), pp. 315–70.

"Il filosofo, il principe e la virtù. Note sulla recezione e l'uso dell'*Etica Nicomachea* nel *De regimine principum* di Egidio Romano." *Documenti e studi sulla tradizione filosofica medievale* 2 (1991), pp. 239–79.

"'Philosophus videtur tangere tres rationes.' Egidio Romano lettore ed interprete della *Politica* nel terzo libro del *De regimine principum*." *Documenti e studi sulla tradizione filosofica medievale* 1 (1990), pp. 277–325.

Lawler, T. "On the Properties of John Trevisa's Major Translations." *Viator* 14 (1983), pp. 267–88.

Lawton, L. "The Illustration of Late Medieval Secular Texts, with Special Reference to Lydgate's 'Troy Book'." In *Manuscripts and Readers in Fifteenth-Century England: The Literary Implications of Manuscript Studies*, ed. D. Pearsall, pp. 41–69. Cambridge, 1983.

Leader, D. R. *A History of the University of Cambridge*. Vol. 1. Cambridge, 1988.

Leff, G. *Paris and Oxford Universities in the Thirteenth and Fourteenth Centuries: An Institutional and Intellectual History*. New York, 1968.

Le Goff, J. *Medieval Civilization*. Translated by J. Barrow. Oxford, 1988.

"Le vocabulaire des *exempla* d'après l'*Alphabetum narrationum* (début XIVᵉ siècle)." In *La lexicographie du latin médiéval et ses rapports avec les recherches actuelles sur la civilisation du Moyen Age*, pp. 321–32. Paris, 1981.

Lemaire, J. *Introduction à la codicologie*. Louvain-la-Neuve, 1989.

Lester, G. A. *Sir John Paston's "Grete Boke": A Descriptive Catalogue, with an Introduction, of British Library MS Lansdowne 285*. Woodbridge, Suffolk, 1984.

Libera, A. de. *Penser au Moyen Age*. Paris, 1991.

Liddell, J. R. "'Leland's' Lists of Manuscripts in Lincolnshire Monasteries." *English Historical Review* 54 (1939), pp. 88–95.

Lowry, M. "The Arrival and Use of Printed Books in Yorkist England." In *Le livre dans l'Europe de la Renaissance*, ed. P. Aquilon and H.-J. Martin, pp. 449–59. Paris, 1988.

Lusignan, S. *Parler vulgairement: Les intellectuels et la langue française aux XIIIᵉ et XIVᵉ siècles*. Montreal, 1987.

"La topique de la *translatio studii* et les traductions françaises de textes savants au XIVe siècle." In *Traduction et traducteurs au Moyen Age*, ed. G. Contamine. Paris, 1989.

Lyall, R. J. "Materials: The Paper Revolution." In *Book Production and Publishing in Britain, 1375–1475*, ed. J. Griffiths and D. Pearsall, pp. 11–29. Cambridge, 1989.

Mabille, M. "Pierre de Limoges et ses méthodes de travail." In *Hommages à Andre Boutemy*, ed. G. Cambier, pp. 244–51. Brussels, 1976.

Mathew, G. *The Court of Richard II*. London, 1968.

McFarlane, K. B. "The Education of the Nobility in Later Medieval England." Chapter in *The Nobility of Later Medieval England*. Oxford, 1973.

Lancastrian Kings and Lollard Knights. Oxford, 1972.

McKisack, M. *The Fourteenth Century, 1307–1399*. Oxford, 1959.

Michael, M. A. "A Manuscript Wedding Gift from Philippa of Hainault to Edward III." *The Burlington Magazine* 127 (1985), pp. 582–99.

Miethke, J., ed. *Das Publikum politischer Theorie im 14. Jahrhundert.* Munich, 1992.

Minnis, A. J. *Medieval Theory of Authorship: Scholastic Literary Attitudes in the Later Middle Ages.* London, 1984.

Monfrin, J. "Les traducteurs et leur public en France au Moyen Age." *Journal des savants* (1964), pp. 5–20.

Murray, A. *Reason and Society in the Middle Ages.* Oxford, 1978.

Nederman, C. J. "Aristotelianism and the Origins of 'Political Science' in the Twelfth Century." *Journal of the History of Ideas* 52 (1991), pp. 179–94.

Oates, J. C. T. *Cambridge University Library, a History: From the Beginnings to the Copyright Act of Queen Anne.* Cambridge, 1986.

Ong, W. J. *Orality and Literacy: The Technologizing of the Word.* New York, 1982.

The Presence of the Word. New Haven, 1967.

Orme, N. "The Education of the Courtier." In *English Court Culture in the Later Middle Ages,* ed. V. J. Scattergood and J. W. Sherborne, pp. 63–85. London, 1983.

From Childhood to Chivalry: The Education of the English Kings and Aristocracy, 1066–1530. London, 1984.

Ornato, M. and N. Pons, eds. *Pratiques de la culture écrite en France au XVe siècle.* Louvain-la-Neuve, 1995.

Pächt, O. and J. J. G. Alexander. *Illuminated Manuscripts in the Bodleian Library, Oxford.* Vol. III. Oxford, 1973.

Painter, G. D. *William Caxton: A Quincentenary Biography of England's First Printer.* London, 1976.

Pantin, W. A. *Canterbury College Oxford.* Vols. I and IV of 4. Oxford Historical Society, new ser. 6 and 30 (1947 and 1985).

Parkes, M. B. *English Cursive Book Hands, 1250–1500.* Oxford, 1969.

"The Influence of the Concepts of *Ordinatio* and *Compilatio* on the Development of the Book." In *Medieval Learning and Literature: Essays presented to Richard William Hunt,* ed. J. J. G. Alexander and M. T. Gibson, pp. 115–33. Oxford, 1976.

"The Literacy of the Laity." In *Literature and Western Civilization: The Medieval World,* ed. D. Daiches and A. Thorlby, pp. 555–77. London, 1973.

"The Provision of Books." In *The History of the University of Oxford,* vol. II, ed. J. I. Catto and R. Evans, pp. 407–83. Oxford, 1992.

Parkes, M. B. and A. G. Watson, eds. *Medieval Scribes, Manuscripts and Libraries: Essays Presented to N.R. Ker.* London, 1978.

Pearsall, D. "Hoccleve's *Regement of Princes*: The Poetics of Royal Self-Representation." *Speculum* 69 (1994), pp. 386–410.

Petrucci, A. *Writers and Readers in Medieval Italy: Studies in the History of Western Culture.* Edited and translated by C. M. Radding. New Haven, 1995.

Pfander, H. G. "The Mediaeval Friars and Some Alphabetical Reference-Books for Sermons." *Medium Aevum* 3 (1934), pp. 19–29.

Piper, A. J. "The Libraries of the Monks of Durham." In *Medieval Scribes, Manuscripts and Libraries: Essays Presented to N.R. Ker,* ed. M. B. Parkes and A. G. Watson, pp. 213–77. London, 1978.

Pollard, G. "The *Pecia* System in the Medieval Universities." In *Medieval Scribes, Manuscripts* and Libraries: Essays Presented to N. R. Ker, ed. M. B. Parkes and A. G. Watson, pp. 145–61. London, 1978.

"The University and the Book Trade in Medieval Oxford." In Beiträge zum Berufsbewusstsein des mittelalterlichen Menschen, ed. P. Wilpert, pp. 336–44. Miscellanea Mediaevalia 3. Berlin, 1964.

Potthast, A. Bibliotheca Historica Medii Aevi. Berlin, 1896.

Prestwich, M. Armies and Warfare in the Middle Ages: The English Experience. New Haven, 1996.

Reynolds, C. "The Shrewsbury Book, British Library, Royal MS 15.E.VI." In Medieval Art, Architecture and Archaeology at Rouen, ed. J. Stratford, pp. 109–16.

Rickert, E. "King Richard II's Books." The Library, 4th ser., 13 (1933), pp. 144–7.

Ridder-Symoens, H. de, ed. A History of the University in Europe. Cambridge, 1992.

Robinson, J. A. and M. R. James. The Manuscripts of Westminster Abbey. Cambridge, 1909.

Roskell, J. S. The Commons and Their Speakers in English Parliaments, 1376–1523. Manchester, 1965.

Roth, F. The English Austin Friars, 1249–1538. New York, 1966.

Rouse, M. A. and R. H. Rouse. Authentic Witnesses: Approaches to Medieval Texts and Manuscripts. Notre Dame, Ind., 1991.

"The Texts called Lumen Anime." Archivum Fratrum Praedicatorum 41 (1971), pp. 5–113.

Rouse, R. H. and M. A. Rouse. Preachers, Florilegia and Sermons: Studies on the "Manipulus florum" of Thomas of Ireland. Toronto, 1979.

Salter, E. and D. Pearsall. "Pictorial Illustration of Late Medieval Poetic Texts: The Role of the Frontispiece or Prefatory Picture." In Medieval Iconography and Narrative: A Symposium, ed. F. G. Andersen et. al., pp. 100–23. Odense: Odense University Press, 1980.

Sandler, L. F. Gothic Manuscripts, 1285–1385. A Survey of Manuscripts Illuminated in the British Isles, ed. J. J. G. Alexander. Vol. II. London, 1986.

Scanlon, L. Narrative, Authority, and Power: The Medieval Exemplum and the Chaucerian Tradition. Cambridge, 1994.

Scattergood, V. J. "Literary Culture at the Court of Richard II." In English Court Culture in the Later Middle Ages, ed. V. J. Scattergood and J. W. Sherborne, pp. 29–43. London, 1983.

Scattergood, V. J. and J. W. Sherborne, eds. English Court Culture in the Later Middle Ages. London, 1983.

Schmitt, C. B. and D. Knox. Pseudo-Aristoteles Latinus: A Guide to Latin Works Falsely Attributed to Aristotle before 1500. London, 1985.

Scott, K. L. "Caveat Lector. Ownership and Standardization in the Illustrations of Fifteenth-Century Manuscripts." English Manuscript Studies, 1100–1700 1 (1989), pp. 19–63.

"Design, Decoration and Illustration." In Book Production and Publishing in Britain, 1375–1475, ed. J. Griffiths and D. Pearsall, pp. 31–64. Cambridge, 1989.

Sears, H. L. "The Rimado de Palaçio and the 'De regimine principum' Tradition of the Middle Ages." Hispanic Review 20 (1952), pp. 1–27.

Seaton, E. Sir Richard Roos, c. 1410–1482, Lancastrian Poet. London, 1961.

Sherborne, J. W. "Aspects of English Court Culture in the Later Fourteenth Century." In English Court Culture in the Later Middle Ages, ed. V. J. Scattergood and J. W. Sherborne, pp. 1–27. London, 1983.

Sherman, C. R. Imaging Aristotle: Verbal and Visual Representation in Fourteenth-Century France. Berkeley, 1995.

"Les thèmes humanistes dans le programme de traduction de Charles V: Compilation des textes et illustrations." In *Pratiques de la culture écrite en France au XVᵉ siècle*, ed. M. Ornato and N. Pons, pp. 527–37. Louvain-la-Neuve, 1995.

Sherwood, F. H. "Studies in Medieval Uses of Vegetius' *Epitoma rei militaris*." Ph.D. dissertation, University of California at Los Angeles, 1980.

Shrader, C. R. "A Handlist of Extant Manuscripts Containing the *De re militari* of Flavius Vegetius Renatus." *Scriptorium* 33 (1979), pp. 280–305.

Smalley, B. *English Friars and Antiquity in the Early Fourteenth Century*. Oxford, 1960.

Somerset, F. *Clerical Discourse and Lay Audience in Late Medieval England*. Cambridge, forthcoming.

Talbot, C. H. "The Universities and the Mediaeval Library." In *The English Library Before 1700*, ed. F. Wormald and C. E. Wright, pp. 66–84. London, 1958.

Tuck, A. *Richard II and the English Nobility*. New York, 1974.

Tudor-Craig, P. *Richard III*. 2nd edn. Ipswich, 1977.

Vale, J. *Edward III and Chivalry: Chivalric Society and Its Context, 1270–1350*. Woodbridge, Suffolk, 1982.

Wagner, A. R. "The Swan Badge and the Swan Knight." *Archaeologia* 97 (1959), pp. 127–38.

Waldron, R. A. "John Trevisa and the Use of English." *Proceedings of the British Academy* 74 (1988), pp. 171–201.

"The Manuscripts of Trevisa's Translation of the *Polychronicon*: Towards a New Edition." *Modern Language Quarterly* 51 (1990), pp. 281–317.

"Trevisa's Original Prefaces on Translation: A Critical Edition." In *Medieval English Studies Presented to George Kane*, ed. E. D. Kennedy, R. Waldron, and J. S. Wittig, pp. 285–95. Wolfeboro, N.H., 1988.

Walther, H. G. "'Verba Aristotelis non utar, quia ea iuristae non saperent.' Legistische und aristotelische Herrschaftstheorie bei Bartolus und Baldus." In *Das Publikum politischer Theorie im 14. Jahrhundert*, ed. J. Miethke, pp. 111–26. Munich, 1992.

Watson, A. G. *Medieval Libraries of Great Britain: Supplement to the Second Edition*. London, 1987.

Watson, N. "Censorship and Cultural Change in Late-Medieval England: Vernacular Theology, the Oxford Translation Debate, and Arundel's Constitutions of 1409." *Speculum* 70 (1995), pp. 822–64.

Weisheiple, J. A. "The Classification of the Sciences in Medieval Thought." *Mediaeval Studies* 27 (1965), pp. 54–90.

Weiss, R. *Humanism in England during the Fifteenth Century*. 3rd edn. Oxford, 1967.

Welter, J.-T. *L'exemplum dans la littérature religieuse et didactique du Moyen Age*. Paris, 1927; reprint, New York, 1973.

Wenzel, S. "The Classics in Late-Medieval Preaching." In *Mediaeval Antiquity*, ed. A. Welkenhuysen, H. Braet, and W. Verbeke, pp. 127–43. Louvain, 1995.

Macaronic Sermons: Bilingualism and Preaching in Late-Medieval England. Ann Arbor, 1994.

Winter, P. M. de. *La bibliothèque de Philippe le Hardi, Duc de Bourgogne (1364–1404)*. Paris, 1985.

Wisman, J. "L'*Epitoma rei militaris* de Végèce et sa fortune au Moyen Age." *Le Moyen Age* 85 (1979), pp. 13–31.

Witty, F. J. "The Beginnings of Indexing and Abstracting." *The Indexer* 8 (1973), pp. 193–8.

Wormald, F. and C. E. Wright, eds. *The English Library before 1700*. London, 1958.

Wright, C. E. "The Dispersal of the Libraries in the Sixteenth Century." In *The English Library before 1700*, ed. F. Wormald and C. E. Wright, pp. 148–75. London, 1958.

Fontes Harleiani. London, 1972.

Zumkeller, A. *Manuskripte von Werken der Autoren des Augustiner-Eremitenordens in mitteleuropäischen Bibliotheken.* Cassiciacum, Band 20. Würzburg, 1966.

Index of manuscripts

General index

Abendon, Thomas, OESA, 103
abridgments, 15, 16, 43, 91–2, 108, 116–28
Alexander the Great, 21, 59, 60, 150
Alne, Thomas, 97
alphabetical indexes, 43, 70, 95, 100, 101–6, 121,
    128–42, 180–6
Aquinas, Thomas, 9, 10, 20, 76, 148
Arderne, Mary, daughter of Peter Arderne, 67
Arderne, Sir Peter, 67
Aristotle, 21, 33, 45, 58, 59–60, 150
    influence on *De regimine principum*, 11, 12–13
    moral philosophy of, 2, 10–11, 50, 91, 107,
      146–8, 149, 151
    Economics of, 115, 148
    Ethics of, 11, 75, 113–15, 148
    Politics of, 11, 75, 113–15, 148
    Rhetoric of, 11, 148
Ashridge (Herts.), priory of Bonshommes (Boni
    Homines), 101, 170
audience
    definition of and evidence for, 6–8
    clerical, 14–15, 93–4
    gentry and middle-class, 67–8, 76
    monastic and mendicant, 15–16, 93–4
    reading habits of, 44–52
    royal and aristocratic, 16–18, 53–66, 68–70, 76
Augustinian friars, 15, 35, 52, 95, 100, 101–3, 129,
    131, 150, 171
authority, 35, 39, 58–9, 148–9; *see also* Giles of
    Rome, authorial status of
Avis aux roys, 18

Baldock, Ralph de, bishop of London, 14, 55, 94,
    95
Barletta, Gabriel, OP, 145
Bartolomeo Capodilista, OP, 16
Bartolomeo Carusi da Urbino, OESA, 15
Bartolomeo da San Concordio, OP, 16, 91–3
Bartolus of Sassoferrato, 18, 95

Beauchamp, Elizabeth Berkeley, daughter of
    Thomas Berkeley, 85, 88, 167
Beauchamp, Richard, earl of Warwick, 85, 88–9
Beauchamp, Thomas, earl of Warwick, 88–9,
    167
Benedictines, 15, 95, 100, 103, 129, 131
Beraud, count of Sancer, 17
Berges, W., 18–19, 45
Berkeley, Thomas fourth Lord, 17, 61, 62, 65,
    77–82, 84–90, 99, 151, 167
Boniface VIII, pope (Benedetto Caetani), 10
book trade
    at the universities, 13–15, 24–6, 51–2, 94,
      97–100
    in London, 87, 98
    see also De regimine principum, textual
      transmission and manuscript dissemination
      of
books of knighthood, 45, 63–6, 71, 128
Bouvet, Honoré de, 18, 45
Broughton, John, 67, 162
Brown, E. A. R., 9
Bruni, G., 4
Budé, Jean, 17
Bukwode, John, OESA, 101
Bullington (Lincs.), Gilbertine priory, 101
Burley, Sir Simon de, 61–2
Bury, Richard de, bishop of Durham, 58–60, 94
Bury St. Edmunds, 106, 107, 156

Cambridge, Augustinian convent, 171
Cambridge University, colleges
    Corpus Christi, 96
    Peterhouse, 97, 157
    Pembroke, 97, 157
Cambridge University Library, 99
Canterbury, Christ Church priory, 95, 103, 158
Capgrave, John, 53
Castigos e documentos del rey don Sancho, 18

Lavenham, Thomas, 97, 157
Lay, Thomas, 97, 165
Lecche, John, 1, 96, 109, 163
Leonino da Padova, OESA, 15
Limoges, Peter of, 113 n.10
Lloyd, Owen, 98, 111, 160
loan-chests, 97, 168
Lollardy, 83
London, Franciscan convent, 100, 161
López de Ayala, Pedro, 18
Louis, duke of Orleans, 56
Louvre, French royal library, 16, 54
Luna, C., 5, 30
Lusignan, S., 68

manuscripts
    contents of, 41, 44–5, 48–51
    dates and places of origin of, 21–6
    English Group defined, 21
    iconography of, 32–40, 57, 89–90
    illumination of, 30–40, 56–8, 68–9, 89–90
    marginalia in, 109–16
    size and material support of, 26–9
Marcellus II, pope (Marcello Cervini), 170, 171
Margaret of Anjou, queen of Henry VI, 66, 163
Margaret, duchess of Burgundy, 17
Markaunt, Thomas, 96
Marshall, John, 96
Masham, Robert, OSB, 104–5, 106
Meffreth, 145
Mézières, Philippe de, 18
Milemete, Walter de, manuscripts of, 57, 59–60
mirrors of princes, 20–1, 44–5, 71
moral philosophy, 92, 93; see also Aristotle, moral
    philosophy of
Mortain, count of, 17
Molet, John, OSB, 106, 155
Mosie, Henry, 99, 162

Newton, John, 97
Norham, William of, OP, 100, 111, 169
Norwich, cathedral priory, 105, 106–7, 155

Ong, W., 129
Oresme, Nicole, 75, 148
Oxford, colleges
    All Souls, 97, 165
    Balliol, 97, 130
    Canterbury, 104, 138, 166
    Durham, 107, 138
    Exeter, 99
    Gloucester, 103, 107, 138
    Jesus, 98
    Lincoln, 96
Oxford, university library, 99

Parkes, M. B., 5
Paxton, Thomas, 99
Pearsall, D., 63
Percy, Henry fifth Lord, 66, 100, 169
Pert family, 67, 156, 175, 179
Peter, duke of Bourbon, 17
Philip III, king of France, 9, 13
Philip IV "the Fair," king of France, 9, 32
Philip the Bold, duke of Burgundy, 17
Philippa of Hainault, queen of Edward III,
    54–5
Pizan, Christine de, 18, 45, 65, 148 n.6, 150
printing, 142, 149–50
Prise, Sir John, 98
Pye, John, 98, 162

Queen Mary group of artists, 56–7, 60

Reading, Benedictine abbey, 106, 166
Rice, David, 98, 169
Richard II, king of England, 60–2, 71
Richard III, king of England, 70, 72, 164
Richard, duke of York, 68–9, 72, 102, 142, 164
Roos, Sir Robert, 66, 68, 154
Rotherham, Thomas, archbishop of York, 99,
    154
Rouse, Richard and Mary, 5, 129

St. George's, Windsor, collegiate church, 93 n.6,
    167
St. Paul's, London, cathedral, 94
Saint-Yon, Garnier de, 177
Sarysbury, John, OSB, 104, 106, 158
Scattergood, V. J., 55
Scott, K. L., 32
Secretum secretorum, 21, 59, 71, 77, 150
Semer, Robert, 97
Sertum florum moralium, 144
Sherborne, J. W., 55
Sherman, C. R., 32
Sidney, Sir Philip, 175 n.1
Somerset, F., 81, 84
Sonnyng, William, 67–8, 164
Sory, John, 99, 162
Stapeldon, Walter de, bishop of Exeter, 54, 55, 94,
    95, 99
Strangways, Sir James, 67, 154
Strayer, J. R., 9
Swalwell, Thomas, OSB, 159

Talbot, John, earl of Shrewsbury, 66, 68, 72, 163
Tapton, Hugh, 98, 169
Thomas, duke of Clarence, 2
Thomas of Woodstock, duke of Gloucester, 61,
    62, 63

General index

Thorp, William Lord, of Northampton, 60, 117, 166

Tractatus de regimine principum ad Regem Henricum Sextum, 68, 148

translations
  Castilian, 14, 17, 43
  Catalan, 17, 43
  English, of John Trevisa, 6, 17, 43, 61, 65, 77–90
  Flemish, 18, 43
  French, of Henri de Gauchy, 8, 9, 13, 16–17, 26, 32, 43, 44, 75–6; other, 16, 43, 76, 84
  German, 15, 17, 43
  Hebrew, 43
  Italian, 13, 17, 43
  Portuguese, 17–18, 43
Trevisa, John, 17, 61, 77–82, 99; *see also* translations, English

Vegetius, Flavius Renatus, *De re militari* of, 11, 45, 65–6, 71, 72, 77, 85, 87, 127, 149
vernacularization, 74–83; *see also* English language; French language; translations

Waterhouse, Thomas, 170
Westminster Abbey, 16, 106, 107, 164
Whelpdale, Roger, bishop of Carlisle, 97
Whytefeld, John, OSB, 105–6
Worcester, cathedral priory, 106, 107
Wyclif, John, 77
Wydenroyde, Johannes, 145, 169

York, Augustinian convent, 101
York Minster, 97

Zainer, Günther, 149
Zumkeller, A., 5, 22